HUMAN RIGHTS WORLDWIDE

A Reference Handbook

Other Titles in ABC-CLIO's
**CONTEMPORARY
WORLD ISSUES**
Series

Books in the Contemporary World Issues series address vital issues in today's society such as genetic engineering, pollution, and biodiversity. Written by professional writers, scholars, and nonacademic experts, these books are authoritative, clearly written, up-to-date, and objective. They provide a good starting point for research by high school and college students, scholars, and general readers as well as by legislators, businesspeople, activists, and others.

Each book, carefully organized and easy to use, contains an overview of the subject, a detailed chronology, biographical sketches, facts and data and/or documents and other primary-source material, a directory of organizations and agencies, annotated lists of print and nonprint resources, and an index.

Readers of books in the Contemporary World Issues series will find the information they need in order to have a better understanding of the social, political, environmental, and economic issues facing the world today.

HUMAN RIGHTS WORLDWIDE

A Reference Handbook

Zehra F. Kabasakal Arat

**CONTEMPORARY
WORLD ISSUES**

A B C 🟰 C L I O

Santa Barbara, California
Denver, Colorado
Oxford, England

Library of Congress Cataloging-in-Publication Data
Kabasakal Arat, Zehra F.
    Human rights worldwide : a reference handbook / Zehra F.
Kabasakal Arat.
        p. cm. — (Contemporary world issues)
    Includes bibliographical references and indexes.
    ISBN 1-85109-762-7 (hard cover : alk. paper) — ISBN 1-85109-767-8
(ebook) 1. Human rights.   2. Human rights—Information resources.
I. Title.   II. Series.

    JC571.K23 2006
    323—dc22
                                              2006008989

09 08 07 06   10 9 8 7 6 5 4 3 2 1

This book is also available on the World Wide Web as an eBook.
Visit abc-clio.com for details.

ABC-CLIO, Inc.
130 Cremona Drive, P.O. Box 1911
Santa Barbara, California 93116-1911

This book is printed on acid-free paper. ∞
Manufactured in the United States of America

To the millions of advocates
whose names missed here . . .

To live like a tree, lone and free
and like a forest, brotherly;
this longing is ours.

Nazım Hikmet, 1947

Contents

Tables

Preface

The notion that people would have some "rights" may be traced back to the earliest civilizations, but the development of the concept of "human rights" has been rather new. Although the twentieth century witnessed some major events that established a common notion of international human rights and human rights gained popularity, there is no complete agreement on the content and domain of human rights. The Universal Declaration of Human Rights, adopted by the General Assembly of the United Nations in 1948, marks a turning point, because by providing a list of human rights it defines the meaning and scope of the concept. The subsequent human rights covenants and conventions of the United Nations elaborate on the content of human rights, define states' obligations, and establish monitoring mechanisms.

In addition to the United Nations, which has global membership, there are several regional and other intergovernmental organizations that include the protection of human rights among their missions or common goals. The Council of Europe, the African Union (formerly known as the Organization of African Unity), and the Organization of American States are such intergovernmental organizations that have issued human rights documents that are binding for the member states. Other intergovernmental organizations such as the Organization for Security and Cooperation in Europe and the Organization of Islamic Conference also showed their human rights concern and commitments by adopting the Helsinki Final Act (1975) and the Cairo Declaration (1990), respectively.

Moreover, people all around the world have established national and international organizations, which are independent from their governments, with the purpose of promoting human rights, monitoring states' behavior, publicizing the violations of human rights, or assisting the victims. Amnesty International and Human Rights Watch are the best-known international human rights organizations.

Despite these governmental and nongovernmental efforts, at both national and international levels, there are still debates about what constitutes human rights. There are also challenges to the notion of universal human rights, and human rights continue to be violated all around the world.

This book was originally conceived to introduce basic information about the development of international human rights and main issues and to assist readers in finding more information on material in which they may have a deeper interest. The revised edition, however, is written with a broader mission. While it will serve as an introductory book to those who are new to the field of human rights, it is designed to speak to a larger and more diverse audience. Thus, instead of offering just descriptive and factual data, I included arguments on issues surrounding the human rights concept. By bringing up controversial issues and argumentative statements, I intend to inform the newcomer and engage the expert at the same time. Thus, a change from the previous edition involves expansion of the analytical content and an increase in the number of such chapters from one to four. This change was enabled also by recent advancements in information technology. For example, since all human rights conventions and declarations can now be accessed through the Internet, I provided a brief summary and included the web addresses of the organizations that post the documents instead of printing their full texts. Consequently, more space could be allocated to the discussion of human rights events, issues, and controversies.

Chapter 1 provides an overview of the concept of human rights in different cultural and historical contexts, discusses the notion of "universal" human rights, and offers a brief history of the internationalization of human rights. The emphasis is placed on the role of the United Nations and the Universal Declaration of Human Rights.

Debates on the meaning of human rights and their classification into different generations or types are covered in Chapter 2. This chapter also addresses the arguments against the universality and interdependency of human rights.

Chapter 3 highlights some areas where human rights violations have been persistent or increasing. The discussion of these issues often brings up the United States as an influential global actor. Thus, the United States is treated separately in Chapter 4, in terms of its global human rights impact as well as with regard to its domestic policies and human rights conditions.

Chapter 5 contains a chronology that lists some of the key dates and events in the development of human rights since the beginning of the twentieth century. Chapter 6 is a selection of biographical sketches of people who are known for their human rights advocacy. The list is far from being exhaustive; the advocates of human rights are numerous and many of them are ordinary people who work for the cause by risking their lives and are never known beyond their immediate community. The biographical material is compiled primarily for those who are new to the field of human rights and intends to make them familiar with a sample of people who are internationally recognized for their contribution to the promotion and advocacy of human rights in different ways.

A brief summary of major human rights documents and websites that contain the full texts are provided in Chapter 7. (The full text of the Universal Declaration of Human Rights is included as an Appendix.) Two tables that show the ratification status of the major United Nations and International Labour Organization conventions are also included in this chapter.

Intergovernmental and nongovernmental organizations that assume the responsibility of promoting human rights or are engaged in human rights monitoring and advocacy are listed and briefly described in Chapter 8. Finally, Chapter 9 provides a selected list of sources that can be consulted for further information and research on human rights. Among the print material, reference material, such as encyclopedias and major human rights periodicals, are listed, but books and other monographs are omitted because of their large numbers. Each of the first four chapters has a reference list at the end. Together these provide a fairly comprehensive list of books and journal articles that are informative on the topics addressed and can be consulted by the reader for further research.

Writing is a rather lonely pursuit, but sometimes the hermetic process can be subject to pleasant and helpful interventions. I am grateful to my student assistants, Kathryn Eaker, Patricia Jasso, Anna Sargsyan, and Sharon Simons, who helped me in gathering and organizing information for different parts of the book. I would also like to acknowledge the work of Nina

Redman, who wrote the previous edition. Coming from different fields, our approaches have been naturally very different; nevertheless, her work set the foundation that I could reshape and build upon.

Several colleagues served as sources of information and constructive critics. Claudia Dahlerus and David Cingranelli responded to my request and kindly brought to my attention some sources important to Chapter 9. I am particularly grateful to Peter Juviler and George Andreopoulos for their friendship and continuous support, and for enriching my intellectual life with their knowledge and wisdom. Our collaboration over the years has been most rewarding, but by sparing their valuable time to read and offer invaluable and detailed comments on the first four chapters, they helped the preparation of this volume directly and definitely improved its quality. Of course, all remaining mistakes and weaknesses reflect only my own shortcomings.

Last, my thanks go to my husband Serdar Arat for his patience with my ever-expanding work schedule and for his constant support for this project and others.

1

The Origins and Development of the Concept of Human Rights

Human rights is a relatively new concept but has a long and mixed lineage. Every human interaction creates some expectations and commitments for the involved individuals, and some of them are standardized and recognized as rights by the community. Thus, in all communities people have certain entitlements and rights, albeit under different names (An-Na'im, 1992; Ishay, 2004, 1997; Lauren, 1998; Wronka, 1998). Moral codes, expressed in philosophical or religious texts, as well as legal codes developed to organize social life and maintaining order in earlier, premodern times addressed duties of people toward each other rather than their rights. As argued by several philosophers and human rights advocates, such as Mahatma Gandhi, E. H. Carr, and Henry Shue, the realization of all rights also invoke correlative duties (Freeman, 2002:58; Sen, 1999:227–231; Shue, 1980:52). Thus, some cultural norms and practices that specify people's obligations and duties toward each other can be taken as implicit references to rights that served as preludes to the modern notions of human rights. What is special about the current usage of the term "human rights" is the universalism reflected in its modern expression, that these are rights that belong to all *human* beings and are claimed on the sole criterion of being human. The idea of rights, with implicit or explicit references, has existed for a long time, but the notion that rights are held and claimed by each person by the virtue of being human is a fairly recent development. This idea gained wide acceptance at the global level first in the

United Nations Charter (1945) and later in the United Nations' Universal Declaration of Human Rights (1948).

Although the Universal Declaration of Human Rights is an important milestone in the advancement of *universal* human rights, and the United Nations Charter and human rights treaties mark important progress for putting human rights under international protection, they were not the first attempts to secure such rights, and they have not been particularly effective. This chapter focuses on the historical and cultural foundations of the concept of human rights, examines the development of international efforts and the role of the United Nations, introduces the Universal Declaration of Human Rights, and discusses the nature and limitations of the international human rights laws.

Sources of Human Rights

Human rights are held by *individuals* and claimed upon the *state* and *society*. They derive from moral and ethical sources and can enjoy legal and political support. Human rights, both moral and legal, are promoted to ensure the dignity of every human being without discrimination. As moral rights, they are inherent rights to which each human being is entitled. As legal rights, they are established in local, national, and international laws and enforced by governments and intergovernmental organizations. Expressed in ethical codes and customs or articulated in legal documents, which are all subject to change, human rights have never had a "fixed" content and evolved over time (Bobbio, 1995; Humana, 1992; Nickel 1987).

Moral and Philosophical Foundations of Human Rights

As moral rights, human rights are mainly expressed in philosophical arguments and belief systems, both religious and secular. One can argue that all world religions have a humanist dimension that supports human rights, even though the vocabulary used may not correspond to the contemporary terminology (Rouner, 1988). The notion of a creator that created all people on earth implies that all peoples deserve dignity and respect (and in some religions such as Jainism, this respect can be expanded to all creatures), though not necessarily equally. The religious prohibitions against killing may be taken as the first recognition of an attempt to protect one's right to life, the most fundamental of all rights, without which other rights would be void. In Abrahamic religions (i.e., Judaism, Christianity, and Islam), both the Old and New Testaments, as well as the Qur'an, introduce various moral codes that have human rights implications. Calls for compassion, love, and care, especially for the weaker and needy segments—such as the poor, slaves, and orphans—the emphasis on justice, and the promises of divine rewards for charitable acts, most explicitly stated in the Qur'an, are expressions of social responsibility toward respecting others' social and economic rights (Said, 1982). These religious texts also order the believers not only to serve their immediate communities but also to respect the people of all nations (Ishay 1997, 2004; Lauren, 1998).

S. V. Puntambekar, who advised the UNESCO (United Nations Educational, Scientific, and Cultural Organization) committee at the drafting of the Universal Declaration of Human Rights, argued that Hinduism and Buddhism "propounded a code as it were of ten essential human freedoms and controls or virtues of good life"; the five freedoms included "freedom from violence (Ahimsa), freedom from want (Asteya), freedom from exploitation (Aparigraha), freedom from early death and disease (Armritatva and Adroha)," and the five controls or virtues that corresponded to the freedoms included "absence of intolerance (Akrodha), compassion (Bhutadaya, Adroha), knowledge (Jnana, Vidya), freedom of conscience and freedom from fear, frustration and despair (Pravrtti, Abhaya, Dhrti)" (as quoted in Ishay, 2004:20). By rejecting the caste system of Hinduism, Buddhism further emphasized equality.

Although they fell short of providing a comprehensive and coherent view of human rights, ancient and classical philosophies also rendered certain notions of ethical and right behavior that have served as building blocks for the development of a more sophisticated human rights concept. The Chinese philosopher Confucius (K'ung Fu Tzu, 551–479 B.C.E.) emphasized the rationality of all human beings and considered education a way to cultivate the intellectual potential inherent in all (Confucius, 1956). He recognized people's right to rebel against unjust rulers, despite the high value he attached to order and stability. He also found that maintaining order was dependent on reciprocal obligations and obliged the strong to look after and care for the weak (Confucius, 1956; De Bary and Weiming, 1998). Asian philosophies, Buddhism and Taoism in particular, also emphasize humans' harmonious existence in nature and the need to protect and respect our natural environment (Rouner, 1988).

Ancient Greek philosophers, such as Plato (427–348 B.C.E.) and Aristotle (384–322 B.C.E.), emphasized the common good and defined good governance, or the just ruler, as the one that sought the common good instead of promoting self or class interest. According to Plato, ethical conduct had to be followed in dealing with all people, including foreigners, even in warfare, and the guardians of nations could not "ravage lands or burn houses" (Ishay 1997:xvi). In fact, many Greek philosophers, especially Stoics, subscribed to the notion that there was an eternal and universal natural law that governed the entire universe; human beings were all born with the ability to reason, and they should harmonize their conduct with this universal law. These philosophers followed the universalism of law by equality in various aspects of life: "equal respect for all citizens (*isotimia*), equality before law (*isonomia*), equality in political power (*isokratia*) and suffrage (*isopsephia*), and equality of civil rights (*isopoliteia*)" (Lauren, 1998:12).

Antigone, the classical Greek play by Sophocles (469–406 B.C.E.), presents characters who are willing to break the state's rules for what they believe in; this play is often considered one of the first examples of advocacy for the individual's right to freedom of consciousness and expression (Wronka 1998:45). The Roman statesman Cicero (106–43 B.C.E.) invoked the natural law theory of the ancient Greeks—best articulated in Stoicism that emphasized reason both as the governing source of the universe and as a quality held by all human beings—in *The Laws* (52 B.C.E.) and argued that there should be universal laws that would transcend customary and civil laws (Ishay, 1997). In medieval Europe, some church leaders like St. Thomas Aquinas (c. 1225–1274) emphasized the value of the individual and advanced the natural law theory (Ishay, 1997) by identifying reason and natural law with God and divine wisdom. This led to a conception of natural rights, that all human beings are created with certain inalienable rights. The humanist aspects of Aquinas's teaching were largely informed by the Muslim philosophers Avicenna (Ibn Sina, 980–1037) and Averroes (Ibn Rushd, 1126–1198), who studied ancient Greek philosophy, reconciled reason with faith, and championed equality and religious tolerance. More egalitarian than his predecessors, contemporaries, and even some successors, Averroes was also critical of the unequal treatment of sexes and considered the reduction of women's value to childbearing and rearing as detrimental to the economic advancement of the society and a cause of poverty (Averroes, 1969; Fakhry, 2001).

During the Age of Enlightenment, several philosophers refined and extended the theoretical basis for human rights as expressed in the natural rights doctrine. Thomas Hobbes (1588–1679) defined the state as an entity that was created by a social contract to protect individuals' natural rights to life and to provide security. John Locke (1632–1704) built on Hobbes's arguments and reasoning on natural rights, albeit with a forceful treatise against his "divine right of kings" theory that basically justified absolutism. Locke asserted that the sole purpose of the state was to protect individuals' right to life, liberty, and estate (property), and that these God-given rights could be protected effectively only by a representative government. Arguing for an elected government that would be limited in its power and responsible to the electorate, Locke paved the way for the articulation of political rights (Locke, 1952). Later, John Stuart Mill (1806–1873) defined the essential components of liberty as the freedom of thought, expression, association, and living according to one's taste (Mill, 1974). His collaboration with his wife Harriet Taylor Mill (1807–1858) yielded writings that advocated women's rights and political equality (Mill and Mill, 1970). The French philosopher Jean-Jacques Rousseau (1712–1778) promoted political freedoms and rights, though he belittled the advocacy of women's rights by his contemporaries. Nevertheless, the French playwright and essayist Olympe de Gouges (1748–1793) issued *The Declaration of the Rights of Woman* (1790) to criticize the sexist approach of the *The French Declaration of the Rights of Man and Citizen* (1789), and the English philosopher Mary Wollstonecraft (1759–1797) advocated women's equality and rights in *A Vindication of the Rights of Women*, written in 1791 and published in 1792 (Ishay, 1997; Wollstonecraft, 1993).

On the other side of the Atlantic, Thomas Paine (1737–1809) wrote *The Rights of Man* (1791–92). Emphasizing reason as a human quality, he defined rights in more universalistic terms than his contemporaries in Europe, considering them applicable to all men, regardless of time and place (Paine, 1988:171)—though he, too, failed to recognize women as equals of men who could claim political rights. His notion of common good, however, set him apart from other classical liberal theorists; Paine's proposal of a progressive tax system for the sake of public welfare made him an early advocate of social and economic rights (Philp, 1989).

Precolonial African communities devised several cultural norms and practices that cherished social responsibility and care for community members. Moreover, certain principles that would correspond to the current notions of civil and political rights were recognized and respected in many communities in precolonial Africa (Wai, 1982).

Universalism has also been advanced in discussions of the proper conduct in time of war, when the dehumanization of the enemy is most likely to lead to the worst atrocities. The famous Dutch jurist Hugo Grotius (1583–1645), considered the father of international humanitarian law, specified the conditions for just and unjust wars. In *On Laws and Peace* (1625), he introduced international laws that could set forth the standards of permissible actions and thus would offer greater protection to the citizens of the world. Only the wars waged in compliance with these standards could be considered just (Ishay 1997:73–83).

Grotius's conception of just war and humanitarian conduct was based on the ancient Greek and Roman philosophies of natural law. In fact, his arguments were predated by various other philosophies and traditions. The Chinese military theorist Sun Tzu wrote about the obligation to care for the wounded and prisoners of war, as early as the fourth century B.C.E. in his *The Art of War* (Lauren, 1998:57). The humanitarian principles were incorporated also into the Islamic law of nations, *siyar*. Beginning with the rule of the Prophet Mohammad (622–632 C.E.), Muslim leaders, rulers, and jurists introduced codes of conduct that included the protection of noncombatants, human life, property, and environment; warnings against the unnecessary use of violence, employing starvation as a weapon, and ill treatment of prisoners of war; and punishment of the soldiers who violated these codes (Bennoune, 1994).

Legal and Political Foundations of Human Rights

The Code of the Babylonian king Hammurabi is the oldest known or surviving collection of laws. This ancient code includes moral principles and rules "sanctioning punishments for those who transgress the law; discussing how one should marry, divorce, and work the land; proposing ways to regulate the wages of agricultural laborers and craftsmen; and establishing duties and fees for doctors, veterinary surgeons, builders and sailors"; it would definitely have informed the subsequent Mesopotamian and Middle Eastern polities, influencing the rulers in societies that followed the Abrahamic traditions (Ishay, 2004:19). As already noted in this chapter, these religious codes mainly specified obligations. The legal articulation and recognition of "rights," which could be claimed by the holders against the duty bearers, were developed largely in relation to people's struggle against the absolute power of monarchs. Thus, the early *legal* expressions of human rights tend to correspond to the protection of individuals (and often the economically powerful ones) against the arbitrary use of state power.

The English Magna Carta (1215), for example, was created in response to the heavy taxation burden created by the third Crusade and the ransom of Richard I, who had been captured by Henry VI of Germany. The English barons, who protested the heavy taxes, were unwilling to support the rule of King John unless he recognized their rights. Thus, the Magna Carta was drafted to protect their property, prevent arbitrary acts by the king, and constrain the king's power; but it also included various rights that offered further protections. Land and property could no longer be seized, judges had to know and respect laws, taxes could not be imposed without common council, there could be no imprisonment without a trial, and merchants were granted the right to travel freely within England and outside. Article 39 is particularly noteworthy for stating, "No freeman shall be arrested, or detained in prison, or deprived of his freehold, or outlawed, or banished, in anyway molested; and we [the sovereign] will not set forth against him nor send against him, unless by the lawful judgment of his peers and by the law of the land" (Ishay, 1997:58). During the seventeenth century, the Magna Carta was invoked in debates about rights, gave way to the Petition of Rights (1628) and the Habeas Corpus Act (1679), and became a part of the English common law (Davidson, 1993:12).

Habeas corpus, which literally means "you should have the body," entitled prisoners to a justification of their imprisonment and established appropriate processes to prevent illegal imprisonment of people. Such requirements are now referred to as due process of law. The Glorious Revolution in England, which affirmed the notion that the monarch, too, is subject to law and has to share his power with the parliament, transformed the political system of the country into a constitutional monarchy and gave birth to the English Bill of Rights (1689). In addition to exerting the rights of the parliament and reiterating main tenets of the Habeas Corpus Act, the English Bill of Rights recognized the freedom of speech and the right to free elections.

In the American colonies, the struggle against the English monarch led to the Virginia Declaration of Rights (1776), which indicated that no one should be deprived of freedom without due process of law; it also specified freedom of the press and the right to exercise religion freely as liberties that should be protected from interference by the state. A month later, the American Declaration of Independence was issued with similar safeguards. The Founding Fathers of the United States borrowed heavily from the writings of John Locke, Jean Jacques Rousseau, and other liberal philosophers during their struggle for independence and through the drafting of the U.S. Constitution in the 1780s. In 1791, the Bill of Rights, which included various freedoms and the right to due process of law, was enacted as the first ten amendments to the Constitution. However, the most influential human rights document issued prior to the twentieth century is the French Declaration of the Rights of Man and Citizen, adopted during the 1789 French Revolution. Despite the nationalist fervor of the time, this document specified rights that were fundamental to the individual and therefore universally applicable (Ishay 1997:xxiii; Marks, 1998). Although it failed to offer protection to the French at the time, it became an inspirational text for oppressed people throughout the world. During the twentieth century, in many countries, people and their leaders who struggled against colonialism, despotism, and oppression invoked the principles expressed in the French Declaration to further their nationalist aspirations.

Starting in the nineteenth century, various socialist ideologies, including Anarchism (not to be confused with anarcho-syndicalism or other ideologies and movements that take the "anarcho" prefix), Marxism, Fabian Socialism, and post-Marxist Social Democracy, evolved as protests against the violation of human dignity and freedoms that was becoming more and more apparent with the rise of industrial capitalism (Ishay, 1997:175–232, 277–280, 325–344; Ishay, 2004:117–172). The emphasis on class analysis and oppression by these socialist ideologies appear to be different from the "individual rights" emphasis of the human rights language; in fact, some socialists were overtly critical of the liberal human rights theorists whose main concern was the protection of property. However, socialist struggles have been mainly against the indignity and inhuman conditions faced by *individual* workers, albeit as members of an oppressed class. The goal has been individual freedom that is deemed possible only through collective, class action. In addition to their philosophical contributions, socialists mobilized workers to claim their rights, and by posing a revolutionary threat, they forced the prevailing regimes to compromise and move toward recognizing and protecting labor rights.

Although the belief systems and philosophies covered in this section have all had a bearing on furthering universal human rights, they also posed problems. Various notions that geared toward protecting human life, dignity, and rights co-existed with elements that undermine certain aspects of human rights or endorse discrimination. These inconsistencies have often been exploited by those in power, who tended to uphold the discriminatory and repressive components more than the humanitarian ones. Consequently, history has recorded more incidents of human rights violations, discrimination, and warfare—often conducted in the name of this or that religion—than incidents that supported universal human rights. Nevertheless, there were always individuals and groups who struggled against discrimination and oppression and were willing to risk their own lives to protect the rights and dignity of others.

Development of International Human Rights

The effort to create common, internationally recognized human rights norms can be traced back in history, at least to the beginnings of the antislavery movement, which targeted first the abolishment of the trans-Atlantic slave trade and then the practice of holding slaves. In addition to the abolitionists, who opposed slavery on moral grounds and considered it the ultimate indignation, the movement was also supported by political and economic leaders from industrializing regions, who could no longer consider slave labor as relevant or profitable. The struggle lasted over a century and eventually yielded a treaty to end international slave trade in 1890, but it fell short of ending the use of slave labor. The efforts to eradicate slavery would continue well into the twentieth century. In the meantime, in the mid-1800s, the humanitarian J. H. Dunant proposed creating an international relief agency of trained and dedicated volunteers from all countries to care for those wounded in wars without any distinction as to their nationality, race, class, or any other difference. His vision led delegates from fourteen countries to meet in Geneva in 1863. Although they had no authority to make decisions binding for their states, these delegates agreed to establish medical societies in their countries that would function as the auxiliary of a private humanitarian organization that would be based in Geneva and called the International Committee of the Red Cross. Knowing that the Committee's services could not be carried out without the cooperation of countries, they called for a second conference in 1864, which brought sixteen government representatives to Geneva. The negotiations at this conference yielded the Geneva Convention for the Amelioration of the Condition of the Wounded in Armies in the Field, which is considered "the first multilateral treaty in history designed to protect the individuals in times of war" (Lauren, 1998:60). In addition to the Red Cross societies, the war between the Russian and Ottoman empires in 1877–1878 brought about the Ottoman Red Crescent Society, which was based on the same principles and reinforced universalism in caring for the wounded (Lauren, 1998:61).

Humanitarian concerns and the "rights" language are employed also in addressing the condition of minorities in some nations. Starting in the late seventeenth century, the major powers of Europe often pressured the Ottoman government about the treatment of the non-Muslim subjects living under Ottoman rule (Laqueur and Rubin, 1989). However, they tended to use the protection of non-Muslims as an excuse to interfere in the affairs of the Ottoman Empire and advance their own economic and political interests (Braude and Lewis, 1982; Davison, 1973). The condition of minorities within their own borders and the plight of those in their colonies were treated as a nonissue. A legacy of these interventions and double standards has been skepticism about the actual intentions of Western states that claim to be an advocate and protector of the human rights of people in other countries.

International concerns over the promotion and protection of human rights became more noticeable in the twentieth century— though not always for the right reason. Arguments about human rights began to gain diplomatic currency during the World War I era. The International Labour Organization (ILO) was created by the Versailles Peace Treaty in 1919, to address labor rights and conditions. Its constitution was further developed with the Declaration of Philadelphia (1944), and the ILO has become a significant apparatus for the articulation of common labor standards, especially after it became affiliated with the United Nations in 1945.

The League of Nations also had its covenant within the Treaty of Versailles; it came into existence when the Treaty entered into force on January 10, 1920. The League's covenant had no specific human rights references but committed its member states to work toward establishing humane working conditions, prohibited trafficking in women and children, worked to prevent and control disease, and called for the just treatment of minorities and colonized peoples (Davidson, 1993; Lauren, 1998). However, controlled by the European colonial powers, the League failed to take any steps against racism, despite the efforts of the Japanese; in fact, it ended up serving the Western imperialist interests and expansionism rather than upholding human rights principles (Lauren, 1998). The Mandate System created by the League left a legacy that has been particularly problematic for the "international advocacy" of human rights. Under the Mandate System, territories belonging to the states defeated in the First World War were brought under the control of the victorious Western powers (Britain and France, in particular) under the pretext of assisting the newly established states in self-governance. Although the Mandate Commission, an expert group whose membership was drawn largely from countries that did not hold mandates, worked toward improving workers' rights in mandate states and tried to secure the independence of a group of such states, the entire system was tainted by the hegemonic power of and double standards pursued by the leading countries. Nevertheless, the League should be credited for issuing some important human rights documents such as the Declaration of the Rights of the Child (1924), the 1925 Geneva Protocol that prohibited the use of poisonous gases and bacteriological agents in war, and the 1929 Geneva Convention Relative to the Treatment of Prisoners of War, which required the humane treatment and protection of the wounded and prisoners of war and stipulated their rights to receive medical care, food, and clothing.

More genuine efforts toward the recognition and protection of human rights were displayed by private individuals and non-governmental organizations. Leagues for the international defense of human rights started to emerge in different countries. Italian and Chinese efforts led to the creation of the Fédération Internationale des Droits de l'Homme in 1922, which had the purpose of advancing human rights across borders and included the preparation of a declaration of human rights for all people in its program. Such a declaration had already been drafted by the Institut de Droit International in 1921. After eight years of debate, in 1929, the Institute adopted the Declaration of the International Rights of Man. Asserting in its preamble that "it is essential to extend international recognition of the right of man to the entire world," the Declaration continued with articles that identified the rights and specified that each state has the duty to protect these rights "without distinction of nationality, sex, race, language, or religion" (Lauren, 1998:111).

There is no doubt that the goal of advancing human rights entered a special phase after the Second World War. The United Nations (UN) played the key role: by incorporating the promotion of human rights into its Charter (1945); by adopting the Universal Declaration of Human Rights (1948), two covenants on civil and political rights and economic, social, and cultural rights (1966), and numerous other conventions; by creating monitoring agencies; and by holding global conferences on human rights. The cumulative effect of these has been the formation of an international human rights regime. Most scholars agree that the momentum for the creation of the United Nations came from the desire to secure peace after World War II, and concern over protecting human rights was largely a response to the Nazi atrocities that had been committed during that war (Henkin, 1990; Morsink, 1999).

Work toward establishment of the United Nations started during the war, and the human rights concerns of the UN Charter were brought up in preceding meetings and documents, such as the Atlantic Charter (August 14, 1941), the Declaration by United Nations (January 1, 1942), and the Dumbarton Oaks Proposals of September and October 1944. The U.S. president Franklin Roosevelt had already informed the United States public about the need to recognize and protect human rights when he addressed Congress on January 26, 1941. This famous speech specified "four freedoms": freedom of speech and expression, freedom of religion, freedom from want, and freedom from fear (Ishay, 1997:403–406).

On January 11, 1944, his State of the Union address to Congress introduced an "Economic Bill of Rights," which he referred to as "a second Bill of Rights under which a new basis of security and prosperity can be established for all—regardless of nation, race, or creed." Among the rights he spelled out were the right to a useful and remunerative job; the right to earn enough to provide adequate food and clothing and recreation and allow families to have a decent living; the freedom from unfair competition and domination by monopolies at home or abroad; the right of every family to a decent home; the right to adequate medical care and the opportunity to achieve and enjoy good health; the right to adequate protection from the economic fears of old age, sickness, accident, and unemployment; and the right to a good education (Laqueur and Rubin,1989:313–314).

While Roosevelt was an advocate of human rights, to include human rights in the charter of the United Nations was not his idea nor that of any other Western statesmen. In fact, when the Chinese government and delegation to the Dumbarton Oaks meetings proposed that the new international organization, with its universal membership, should work toward securing social welfare, support self-determination of peoples, and uphold the principle of equality of all races, the delegations of the other three participating countries (the United Kingdom, the United States, and the USSR) opposed the proposal immediately (Lauren, 1998:167). Including a bill of rights in the UN Charter was the proposal advanced by civil society organizations, not governments. Specifically, a number of nongovernmental organizations had been invited to the San Francisco conference by the state department of the United States to act as consultants, and the persistent pressure of this group led the governments to incorporate the promotion of human rights into the Charter (Korey, 1998:29–41).

Starting with its charter, the United Nations (UN) initiated a movement toward an international political system that redefined not only interstate relationships but also relationships between states and individuals. The UN Charter placed the promotion of human rights among the purposes of the UN, theoretically on the same footing as maintaining international peace and security (Article 1); the charter assigned its members the responsibility of promoting "universal respect for, and observance of human rights and fundamental freedoms for all without distinction as to race, sex, language or religion" (Article 55). It also required that "All members pledge themselves to take joint and separate action in cooperation with the Organization for the achievement of the purposes set forth in Article 55" (Article 56). This was not the first assertion of "internationalism" in human rights protection, since a decree by the French Convention, dated November 19, 1792, declared that the French would "come to the aid of all peoples who are seeking to recover their liberty" (Lazreg, 1982:42, n. 25).

What was initiated with the UN Charter and later reinforced by the Universal Declaration of Human Rights, which defined the content of human rights mentioned in the Charter, was a new normative foundation for international politics. The Declaration, referred to as "a common standard of achievement for all peoples and all nations" by its Preamble, was adopted by the UN General Assembly on December 10, 1948, by forty-eight votes to zero, with only eight abstentions. The subsequent human rights treaties and treaty bodies further expanded the human rights obligations of states and created an international human rights regime.

The Universal Declaration of Human Rights

Technically, the Universal Declaration of Human Rights is not legally binding. However, over the years it has been transformed into a potent legal instrument and invoked in many treaties and national laws. While its precise legal status is still subject to debate, the current legal interpretations tend to treat it as complementary to the UN Charter, which specifies the member states' human rights obligations but falls short of defining what they are and thus binding as is the Charter (Henkin, 1990). Consisting of a preamble and thirty articles, the Declaration proclaims that "All human beings are born free and equal in dignity and rights" (Article 1) and "Everyone is entitled to all the rights and freedoms set forth in this Declaration without distinction of any kind" (Article 2). It also reiterates equality before the law and the right to equal protection of the law without discrimination (Articles 7–8). Although it does not provide an explicit classification of rights, the rights listed in the Declaration are placed into five categories: civil, political, economic, social, and cultural.

Civil Rights, focusing on the right to life, liberty, and security of the person (Article 3), specify freedoms and rights that cannot be restricted or violated. They include the right to freedom from slavery and servitude (Article 4); the right to freedom from torture and cruel and inhuman or degrading treatment or punishment (Article 5); the right to freedom from arbitrary arrest, detention, or exile (Article 9); the right to fair and public trials, and to be presumed innocent until proven guilty, to defense, and to freedom from undue penalties (Articles 10–12); the right to privacy (Article 12) and to freedom of movement within and between countries (Article 13); the right to asylum and nationality (Articles 14–15); equal rights and freedoms in entering and ending marriages (Article 16); the right to own property (Article 17); the right to freedom of thought, conscience, and religion (Article 18) and to freedom of opinion and expression (Article 19); and the right to freedom of peaceful assembly and association (Article 20).

Political Rights refer to the right to participate in the government of one's country and include the rights to hold public office and to vote in free and periodic elections (Article 21). Freedoms of opinion, expression, assembly, and association, listed under civil rights, can be also treated as political rights, since they involve the means of participation in governance.

Economic and Social Rights, centering on social security, identify rights in the areas of work, basic needs, and education that would protect dignity and enable the development of the person. Article 22 of the Declaration notes that "Everyone, as a member of the society, has the right to social security and is entitled to realization, through national effort and international cooperation and in accordance with the organization and resources of each State, of the economic, social and cultural rights indispensable for the dignity and the free development of his personality."

Then, several paragraphs of Articles 23–26 specify these rights. They include the right to work, free choice in employment, equal pay for equal work, sufficient pay to ensure dignity, and the freedom to form and join trade unions for the protection of one's interests (Article 23). Also related to work, the Declaration recognizes the right to rest and leisure as well as the right to reasonable working hours and periodic paid holidays (Article 24). The right to a standard of living adequate for the healthy existence of all family members is addressed in Article 25, which includes the right to food, clothing, housing, medical care, social services, and social security in the event of unemployment, sickness, disability, widowhood, old age, and other circumstances beyond one's control. This article also entitles mothers and children to special care and assistance. Finally, the right to education is addressed in Article 26, which requires that elementary education be free and mandatory, technical education be accessible, and the content of education be geared toward personal development and tolerance. It also recognizes parents' right to choose the kind of education they want for their children.

Cultural Rights include the right to freely participate in the cultural life of the community, to enjoy the arts, and to share in scientific advancement. Also recognized is copyright protection for the intellectual property of those who are engaged in scientific, literary, and artistic productions.

Article 28 reads: "Everyone is entitled to a social and international order in which the rights and freedoms set forth in this declaration can be fully realized." This article calls for a peaceful and collaborative international environment. It is taken as a prelude to the third generation rights that include the rights to development, peace, disaster relief, and a healthy environment and require international solidarity to fulfill them. (See next chapter on generations of rights.)

The Declaration also notes that rights cannot be realized unless all people fulfill their duties to the community, the rights can be subject to limitations only by law to protect the public, and the rights and freedoms cannot be exercised in any way contrary to the UN purposes and principles (Article 29). Finally, the last article speaks to the sanctity of rights and objects to the misuse of rights and freedoms: "Nothing in this Declaration may be interpreted as implying for any State, group or person any right to engage in any activity or to perform any act aimed at the destruction of any of the rights and freedoms set forth herein" (Article 30).

The UN, International Bill of Rights, and Human Rights Agencies

The United Nations is a complex intergovernmental organization that includes a network of bodies, agencies, and affiliates (Roberts and Kingsbury, 1993). Its charter has given all principal organs a direct or indirect role in the field of human rights (*United Nations and Human Rights,* 1995:9). The General Assembly is the main body that grants each member state one vote. It is an important discussion forum, and declarations and treaties are adopted only after they have been voted on in the General Assembly. It can also issue recommendations and pass resolutions, but the General Assembly has no powers to compel member states to act. Nevertheless, in addition to the proclamation of the Universal Declaration of Human Rights, the General Assembly was crucial in setting the principles with regard to war crimes and crimes against humanity, which were included in the Charter of the International Military Tribunal (1945) that tried Nazi criminals in Nuremberg. In 1946, the General Assembly affirmed that genocide was a crime against international law. This was an important step toward the Convention on the Prevention and Punishment of the Crime of Genocide, which was adopted on December 9, 1948.

A less egalitarian but more powerful body of the UN is the Security Council. It includes five permanent members—China, France, Russia, the United Kingdom, and the United States—each of which has veto power on any Security Council resolution. It also includes ten rotating members elected for two-year terms by the General Assembly, in a manner that would reflect a balance in the representation of major geographic regions. Article 24 of the UN Charter entrusts the primary responsibility of maintaining international peace and security to the Security Council. The Security Council is expected to resolve disputes by peaceful means but is also empowered to impose binding economic and military sanctions to enforce UN resolutions and international law.

The Economic and Social Council is an intergovernmental body charged by the UN Charter to undertake studies and make recommendations on a broad spectrum of issues, including human rights. Authorized by Article 68 of the UN Charter, which notes that the Security Council (SC) "shall set up commissions in economic and social fields and for the promotion of human rights," the SC established the Commission on Human Rights in 1946. The Commission originally consisted of nine members who acted as experts in their individual capacity, but at the second session of the Security Council its membership was expanded to eighteen who would serve as representatives of their states. (Later, the size of the membership was expanded again, into fifty-three.) The Commission was given "the mandate of submitting proposals, recommendations, and reports to the Security Council regarding

1. An international bill of rights;
2. International declarations or conventions on civil liberties, the status of women, freedom of information and similar matters;
3. The protection of minorities;
4. The prevention of discrimination on grounds of race, sex, language or religion;
5. Any other matter concerning human rights not covered by the other items" (*United Nations and Human Rights,* 1995:14).

The Commission of Human Rights drafted the Universal Declaration of Human Rights. It also drafted the two covenants: (1) International Covenant on Civil and Political Rights (ICCPR); and (2) International Covenant on Economic, Social and Cultural Rights (ICESCR). The Universal Declaration and these two covenants, both adopted in 1966 and entered into force in 1976, constitute the International Bill of Rights. As implied by their titles, these covenants correspond to the different parts of the Universal Declaration, focusing on civil-political and social-economic rights, respectively.

The original intention was to create a single covenant specifying the obligations of states in upholding the rights spelled out in the Declaration; later, however, the arguments in favor of two covenants prevailed. Those who had argued in favor of a single covenant maintained that human rights should be promoted and protected together because there are no clear distinctions between the categories of rights, they could not be ranked in order of importance, and the enjoyment of rights depended on each other. Without economic, social, and cultural rights, civil and political rights would exist only in name; similarly, social, economic, and cultural rights could not be guaranteed in the absence of civil and political rights. Those who pushed for two covenants argued for the difference in the nature of the two categories of rights; they maintained that while civil and political rights could be protected through litigation, economic, social, and cultural rights could not be protected through the courts. Moreover, while the former group included individual rights that would be protected against the unlawful action by the state, the latter group would require positive action by the state. (See positive versus negative rights in Chapter 2). Finally, they contended that whereas civil and political rights were immediately applicable, the social, economic, and cultural rights had to be achieved gradually (*United Nations and Human Rights*, 1995:44).

In fact, while the two covenants embody some of the same rights and provisions, such as "people's right to self-determination," they differ not only in terms of the lists of rights they protect but also in regard to the monitoring and enforcement mechanisms that apply to them. Pursuant to Articles 28–45 of the ICCPR, a Human Rights Committee, composed of independent experts selected by states parties, is established to oversee the implementation of the ICCPR. The Committee considers the periodic reports submitted by states parties and issues recommendations. An Optional Protocol to the ICCPR also permits the Committee to accept complaints from individuals, although the Human Rights Committee cannot pursue these complaints beyond a fact-finding mission.

The ICESCR, on the other hand, was devised without a similar monitoring agency. The periodic reports submitted by states parties are transmitted to the Economic and Social Council, which is composed of state representatives. However, the Economic and Social Council was given the option of establishing an expert committee; and in 1987, it finally acted on this provision and established a committee of eighteen experts. It should be noted that all major human rights treaties of the United Nations, except for the ICESCR, provide for the establishment of a treaty body of experts as a monitoring and follow-up mechanism. In addition to the ICCPR, these include the International Convention on the Elimination of All Forms of Racial Discrimination, the Convention on the Elimination of All Forms of Discrimination against Women, the Convention against Torture and Other Cruel, Inhuman or Degrading Treatment or Punishment, the Convention on the Rights of the Child, and the International Convention on the Protection of the Rights of All Migrant Workers and Members of Their Families.

Another aspect of the ICESCR that separates it from the ICCPR involves the issues of standard setting and state obligations. Instead of setting standards for the rights covered, the ICESCR provides a loophole to states parties by seeking gradual realization of economic, social, and cultural rights. As specified in Article 2, Paragraph 1:

> Each State Party to the present Covenant undertakes to take steps, individually and through international assistance and cooperation, especially economic and

technical, to the maximum of its available resources, with *a view to achieving progressively* the full realization of the rights in the present Covenant by all appropriate means, including particularly the adoption of legislative measures (emphasis added).

In addition to monitoring the implementation of the provisions of the treaty by states parties, by demanding periodic reports from them, the treaty bodies also issue general recommendations or comments. Issuing general recommendations or comments in relation to a treaty may involve the interpretation of the treaty to clarify its intent. This allows the treaty to be a "living document," responsive to new questions and concerns that were not evident at the time of its creation.

The Vienna Declaration, adopted at the 1993 World Conference on Human Rights, recommended the creation of "a High Commissioner of Human Rights for the promotion and protection of all human rights." Later in the year, in December 1993, the UN General Assembly adopted resolution 48/141 and created the post of United Nations High Commissioner of Human Rights, holding the rank of Under-Secretary General. Serving for a renewable four-year term, the High Commissioner has a mandate that covers six broad areas: "promotion and protection of human rights throughout the world, the reinforcement of international cooperation in the field of human rights, the establishment of a dialogue with Governments with a view of ensuring respect for human rights, the coordination of efforts made in this area by the different United Nations organs, the adaptation of the United Nations machinery in this area to current and future needs and supervision of the Centre for Human Rights" (*United Nations and Human Rights*, 1995:110).

In addition to the above-mentioned main organs and special human rights offices, the UN Commission on Human Rights also appoints special rapporteurs (e.g., special rapporteur on violence against women; special rapporteur on the right to education) who gather information on their designated issue areas in all member states; in connection to their fact-finding mission, they issue reports and recommendations.

At the 2005 World Summit, held in New York in September, the member states resolved to create a Human Rights Council, which would replace the Commission of Human Rights, to strengthen the human rights machinery of the United Nations.

However, neither its specific mission, its membership, nor its place on the organizational chart of the UN has been determined (A/RES/60/1).

The UN has several other agencies and affiliated organizations that are involved in human rights, including the High Commissioner for Refugees, which sets standards and provides humanitarian aid for refugees; the United Nations Children's Emergency Fund (UNICEF), which works to improve the well-being of children worldwide; the International Labour Organization (ILO); and the World Health Organization (WHO). Established for the purpose of economic development, United Nations Development Programme undertakes several activities and issues reports that are relevant to human rights, especially to economic and social rights and sustainable development.

The Regional and Cultural Human Rights Regimes

In addition to the United Nations, there are regional systems that work for the promotion and protection of human rights (Forsythe, 2000:110–138). Compared to the other regions of the world, Europe maintains a more developed institutional structure that may partially account for the relatively higher standard of human rights maintained in this region. The Council of Europe has issued numerous human rights documents. The principal documents include the European Convention for the Protection of Human Rights and Fundamental Freedoms, which cover civil-political rights, and the European Social Charter, which focuses on social and economic rights. The provisions of both documents also include the creation of monitoring bodies, and the Convention further enjoys the enforcement power of the European Court of Human Rights.

In the early 1970s, at the height of the Cold War, increased concerns over the escalating arms race between the two superpowers led to a Conference for the Security and Co-operation in Europe in 1973. The Conference later evolved into the Organization for the Security and Co-operation in Europe (OSCE). The Helsinki Final Act, adopted at the summit meeting of the OSCE on August 1, 1975, included provisions for the protection of human rights, in addition to its détente measures. The Helsinki

Final Act is not a binding treaty, but it reiterates the human rights obligations of states and was instrumental in bringing the Eastern Bloc countries to accept a range of human rights commitments. It is argued that the Helsinki-based human rights advocacy groups that emerged in the Soviet Union and other Eastern Bloc countries such as Czechoslovakia were instrumental in the breakdown of these regimes (Donnelly, 1998; Forsythe, 2000).

The Organization of American States (OAS) has demonstrated its commitment to human rights by issuing not only a Declaration of Human Rights but also by adopting first the American Convention of Human Rights, which covers civil and political rights, and later a Protocol on social, economic, and cultural rights. The implementation of both the Convention and the Protocol is monitored by the Inter-American Commission on Human Rights. Moreover, the Inter-American Court of Human Rights, created by the Convention, charges its seven elected judges with the enforcement of the Convention.

The African Charter on Human and Peoples' Rights was adopted by the members of the Organization of African Unity, which later assumed the name of the African Union. The African Charter also includes a treaty body, known as the African Commission on Human and Peoples' Rights, that oversees the implementation of its provisions, but it lacks the support of a court. Although not created in the Charter, the African Court on Human and Peoples' Rights was sought in a Protocol signed in 1998. This Protocol created the Court and entered into force on January 1, 2004, after its ratification by fifteen member states.

There are no regional human rights organizations or treaties in Asia. However, most Asian states are parties to the United Nations' human rights treaties. Some Muslim-populated countries, mostly from the Middle East but also including some Asian states, are members of the Organization of Islamic Conference (OIC). At its 1990 meeting, under the leadership of the Iranian Minister of Foreign Affairs, the OIC adopted the Cairo Declaration of Human Rights as an Islamic alternative to the International Declaration of Human Rights. The actual impact of this declaration, especially since it poses a challenge to the universalism of the International Bill of Rights, is yet to be seen. Another regional organization, the Arab League, has established a Human Rights Commission, but this organization has very little effect beyond protesting the Israeli government's violations of the Palestinian rights in the occupied territories.

International Law and Human Rights

International laws in general and the international human rights laws in particular lack effective enforcement mechanisms. International human rights instruments include declarations and conventions as well as optional protocols issued in connection with some conventions.

International human rights declarations do not impose legal obligation on the accepting states; they set out the principles to be upheld and goals to be pursued. A covenant or convention (or alternatively referred to as treaty or pact), on the other hand, obliges the state that becomes a party to the convention to abide by its provisions and take measures toward implementing them within its jurisdiction. Treaties also call states to collaborate with each other to promote human rights outside of their jurisdictions. Just voting for the convention, or signing it, however, does not make the state a party to the convention. The state has to pursue the document through its necessary legislative procedures and *ratify* it in order to be considered a party to it. (See Chapter 5 for major human rights conventions and states' status and position on each.)

In international law, when a state becomes a party to a treaty, it is obliged to follow the provisions of that treaty unless it decides to breach the treaty, in which case the treaty is generally canceled. A distinguishing feature of human rights treaties is that they are not canceled when a breach occurs. This provision is allowed with the understanding that there would be no protective character to human rights treaties if a single human rights violation nullified the agreement. States may also denounce human rights treaties by following certain procedures spelled out in the treaty, but states are still held responsible for any violations committed before the denouncement.

A state may also ratify a convention with some reservations. In placing reservations, the state would indicate in what areas and for what reasons it would fall short of implementing the convention. Reservations are permitted with an understanding that they would be temporary (to be removed in time) and would not be incompatible with the object and purpose of the convention.

Treaties may also specify the conditions under which states parties would not be obligated to honor some treaty provisions. This involves the question of limitations and is called derogation.

The issue of derogation was discussed during the drafting of both UN covenants, but only the ICCPR contains such a disabling clause. Article 4 acknowledges the need for exceptions in times of emergency. Only if the situation "threatens the life of the nation" can the disabling clause be applied to *certain rights*. For example, freedoms of movement or association might be derogated in a time of war. However, certain rights, including the right to freedom from torture, slavery, or freedom of thought, conscience, and religion, may never be derogated.

While most human rights are covered and protected by treaties, certain violations of human rights are regarded as "crimes against humanity" that cannot be tolerated at all. Crimes against humanity, which include genocide, apartheid, and summary executions, can be tried regardless of the nationality and position of the perpetrator, and punishment is not subject to the limitation of time. In other words, these crimes fall under universal jurisdiction. Genocide was recognized as a crime against humanity by the Convention on the Prevention and Punishment of the Crime of Genocide, which was adopted by the UN General Assembly on December 9, 1948, one day before the adoption of the Universal Declaration of Human Rights, and entered into force on January 12, 1951. The Genocide Convention, as a legacy of the Nuremberg Tribunal that held Nazis responsible for their acts even when they were following orders, does not allow following orders as a legitimate defense if the charge involves crimes against humanity (Ratner and Abrams, 1997). The Convention confirms that genocide is a crime under international law "whether committed in time of peace or in time of war" (Article 1). It defines genocide as "any of the following acts committed with intent to destroy, in whole or in part, a national, ethnical, racial or religious group, such as:

(a) Killing members of the group;
(b) Causing serious bodily or mental harm to members of the group;
(c) Deliberately inflicting on the group conditions of life calculated to bring about its physical destruction in whole or in part;
(d) Importing measures intended to prevent births within the group;
(e) Forcibly transferring children of the group to another group" (Article 2).

The International Criminal Court

While the Genocide Convention has had international jurisdiction, it lacked the power of a court system that would enforce the law. Although, there is the International Court of Justice, located in the Hague and referred to as the World Court, this court addresses disputes between states. Some regional organizations established judicial systems for human rights violations. The European Court of Human Rights (ECHR), for example, allows individuals in any state under its jurisdiction to apply after all appeal mechanisms available within the person's home country are exhausted, and it can order the state to redress and remedy the situation.

However, there was no court to address human rights violations at the global level, or to try individuals directly responsible for violations. Following the model of the Nuremberg trials, in the 1990s special tribunals were set up to prosecute individuals perpetrating ethnic cleansing and genocide in Yugoslavia and Rwanda. The *ad hoc* tribunal system, however, incurred several organizational problems, such as inadequate funding, failure to arrest and extradite the vast majority of those indicted by the tribunal, shortages of and limited training for qualified personnel, weak investigative procedures, and lengthy lead time needed to set up a tribunal (Carter 1998:165). The lack of a permanent court allowed many perpetrators of gross violations, some reaching the level of genocide, to remain unpunished.

In July 1998, the United Nations convened a diplomatic conference to establish a permanent International Criminal Court (ICC) to prosecute human rights abuses including genocide, crimes against humanity, war crimes, and aggression. Referred to as the Rome treaty, the convention that established the court was adopted by 120 votes, with 7 against (the United States, China, Iraq, Israel, Libya, Sudan, and Yemen), and entered into force on July 1, 2002, after 60 countries ratified it. The Assembly of States Parties to the treaty elected the eighteen judges of the Court during its first session in February 2003; their terms of office are three, six, and nine years. The judges constitute a forum of international experts who represent the world's principal legal systems. States parties, as well as the UN Security Council, can refer cases to the Office of the Prosecutor. The Prosecutor also has power to initiate investigations on his or her own, if the state where the crime is committed is a party to the statute or it is the country of the defendant, after obtaining the approval of the pretrial chamber of the Court. As of November 1, 2005, states parties to the Rome Statute of the International Criminal Court included 100 countries.

Perhaps the most basic concept in international law, and an obstacle to the implementation of international law, is the idea that nations have sovereignty over themselves. Thus individual states have a total right to conduct their internal and external affairs in whatever way they choose. A related concept is nonintervention: no state or states have the right to intervene in the internal or external affairs of any other state. In other words, international law presents a paradox. While states monitor each other and have the obligation of intervening if a state violates the rights of people within its own borders, the sovereignty rights of the state prevent foreign intervention. Consequently, the world has been in the position of witnessing many atrocities carried out by various states, even after the Second World War, when the world entered the "Age of Rights," without taking any effective action to stop them.

One of the main missions of the United Nations is maintaining peace. Although Article 42 of the UN Charter authorizes the Security Council to sanction military action in situations that threaten international peace and security, the UN has tried to avoid military intervention, even in cases that qualified as genocide. The paradoxical principles, combined with a lack of political will and rivalries among the states, caused a stalemate and prevented the international community from taking action in the face of genocidal acts and ethnic cleansing that ravaged Rwanda and Yugoslavia in the early 1990s. Later in the decade, the Serbian aggression in Kosovo was tolerated for a long time, until NATO decided to interfere without an authorization from the UN Security Council. Since then, the interference into the Kosovo case has come to be seen as setting a precedent for military intervention for humanitarian purposes, but the crisis and atrocities in the Darfur region of Sudan were permitted to continue without decisive action well into the first decade of the new millennium.

Some alternative measures taken by the United Nations or individual states, such as imposing sanctions on the violator state, have also proven to be largely ineffective (except perhaps in the case of South Africa, in which trade sanctions imposed by the international community played an important role in pushing the apartheid regime to negotiate). Economic sanctions may also be counterproductive and worsen the conditions. The most problematic outcome would be for the intervention to cause the people of the county to suffer instead of the government in power. The sanctions imposed on Iraq after the 1991 Gulf War had a devastating impact on the Iraqi public; a million Iraqi children are estimated to have died because of the sanctions during the first five years (Clark, 1996). Similarly, the U.S. embargo on Cuba crippled the Cuban economy with dire consequences for its population (Schwab, 1999).

Another source of tension is the dual character of states' role in regard to human rights. On the one hand, states are assigned the main responsibility for protecting human rights. On the other hand, given their coercive power and the potential to abuse that power (as seen in the case of Nazi atrocities), states appear in the category of worst violators. The dilemma—trusting the state with the protection of rights and watching it for the potential threat it poses—has been difficult to resolve. Does the protection of human rights call for a weak or strong state?

The classical liberal notions of human rights focus on the state as a potential violator and call for a state that is limited in power. However, by obliging states parties to take measures toward the realization and protection of human rights, human rights instruments call for a state that is *interventionist*, at least within its own jurisdiction. Moreover, since the state has to be equipped to fulfill these responsibilities, human rights expectations implicitly endorse the notion of a *strong* state. The classical liberal motto, "the best government is the one that governs least," may work against human rights. Unfortunately, still promoted by some powerful states, this approach leads to foreign aid and loan policies that tend to cripple the state in developing countries (Hamm, 2001; Sano, 2000; Udombana, 2000).

A more recently recognized problem is the lack of knowledge; often people are not aware of their human rights or the mechanisms to claim them, and government officials may not know their obligations to respect and protect human rights. In an effort to combat the problem of ignorance, in December 1994 the UN General Assembly proclaimed the ten-year period beginning in January 1995 the United Nations Decade for Human Rights Education. Although most countries adopted national plans to develop educational tools, make curricular changes at schools, and initiate training programs for their law enforcement personnel, at the end of the decade, it was hard to argue that these programs resulted in any significant change or improvement.

Despite the dispiriting outcomes and persistent problems and obstacles, the concept of human rights has become a diplomatic currency and a source of legitimacy during the last six decades. Even if it resists protecting or fails to protect human rights, no government can express an overt opposition to human rights. This progress is largely a result of the relentless work of numerous civil society organizations and networks. Thanks to them, the promotion of human rights was placed among the goals of the United Nations in its Charter in the first place, and their continuous efforts in lobbying, monitoring, reporting, protesting, and shaming states (and more recently intergovernmental organizations and transnational corporations) have ensured that the UN, other intergovernmental organizations, states, and private citizens continue to work toward protecting human rights. In addition to the well-known international human rights organizations—such as Amnesty International, established in 1961, and Human Rights Watch, founded after the Helsinki Final Act—there are numerous international, national, and local organizations and groups that focus on human rights advocacy. They were the force behind many international human rights documents, including the Rome Statute that established the International Criminal Court. They also embrace these treaties and pressure states parties to implement them. A list of these organizations and basic information on their mission and activities are provided in Chapter 8.

References

An-Na'im, Abdullahi., ed. *Human Rights in Cross-Cultural Perspectives.* Philadelphia: University of Pennsylvania Press, 1992.

Averroes. *Averroes' Commentary on Plato's 'Republic.'* New Impression Edition. Cambridge: Cambridge University Press, 1969.

Bennoune, Karima. "As-Salamu 'Aleykum? Humanitarian Law in Islamic Jurisprudence." *Michigan Journal of International Law* 15:2 (Winter 1994): 605–643.

Bobbio, Norberto. *The Age of Rights,* revised ed. Oxford: Blackwell, 1995.

Braude, Benjamin, and Lewis, Bernard, eds. *Christians and Jews in the Ottoman Empire.* New York: Holmes, 1982.

Carter, Jimmy. "A Permanent International Criminal Court Should Be Created." In Mary Williams, ed., *Human Rights: Opposing Viewpoints*. San Diego: Greenhaven Press, 1998. Carter Center Website. http://www .emory.edu/CARTER_CENTER (accessed June 1998).

Clark, Ramsey. *The Children Are Dying: Impact of Sanctions on Iraq*. New York: World View Forum Publishers, 1996.

Confucius. *The Analects*. Edited and translated by Arthur Waley. London: George Allen and Unwin, 1956.

Davidson, Scott. *Human Rights*. Philadelphia: Open University Press, 1993.

Davison, Roderic. *Reform in the Ottoman Empire, 1851–1876*, 2nd ed. New York: Gordian, 1973.

De Bary, William Theodore, and Weiming, Tu., eds. *Confucianism and Human Rights*. New York: Columbia University Press, 1998.

Donnelly, Jack. *International Human Rights*, 2nd ed. Boulder, CO: Westview Press, 1998.

Fakhry, Majid. *Averroes: His Life, Work*. Oxford: Oneworld Publications, 2001.

Forsythe, David P. *Human Rights in International Relations*. Cambridge: Cambridge University Press, 2000.

Freeman, Michael. *Human Rights: An Interdisciplinary Approach*. Cambridge, UK: Polity Press, 2002.

Hamm, Brigitte I. "A Human Rights Approach to Development." *Human Rights Quarterly* 23:4 (November 2001): 1005–1031.

Henkin, Louis. *The Age of Rights*. New York: Columbia University Press, 1990.

Humana, Charles. *World Human Rights Guide*, 3d ed. New York: Oxford University Press, 1992.

Ishay, Micheline R., ed. *Human Rights Reader: Major Political Essays, Speeches, and Documents from the Bible to the Present*. New York: Routledge, 1997.

Ishay, Micheline R. *The History of Human Rights: From Ancient Times to the Globalization Era*. Berkeley: University of California Press, 2004.

Korey, William. *NGOs and the Universal Declaration of Human Rights: "A Curious Grapevine."* New York: St. Martin's Press, 1998.

Laqueur, Walter, and Rubin, Barry, eds. *The Human Rights Reader*. Revised edition. New York: Meridian, 1989.

Lauren, Paul Gordon. *The Evolution of International Human Rights: Visions Seen*. Philadelphia: University of Pennsylvania Press, 1998.

Lazreg, Marnia. "Human Rights, State and Ideology: A Historical Perspective." In Peter Schwab and Adamantia Pollis, eds., *Toward a Human Rights Framework*. New York: Praeger Publishers, 1982:32–43.

Locke, John. *The Second Treatise of Government*. Edited by Thomas P. Peardon. New York: Macmillan, 1952.

Marks, Stephen P. "From the 'Single Confused Page' to the 'Decalogue of Six Billion Persons': The Roots of the Universal Declaration of Human Rights in the French Revolution." *Human Rights Quarterly* 20 (August 1998): 459–514.

Mill, John Stuart. *On Liberty*. Middlesex: Penguin Books, 1974.

Mill, John Stuart, and Mill, Harriet Taylor. *Essays on Sex Equality*. Edited and with an introductory essay by Alice S. Rossi. Chicago: University of Chicago Press, 1970.

Morsink, Johannes. *The Universal Declaration of Human Rights: Origins, Drafting, and Intent*. Philadelphia: University of Pennsylvania Press, 1999.

Nickel, James. *Making Sense of Human Rights*. Berkeley: University of California Press, 1987.

Paine, Thomas. *The Rights of Man*. Harmondsworth: Penguin Books, 1988.

Philp, Mark. *Paine*. Oxford: Oxford University Press, 1989.

Ratner, Steven R., and Abrams, Jason S. *Accountability for Human Rights Atrocities in International Law: Beyond the Nuremberg Legacy*. Oxford: Clarendon Press, 1997.

Roberts, Adam, and Kingsbury, Benedict. *United Nations, Divided World: The UN's Role in International Relations*, 2nd ed. Oxford: Oxford University Press, 1993.

Rouner, Leroy, ed. *Human Rights and World's Religions*. Notre Dame, IN: University of Notre Dame Press, 1988.

Said, Abdul Aziz. "Human Rights in Islamic Perspectives." In Peter Schwab and Adamantia Pollis, eds., *Toward a Human Rights Framework*. New York: Praeger Publishers, 1982:86–100.

Sano, Hans-Otto. "Development and Human Rights: The Necessary, but Partial Integration of Human Rights and Development." *Human Rights Quarterly* 22:3 (August 2000): 734–751.

Schwab, Peter. *Cuba Confronting the U.S. Embargo*. New York: St. Martin's Press, 1999.

Sen, Amartya. *Development as Freedom*. New York, Alfred Knopf, 1999.

Shue, Henry. *Basic Rights: Subsistence, Affluence, and U.S. Foreign Policy*. Princeton, NJ: Princeton University Press, 1980.

Udombana, N. J. "The Third World and the Right to Development: Agenda for the Next Millennium." *Human Rights Quarterly* 22:3 (August 2000): 753–787.

United Nations and Human Rights, 1945–1995. New York: Department of Public Information, United Nations, 1995.

Wai, Dunstan M. "Human Rights in Sub-saharan Africa." In Peter Schwab and Adamantia Pollis, eds., *Toward a Human Rights Framework.* New York: Praeger Publishers, 1982:115–44.

Wollstonecraft, Mary. *A Vindication of the Rights of Women,* reissue ed. New York: Penguin Classics, 1993.

Wronka, Joseph. *Human Rights and Social Policy in the 21st Century: A History of the Idea of Human Rights and Comparison of the U.N. Declaration of Human Rights with United States Federal and State Constitutions,* rev. ed. Lanham, MD: University Press of America, 1998.

2

Issues of
Contention and Debate

The post-Second World War period brought the proliferation of human rights treaties and the advancement of the concept of human rights as a diplomatic and political concern and currency. Human rights became a legitimizing device for governments. Both the United Nations and some regional organizations issued human rights documents and created institutional mechanisms to promote and protect human rights. These human rights regimes' performance in improving people's human rights conditions, however, has been far from impressive. The continuation of violations, despite the noted increase in the claims of commitment to human rights, can be explained by various factors: the lack of commitment by states parties; the lack of enforcement mechanisms; a partial endorsement of rights with preferences assigned to different kinds; the persistent emphasis on state sovereignty; the prevalence of "realism" in international politics, which places the pursuit of power and "national interests" above all humanitarian concerns; the inconsistent and hypocritical policies of hegemonic states; the economic or political weakness of states in developing countries; and the resistance of the privileged and powerful groups.

While the interdependency and indivisibility of rights have been reaffirmed at the UN-organized World Conferences on Human Rights, held in Teheran (1968) and Vienna (1993), and in various UN resolutions, there has been resistance to accepting the full content of the International Bill of Rights. The selective treatment of the concept of human rights, which involves separating

33

rights into distinct categories and assigning priorities to some of them and treating others as secondary (or rejecting them completely), has become an approach frequently taken by state officials or tacitly followed in government policies. Even among human rights advocates, there are those who consider prioritization necessary. They oppose the "proliferation of rights" with the claim that proliferation has a "diluting and distracting effect" and weakens the prospect of protecting what they consider to be the "fundamental" rights (Wellman, 1999).

As philosophical questions about the nature and development of rights yield some analytical categories, these categories are employed for political purposes and prioritization. This chapter introduces some of these typologies, under the heading of generations of rights, individual versus group rights, and positive versus negative rights. Also addressed is the challenge to the universal applicability of human rights posed by cultural relativists, who problematize the philosophical and cultural origins of the International Bill of Rights. The view that the current conceptualization of human rights in international documents is an outgrowth of Western thought, a tool used by Western powers to interfere into the affairs of other states, or as a design of Western cultural imperialism, has been shared by many and frequently expressed by some political leaders in developing countries during the last two decades.

Generations of Rights

As noted in Chapter 1, the concept of human rights has been evolving. The idea of human rights has been expanding not only in terms of the population to which it applies but also in terms of its content. This evolution has taken place largely as a response to the changes in social conditions and technological developments (Bobbio, 1995). Referring to the timing of their recognition, human rights are classified into generations, albeit with some anachronism (Kamenka, 1993). Current discussions refer to three generations of human rights: civil and political rights are referred to as the "first generation" of rights; social, economic, and cultural rights are identified as the second generation; the rights to development and peace, disaster relief assistance, and a healthy and protected environment constitute the third generation. One may argue that the rights of the most vulnerable segments of the world population (e.g., children, women, disabled, migrant workers, and refugees) are waiting to be called the fourth generation (Arat, 1999).

This genealogical formulation largely corresponds to the sequence of events that involved the recognition of various rights in Europe. T. H. Marshall, who studied the advancement of rights in connection to the development of citizenship in Europe, noted that "it is possible without doing much violence to historical accuracy, to assign the formative period in the life of each to a different century—civil rights to the eighteenth, political to the nineteenth and social to the twentieth. These periods must, of course, be treated with reasonable elasticity, and there is some evident overlap, especially between the last two" (Marshall, 1964:74).

Seymour Martin Lipset offered a similar chronology in his discussion of major issues of modern times: the place of religious institutions in the society; extending "citizenship" to the lower strata; and the distribution of national wealth. Writing in the late 1950s, he pointed out that the religious issue "was fought through and solved in most of the Protestant nations in the Eighteenth and Nineteenth Centuries" and the "citizenship," or "political rights," issue was resolved "in various ways around the Twentieth Century." According to him, the "only key domestic issue" still waiting to be resolved was "collective bargaining over differences in the division of the total product within the framework of a Keynesian welfare state" (Lipset 1959:69–105).

Since social and economic rights began to be addressed in European and other industrial societies after the Great Depression, and under the rubric of the welfare state, they came to be known as the second generation of rights. The concept of "third generation human rights" was coined by Karel Vasak, the French jurist and former director of the UNESCO (United National Educational, Scientific, and Cultural Organization) Division of Human Rights and Peace. In a speech delivered in 1977, he drew a parallel between the motto of the French Revolution—"liberty, equality, fraternity"—and the normative themes of human rights. As he put it, the first generation human rights focused on the value of liberty and attempted to counter the state power; the second generation human rights placed the emphasis on equality and made demands on the state's positive duties; and the third generation human rights would focus on fraternity, or solidarity.

Then, he named five related rights to be included in this third category: the right to development; the right to peace; the right to (a healthy and sustainable) environment; the right to the ownership of the common heritage of humankind; and the right to communication (Tseng, 2003; Wellman, 2000).

The first three of the third generation rights listed by Karel Vasak later found some expression in declarations and charters. The Declaration on the Preparation of Societies for Life in Peace, adopted by the UN General Assembly in 1978, asserts that "every nation and every human being . . . has the inherent right to life in peace" (UN Doc. A/Res/33/73, 1978). The right to peace is also specified in the African Charter on Human and Peoples' Rights (1981), which indicates that "all peoples shall have the right to national and international peace and security" (Article 23). Later, on November 12, 1984, the UN General Assembly adopted the Declaration on the Right of Peoples to Peace (UN Doc. A/Res/39/11, 1984).

The Declaration on the Right to Development was adopted by the General Assembly on December 4, 1986 (UN Doc. A/Res/41/128). The Vienna Declaration and Program of Action (1993) reaffirmed "the right to development as established in the Declaration, as a universal and inalienable right and an integral part of fundamental rights" (UN Doc. A/CONF. 157/23).

The first human rights reference to "environment" can be found in the first principle of the Stockholm Declaration of the United Nations Conference on the Human Environment, issued in June 1972: "Man has the fundamental right to freedom, equality, and adequate conditions of life, in an environment of a quality that permits a life of dignity and well-being" (Wellman, 2000:646). However, more direct and clearer articulation of environmental rights appeared in regional documents. The African Charter on Human and Peoples' Rights proclaims that "all peoples have the right to a general satisfactory environment favorable to their development" (Article 27). The Additional Protocol to the American Convention on Human Rights in the Area of Economic, Social and Cultural Rights, opened for signature in 1988, indicates that "everyone shall have the right to live in a healthy environment" (Article 11). The UN initiative in this area was led by the Special Rapporteur to the UN Sub-Commission on Human Rights, who annexed the Draft Principles on Human Rights and the Environment to her report in 1994. The second principle in the draft proclaims that "all persons have the right to a secure, healthy and ecologically sound environment" (Wellman, 2000:647).

Some analysts, such as Johan Galtung, associate different generations of rights to separate classes and political struggles. Using color coding, he attributes the first generation human rights to "the bourgeoisie (blue), the second generation to the working class (red), and the third generation to the social movements (green)" (Sano, 2000:737). However, the third-generation advocacy has not been limited to grassroots movements; the right to development, for example, was promoted by the government officials and political leaders of developing countries as well (Sano, 2000:737).

Both the creation of the categories of generations, in general, and what is claimed to be among the third-generation human rights, in particular, are criticized by many. Michael Freeman itemizes these criticisms:

> (1) the language of 'generations' is inappropriate, because generations succeed each other but so-called generations of human rights do not; (2) the concept of 'generation' presupposes a questionable history of human rights: the supposed first two generations were both recognized in the Universal Declaration; (3) it is not clear whether the holders of these rights are individuals, peoples, states, or some combination of these; (4) it is not clear to what the bearers of these rights have a right; (5) it is not clear who the corresponding duty-bearers are, or what their duties are; (6) these rights-claims provide cover for authoritarian governments to violate established human rights; and (7) what is valid in third-generation rights is already contained in established human rights: for example, the right to development is covered by taking economic and social rights seriously. (Freeman, 2002:48)

These chronologies and the classification of rights into generations can be challenged also by the history of non-Western societies. Arguably, the recognition of economic and social rights in Islamic practices and the respect for the natural environment (and implicitly for environmental rights) in African, American, and Asian civilizations, for example, have preceded the recognition of many civil and political rights.

Individual versus Group Rights

As stated earlier, the notion that human rights are held by individuals and claimed against the state and society has achieved some consensus. However, people can claim rights as individuals or as members of a community or group. While the freedom from torture or the right to vote would be claimed by individuals, for some rights the right-bearer would be groups rather than individuals. Peoples' right to self-determination, which is recognized in both UN covenants, for example, is a group right. Article 1 of both covenants, the ICCPR and the ICESCR, is identical and specifies this right and the states' corollary duties in three paragraphs:

> All peoples have the right of self-determination. By virtue of that right they freely determine their political status and freely pursue their economic, social and cultural development.
>
> All peoples may, for their own ends, freely dispose of their natural wealth and resources without prejudice to any obligations arising out of international economic cooperation, based upon the principle of mutual benefit, and international law. In no case may a people be deprived of its own means of subsistence.
>
> The States Parties to the present Covenant, including those having responsibility for the administration of Non-Self-Governing and Trust Territories, shall promote the realization of the right to self-determination, and shall respect that right, in conformity with the provisions of the Charter of the United Nations.

At the time of the drafting of the two UN covenants, this right had been interpreted as a reaffirmation of states' sovereignty claims, as well as the colonized peoples' right to seek independence and self-rule. Self-determination claims made by peoples living within the boundaries of an already independent state (e.g., the Basque people in Spain, the Chechens in Russia, the Kurds in Iraq or Turkey, the indigenous populations in various states of the Americas and Oceania), however, have been treated as more problematic and often repressed by the state. In addition to the established states' concerns over preserving their territorial integrity, questions such as "what constitutes a people?" and "who decides on behalf of the people?" made the fulfillment of this right difficult for many peoples. However, there have been no philosophical or political objections to the right to self-determination being seen as a collective or group right. Sorting out rights as collective or individual rights, however, is not always easy or even possible. Among work-related rights, for example, while the right to work or the freedom of association (e.g., to form labor unions) can be claimed by individuals, the right to collective bargaining can be claimed only by a group of workers. Thus, collective bargaining rights are considered to be group rights.

Minority rights are also considered by many to be a group right, since "minority" covers a group of people who would claim the right to preserve and follow certain cultural traits such as religion or language. However, minority groups' claims that are raised against discrimination (e.g., in employment, exercising the right to vote) are individual rights, even if the demands are made by a group, as a collective.

The rights that are considered to be within the third-generation human rights are also treated as group rights. The rights to development, peace, and a healthy environment are typically brought up on behalf of the people living in developing countries, who find themselves struggling against poverty, perpetual warfare, and deteriorating environmental conditions. These are seen as rudiments of international injustice stemming from past and present power differentials among the states. This pattern can be observed in the voting behavior of the states. The Declaration of the Right to Development was accepted by the General Assembly with 146 votes; only one country, the United States opposed, and the eight abstentions were mainly from the Western industrial countries (Hamm, 2001:1009)

These third-generation rights, however, can be claimed also by the citizens of industrial countries, who are not immune to the human consequences of industrial pollution, armament, and the threats of nuclear war. What may separate them from other rights is that they involve collective goods. Efforts and measures taken to make some of these rights enjoyable by some people would have a spillover effect on other people. By the same token, a single act of violation—for example, a massive discharge of industrial pollutants into a body of water or the air—can violate the rights of an indefinite collective of individuals spread spatially and extend into the future generations.

As pointed out earlier in this chapter, while some analysts refuse to accept these as rights or consider them as vaguely defined group rights that do not have clear duty-bearers (Donnelly, 1989; Freeman, 2002), others treat them as individual rights claimed upon the international community, which includes individual private actors, states, intergovernmental organizations, and corporate entities as well as nations (Sengupta, 2002; Wellman, 2000). The Declaration of the Right to Development defines this right both as an individual right and a collective right, by employing the wording, "The right to development is an inalienable human right by virtue of which *every human person* and *all peoples* are entitled to participate in, contribute to, and enjoy economic, social, cultural, and political development, in which all human rights and fundamental freedoms can be fully realized" (Article 1, emphasis added).

Positive versus Negative Rights

Those who subscribe to natural rights theories define human rights as the rights that individuals enjoyed in their natural state (at a presociety and prenation stage). Therefore, when individuals enter the state of society, these rights should be protected against violations by the state. Specified as the right to life, liberty, and estate in the Lockean tradition, these rights are presumably enjoyed only if the state does not interfere but constrains its domain of action and power. They are referred to as "negative rights"—rights that are enjoyed as a result of omission or nonaction by the state.

Civil and political rights (e.g., the right to freedom from torture, to freedom of speech and association), along with the right to property, are considered to be negative rights. Some other rights, such as the right to education, employment, and health care, on the other hand, are treated as rights that can be realized only through a positive action by the state and society (Cranston, 1967; Downie, 1980; Mayo, 1967). Thus, the latter group of rights, typically what falls within the International Covenant of Economic, Social and Cultural Rights, is placed in a different and secondary category; they are treated as "aspirations" that do not quite fit the notions of natural rights.

The separation of rights into fixed positive and negative categories is rejected by others for setting a false and misleading dichotomy. The counterarguments point to the similarities among different rights, noting that most civil and political rights would also require positive action by the state. For example, due process rights cannot be enjoyed unless public funds are used to establish a functioning court system. Moreover, whether a right demands an omission of action by the state or the state's active engagement, is contingent upon the social and historical circumstances.

The consequence of the violations of social and economic rights can be as devastating as the violation of civil and political rights; poverty and the lack of access to food, for example, undermine human dignity as seriously as do violations of personal integrity. Economic hardship and inequalities are not natural outcomes but results of public choices and political decisions; they can be adjusted to realize economic and social rights, just as policies are devised to protect civil rights. Those who oppose separating rights as positive and negative also emphasize the interdependency and indivisibility of rights, which means that a right cannot be enjoyed or protected fully if some other rights are violated (Bergmann, 1981; Charvet, 1981; Donnelly, 1989; Gavison, 2003; MacMillan, 1986; Nickel 1987; Okin, 1981; Peffer, 1978; Raphael, 1967; Schneider, 1967; Shue, 1980). Henry Shue argues that there are at least three "basic rights"—security, subsistence, and liberty—the enjoyment of which are "essential to the enjoyment of all other rights" (Shue, 1980:19).

Nevertheless, the Lockean approach seems to be prevailing and there appears to be a stronger commitment to property rights and civil liberties. The United States, for example, has been vehement in its libertarian approach and dismissal of social, economic, and cultural rights. Philip Alston, who held several human rights–related posts within the UN, including the chair of the Committee on Economic, Social and Cultural Rights, notes that "the United States has, [especially] since 1981, frequently sought to characterize these rights as 'goals,' or 'aspirations' but certainly not 'human rights'" (Alston, 1993:61). Even President Carter, whose administration was more willing to accept a larger scope of human rights, was ambivalent and negligent about social and economic rights (Arat, 1999; see also Chapter 4 on the U.S. approach).

Unlike the United States, other Western states do not flatly reject social and economic rights. First, most western European countries have developed comprehensive welfare programs. Even if they were introduced as an appeasement strategy to prevent the radicalization of workers and revolutionary upheavals, welfare programs involve a shift from Classical Liberalism, which emphasizes property rights and individual responsibility, to a compromised position that assigns a broader role to the state than did John Locke. As entitlements, welfare benefits imply a philosophical acceptance of social and economic rights by the state. Moreover, the European Human Rights regime includes a Social Charter that recognizes a set of social and economic rights, along with the European Convention for the Protection of Human Rights and Fundamental Freedoms, which embodies mainly civil and political rights.

Nevertheless, the separation of human rights into two different charters and the time lapse between the adoption of the Convention by the Council of Europe (1950) and adoption of the Social Charter (1961) indicate that the two sets of rights have been subject to different treatment by the European states as well. Furthermore, the Convention has a procedure for filing complaints about violations of its provisions, and the drafters of the Convention created the European Court of Human Rights to enforce its implementation; therefore, the Convention enjoys the support of a judicial system that is not available to the Social Charter.

The preferential treatment of civil and political rights over social and economic rights, or vice versa, has been pursued also by those who considered liberty and equality as essentially irreconcilable values that can be achieved only at each other's expense. By associating civil and political rights with liberty and social and economic rights with equality, the inevitability of a trade-off between the two sets of rights is defended by both the followers of liberal schools of thought and those who try to justify the need for authoritarian rule, at least during the period of transition to a society of equals (Donnelly, 1989). These two positions were demonstrated clearly by the superpowers during the Cold War years, in both their domestic and foreign policy formulations.

However, the experience of several countries shows that liberty and equality, or different rights, cannot be maintained at each other's expense, and they are likely to reinforce each other. Amartya Sen's study of India, for example, concludes that the plight of famine ended in India only after the country gained its independence and established a democratic political system, and he further argues that economic development that secures social and economic rights enhances individual capabilities and enables the enjoyment of freedoms (Sen, 1992, 1999). The reports by the United Nations Development Programme provide further data and arguments that support the link between equality and liberty, as well as the indivisibility and interdependency of human rights (*Human Development Report 2000* and *Human Development Report 2002*).

The Charter of Fundamental Rights of the European Union, proclaimed in December 2000, further attest to the wider acceptance of the indivisibility and interdependency of human rights. In fifty-four articles, this comprehensive document combines all categories of human rights—civil, political, economic, social, and cultural—and addresses potential violations of bio-ethics and privacy that may be caused by the advances in genetics and information/surveillance technologies.

Universalism versus Cultural Relativism

Starting at the drafting stage, the Universal Declaration of Human Rights has faced some challenges about its relevance and applicability in different cultures. In 1947, the American Anthropological Association (AAA) sent a memorandum to the UN Commission on Human Rights and warned it about the problem of ethnocentrism. After posing the question, "How can the proposed Declaration be applicable to all human beings and not be a statement of rights conceived only in terms of values prevalent in the countries of Western Europe and America?" the memorandum continued with arguments that stressed the impossibility of devising a document of *universal* human rights in a world of multiple and diverse cultures (Morsink, 1999:ix).

Four decades later, the AAA changed its position in favor of the Universal Declaration (see the end of this chapter), but not all skeptics were converted. Today, nobody claims to be opposed to human rights, but many of the rights spelled out in the International Bill of Rights and its principles of universalism and interdependency of rights face resistance in different quarters, where cultural differences are pointed out as a justification. A common challenge comes from leaders of developing countries that experienced Western colonial rule or other forms of Western imperialism. They contend that the human rights, in its current international usage, is a Western concept, "individual rights" is a Western notion, the rights articulated in the international documents are based on Western individualism, and the protection of human rights is used by the powerful Western states to interfere in the affairs of smaller countries, just as Western imperialism was justified in the past as a "civilizing mission."

Some of these arguments have support in the Western world, including some human rights advocacy groups. In fact, many advocates of human rights define the main character of the Universal Declaration of Human Rights as Western (Donnelly, 1989, 1998; Howard and Donnelly, 1986; Lakoff, 1990; Parekh, 1992; Pollis and Schwab, 1980). Whereas some of them contend that human rights would apply to all, regardless of their origin, some others, who see the origin of human rights as Western, object to their use in or relevance to non-Western societies. These objections can be discussed under three headings: the argument that Asian values seek collective good over individual rights that are promoted in Western philosophies; the Islamic principle of the complementarity of sexes, as opposed to their equality in assigning rights and responsibilities; and the indigenous peoples' rights to self-determination.

Asian Values

A major challenge to the universality of the rights included in the International Bill of Rights comes from Asia. Subject to criticisms about state repression of civil liberties and use of corporal punishment, the authoritarian leaders of some East Asian countries have presented a certain conceptualization of Asian values in their defense. They argue that Asian values are incompatible with some aspects of the International Bill of Rights, which were shaped by Western values; and as the leaders of Asian societies that favor community welfare and order over the individual's rights, they would emphasize economic development and political stability at the expense of individual freedoms (Bauer and Bell, 1999; Bell, Nathan, and Peleg, 2001; Korey, 1998:469–491).

Although peace, order, and economic development are important to the protection of human rights (see arguments on the third generation of rights at the beginning of this chapter),maintaining them at the expense of individual freedom and personal integrity would violate the essence of human rights. By defining the "right to development" as a communal right and "order" as a social good that can override individual liberty, the Asian values argument takes a utilitarian approach, which has been problematic for the promotion of human rights. Writing that "citizens have personal rights to the State's protection as well as personal rights to be free from the State's interference, and it may be necessary for the Government to choose between these two sorts of rights," Ronald Dworkin acknowledges the dilemma (Dworkin, 1989:104). However, he immediately notes that in its effort to balance the rights of the individual with the demands of the society, the government cannot causally infringe on individual rights under a pretext of maintaining security and order; there should be a distinction between "what may happen" and "what will happen" (Dworkin, 1989). In other words, the individual rights cannot be restricted in the absence of an imminent threat faced by the society.

It should be noted that not all East Asian political leaders and philosophers find "Asian values" incompatible with international human rights values. Government officials in Singapore, Malaysia, China, and Indonesia tend to adhere to the cultural relativist position, but the leaders of Taiwan (e.g., Lee Teng-hui, 1997) reject relativism and adhere to universalism. Many consider a sharp division between individualism and communitarianism a fallacy and contend that Asian traditions neither establish a hierarchy between the two nor assign absolute authority to the state to protect community interests (Bauer and Bell, 1999; Bell, Nathan, and Peleg, 2001; Diamond et al., 1997, Parts 2–3). Others also note that the tension between individualism and community welfare does not run between the Western and Asian cultures but through both of them (Inoue, 2003:128), and cultures that are depicted as communitarian (e.g., Asian, Islamic, or indigenous) may have strong strains of individualism and individual rights references as well (Arat, 2000; Holder and Corntassel, 2002).

Nevertheless, the "Asian values" argument continues to be summoned and similar communal model of social organization and communitarian values are put forward by some individuals and groups in African countries, who see the universalist human rights claims based on the Universal Declaration of Human Rights and other UN conventions as not relevant to or compatible with "traditional African culture" (Welch and Meltzer, 1994). Those who take the universalist position argue that such relativist claims are made only to help the ruling classes to stay in power (Howard, 1986: 25). Yet, like their Asian counterparts, elite groups in Africa are far from establishing a united relativist front.

The African Charter on Human and Peoples' Rights, which was negotiated and adopted by African states and entered into force in 1986, is clearly a universalist document. While its emphasis on collective rights and duties is noteworthy, it also embodies all individual rights included in the Universal Declaration of Human Rights.

Equality of Sexes in Islam

The International Bill of Rights and other human rights instruments stress the principle of equality in maintaining human dignity. The equality principle is reiterated in nondiscrimination clauses of all human rights documents. However, some resistance to the notions of equality and equal treatment of individuals is observed in practices that assign separate notions of dignity to different persons. This is most common among some Muslim clergy and state officials who oppose the equality of sexes as intended in the International Bill of Rights. They argue that in Islam, sexes are equal in terms of their value but the roles of men and women in the society are meant to be complementary, not identical. Having different responsibilities, men and women cannot have the same and equal rights.

Muslims believe that the law is given by God and believers are obliged to follow the divine law, so international human rights treaties would be accepted as binding Muslim states as long as they are compatible with what is considered to be the Islamic Law, the *Shari'ah*. Following this approach led some Muslim statesmen to produce an Islamic Declaration of Human Rights, which serves as an alternative to the Universal Declaration. The Cairo Declaration on Human Rights in Islam was adopted by the foreign ministers of the members of the Organization of Islamic Conference at its Cairo meeting on August 5, 1990. It contains various discriminatory clauses and displays substantial deficiencies with regard to women's rights and equality (Mayer, 1999, 1994). Article 6 of the Cairo Declaration starts with a promising statement that "Woman is equal to man in human dignity, and has rights to enjoy as well as duties to perform," but in stipulating her rights, it says only that "she has her own civil entity and financial independence, and the right to retain her name and lineage." On the other hand, it rejects the principle of equality between husband and wife in the union of marriage and recognizes several rights and freedoms, including the freedoms of movement, selecting residence, and seeking asylum, for men only.

The Cairo Declaration further specifies that "all the rights and freedoms stipulated in this Declaration are subject to the Islamic Shari'ah" (Article 24) and reaffirms that "the Islamic Shari'ah is the only source of reference for the explanation or clarification of any of the articles of this Declaration" (Article 25). Similarly, some Muslim states that became parties to the United Nations' Convention on the Elimination of All Forms of Discrimination against Women placed reservations on several articles of the Convention on the grounds that they would be incompatible with the Islamic Shari'ah or reserved the right to uphold the provisions of the Convention only if they are consistent with the Islamic Shari'ah (Arat, 2003).

The *Shari'ah,* however, is not a uniform code and its sources, the *Qur'an, Hadith* (the sayings of the Prophet Mohammad), and *Sunna* (the tradition set by the Prophet), are subject to interpretation. The traditional and prevailing interpretations have been unfavorable to women, but some Muslim jurists and scholars, such as Sheikh Rached Al-Ghannouchi (in *Islam and Justice,* 1997), Abdullahi An-Na'im (1990), and Mahmoud Mohamed Taha (1987), challenge the traditional method of interpretation and dispute the validity of the sexually discriminatory interpretations (see also Afshari, 1994; Arat, 2000; Barazangi, 1997; Engineer, 1992; Roald, 1998; Stowasser, 1998; Wadud, 1999). The diversity in interpretation and the different applications of religious beliefs to human rights surfaced when the draft declaration was debated by the Third Committee of the UN General Assembly in 1948. The representatives of Muslim countries were far from presenting a consensus, and they took very different positions on articles that maintained the equality of sexes in family relations and the freedom to change one's religion (Glendon, 2001:153–155, 168; Waltz, 2004:813–819).

Indigenous Peoples and Premodern Claims

The concept of human rights has developed gradually in different parts of the world and the scope of human rights has been expanding as a response to social and technological changes. As a product of the twentieth century, the International Bill of Rights responds to the violations of human dignity that have become evident in modern and industrial societies. The rights to employment, fair wages, and equal remuneration for work of equal value, for example, are clearly relevant only to those societies that fashioned economies organized around wage labor—a modern notion. Thus, the relevance of some rights, as well as what constitutes a violation of human dignity, is questioned by some indigenous groups that were left out of the negotiation process in the formulation of human rights declarations and treaties. As noted by Richard Falk, "What human rights and self-determination mean to various indigenous peoples was not at all reflected in the Universal Declaration and the Covenants, which are drafted on the assumption of protecting individuals living in *modern* [industrial] societies" (Falk, 2000:62–63 emphasis added).

In 1957, the International Labour Organization (ILO) drafted Convention No. 106 in an effort to address indigenous populations' concerns, but the measures in this convention followed the nondiscrimination principle and attempted to increase indigenous peoples' access and integration into the larger society. Improving access and integration into modern society may unwittingly lay dangerous traps of assimilation and serve to deny cultural identities of individuals and people. In 1977, a global network of indigenous peoples started to prepare a declaration that would emphasize their various and distinct cultures and status and their right to self-determination. In 1982, a Sub-Commission on the Prevention of Discrimination and Protection of Minorities of the UN Human Rights Commission formed the Informal Working Group of Indigenous Populations, which produced the UN Draft Declaration on the Rights of Indigenous Peoples, in 1994 (UN Doc. e/CN.4/Sub.2/1994/2/Add.1, 20 April 1994).

Indigenous peoples challenge the current understanding of the rights that are articulated in the international documents and consider some definitions as inconsistent with their values, practices, and structures. For example, in international human rights documents corporal punishment is deemed to be a violation of personal integrity and can be treated as a form of torture, but some indigenous populations claim that in their cultures imprisonment as a punishment is considered more torturous than the shame and physical pain inflicted by whipping (Barsh, 1999).

The common cause and concerns of the indigenous populations is noted by a Kanien'kehaka (Mohawk) leader, who has been working on the advancement of the indigenous rights by using the UN system:

We never knew that indigenous people were so global, but we find that we have the same common problems and the same kind of world-view in most cases. That's why, in the drafting of the UN Draft Declaration of the Rights of Indigenous Peoples, it was easy for indigenous people to come to an agreement on what our rights are. It's easy for us to agree. The hard part is to get governments to see the Declaration as necessary and not so threatening. (Holder and Corntassel, 2002:141)

The states resist the indigenous claims with a concern over the fragmentation of rights and with the fear that the self-determination claims may be pretexts for secessionist movements.

However, the indigenous populations' demand for dignity as peoples and their right to self-determination, as well as the alternative conceptualizations of rights, are received mostly with sympathy within the international human rights community. Nevertheless, claims that are based on cultural distinctiveness are also viewed as constituting potential problems for the advancement of human rights. The right to self-determination and preservation of cultures can undermine the equal rights principle, especially if the culture in question embodies hierarchal structures and discriminatory norms. Gender equality and other emancipatory aspects of the international human rights regime can be jeopardized in the name of cultural preservation or celebration of "multiculturalism" (Okin, 1999). Human rights advocates are warned that cultural relativism and the right to self-determination, in undemocratic contexts where community members are not allowed to interpret the cultural sources and determine their own lives, may end up serving only as shields of protection for the privileged (Arat, 2003).

In recognizing diversity, it is crucial also to recognize that cultures are both fragmented and dynamic. Respect for cultural diversity has to be accompanied by cultural freedom, rather than an indiscriminant and forced preservation of traditions. The United Nations Development Programme promotes *cultural liberty*, defined as "the capability of people to live and be what they choose, with adequate opportunity to consider other options," as the way of maintaining cultural diversity, as an alternative to cultural conservativism that focuses on "preserving values and practices as an end in itself with blind allegiance to tradition" (*Human Development Report 2004:4*).

The Construction of Human Rights: Further Support for Universalism

Although the current vocabulary of human rights is rooted in Western philosophical writings, as discussed in Chapter 1, the notion of human rights was not alien to other cultures. If all societies have developed some human rights notions, then to what extent have the non-Western philosophies and understandings of human rights found expression in the international human rights documents? Or, how valid are the arguments that the International Bill of Rights is based on Western philosophy and culture?

Challenges to universalism can be addressed by two arguments that refer to historical records. First, although all societies had human rights notions, they also had discriminatory norms and practices, and many of the rights that are recognized in the International Bill of Rights have been violated in all parts of the world, including the Western countries. Second, international human rights documents, starting with the Universal Declaration of Human Rights, are outcomes of negotiations that involved people from different countries, including representatives of non-Western countries with backgrounds in Asian, Muslim, or other cultural and religious values.

A critical examination of Western philosophical texts would reveal that even the natural rights philosophers, who are revered for supporting universalism, not only recognized fewer rights than those covered in the International Bill of Rights, but they also viewed some humans as not capable of being rights-bearers. For example, in John Locke's writings, the inalienable natural rights—namely life, liberty and estate—are claimed to be held only by land-owning men, and only that small group of people is trusted with the governance of the nation and political rights. His elitism not only disenfranchises landless men and all women but it also justifies slavery (Locke, 1952:47–48, paragraph 85). Though more egalitarian, John Stuart Mill also violates the principle of universalism when he writes about "those backward states of society in which the race itself may be considered as in its nonage" and thus not entitled to claim human rights (Mill, 1974:69). The medieval church, which advanced the natural rights doctrine, repressed freedom of religion and justified hierarchal systems and various forms of discrimination. St. Thomas Aquinas, for example, in the first production of things (*Summa Theologicae,* Question XCII, Article 1), questioned why God would even create a "misbegotten or defective" creature like woman. With the rise of Western imperialism, the dehumanization of "the other" became a common practice (Lauren, 1998). In fact, colonialism, with its policies of exploitation, economic oppression, and political repression, involved violations of all kinds of human rights and the principle of universalism. Finally, even on the domestic front, all forms of abuse, ranging from torture to starvation, were rampant and continued regardless of the humanist values advocated during the "Age of Enlightenment." Discrimination on the basis of sex, race, and ethnicity still prevails today. Even Louis Henkin, who argues that "the idea of rights as a political principle in a political theory prescribing relations between individual and society may have been articulated by some Western philosophers," notes that this idea "is not more congenial to Western societies than to others" (Henkin, 1990:27–28). The U.S. government approach and policies, as well as the human rights conditions in this country, can serve as telling testament to Henkin's point. (See Chapter 4.)

The second argument in favor of the universal relevance of international human rights is that the Universal Declaration and the other human rights documents were formulated through debates that involved participants and input from different cultures. The eighteen-member Human Rights Commission of the UN, which drafted the Universal Declaration, included not only the five Great Powers (China, France, the United Kingdom, the United States, and the USSR) but also thirteen other UN members that would rotate at three-year intervals. The first commission, which was established in 1946, included delegates from Australia, Belgium, Byelorussia, Chile, China, Egypt, France, India, Iran, Lebanon, Panama, the Philippines, Ukraine, USSR, the United Kingdom, the United States, Uruguay, and Yugoslavia (Glendon, 2001:32). Two of the three main intellectual forces in the drafting subcommittee, Charles Malik and Peng-chun Chang, being from Lebanon and China, respectively, had roots in Middle-Eastern and Asian cultures. Both the United Nations Secretariat and UNESCO tried to compile information about the conceptualization and formulation of human rights in different societies and philosophical traditions (Glendon, 2001; Humphrey, 1984; Morsink, 1999). Moreover, once the commission submitted its draft to the "Third Committee" of the General Assembly, the chair of the committee, Charles Malik, deliberately allowed long and tedious discussions of every single article, in order to ensure the development of consensus and "a sense of ownership" among the member states (Glendon, 2001:143–144).

As a good portion of the world population was still under colonial rule at that time, the United Nations, having less than sixty member states, was far from being a global organization when it adopted the Universal Declaration. However, the transcripts of the debates show that the representative of non-Western states were very active and made their views known (Morsink, 1999; Waltz, 2001, 2002, 2004). Later, the de-colonization process that peaked in the early 1960s expanded the membership of the United Nations and allowed more diverse views to be expressed during the drafting of the two covenants (Humphrey, 1984). In fact some items ultimately included in the Declaration and the two covenants were not proposed or embraced by the representatives of Western states; several rights and their wording in the documents faced resistance from the major powers (Glendon, 2001; Morsink, 1999).

Thus, arguments claiming that the International Bill of Rights is an expression of Western philosophy or culture are not based on empirical evidence. Yet it is still worth mentioning that when the draft declaration was debated at the Third Committee, some delegates expressed interest in specifying the spiritual or theoretical foundations of the rights, but others, including P. C. Chang (China), Mrs. Lakshmi Menon (India), and Salomon Grumbach (France), argued against it. The point was made that "the nations should and could reach practical agreement on basic principles of human rights without achieving a consensus on their foundations" (Glendon, 2001:147).

In addition to the interrelatedness and interdependency of human rights, the principles of universalism have been accepted and underscored in various international declarations and conventions. The Vienna Declaration and Programme for Action of 1993 asserts: "All human rights are universal, indivisible, and interdependent and interrelated. The international community must treat human rights globally in a fair and equal manner, on the same footing, and with the same emphasis" (UN Doc. A/CONF.157/23 [12 July 1993]). The same principles were reiterated in the outcome document of the 2005 World Summit, in paragraph 13, which reads: "We reaffirm the universality, indivisibility, interdependence and interrelatedness of all human rights," and in paragraph 121:

We reaffirm that all human rights are universal, indivisible, interrelated, interdependent and mutually reinforcing and that all human rights must be treated in a fair and equal manner, on the same footing and with the same emphasis. While the significance of national and regional particularities and various historical, cultural and religious backgrounds must be borne in mind, all States, regardless of their political, economic and cultural systems, have the duty to promote and protect all human rights and fundamental freedoms. (A/RES/60/1)

A recent declaration by the American Anthropological Association, issued in 1999, defines the Universal Declaration of Human Rights and related international law as the baseline of human rights that includes "collective as well as individual rights, cultural, social and economic development, and a clean and safe environment" as having universal relevance, yet with an understanding that "human rights is not a static concept" but one that is constantly evolving as we come to know more about the human condition" (AAA, 1999).

References

AAA. "Declaration on Anthropology and Human Rights." Committee for Human Rights, American Anthropological Association. June 1999. http://www.aaanet.org/stmts/humanrts.htm (accessed September 16, 2005).

Afshari, Reza. "An Essay on Islamic Cultural Relativism in the Discourse of Human Rights." *Human Rights Quarterly* 16:2 (1994): 235–276.

Alston, Philip. "The Importance of the Inter-play between Economic, Social and Cultural Rights, and Civil and Political Rights." In *Human Rights at the Dawn of the 21st Century*, Proceedings of the Interregional Meeting organized by the Council of Europe in advance of the World Conference on Human Rights, palais de l'Europe, Strasbourg, January 28–30, 1993. Strasbourg: Council of Europe Press, 1993:59–74.

An-Na'im, Abdullahi. *Toward an Islamic Reformation: Civil Liberties, Human Rights, and International Law.* Syracuse, NY: Syracuse University Press, 1990.

Arat, Zehra F. "Human Rights and Democracy: Expanding or Contracting." *Polity* 32:1 (Fall 1999): 119–144.

Arat, Zehra F. "Women's Rights in Islam: Revisiting Qur'anic Rights." In Peter Schwab and Adamantia Pollis, eds., *Human Rights: New Perspectives, New Realities*. Boulder, CO: Lynne Rienner, 2000:69–93.

Arat, Zehra F. Kabasakul. "Promoting Women's Rights against Patriarchal Claims: The Women's Convention and Reservations by Muslim States." In David Forsythe and Patrice McMahon, eds., *Global Human Rights Norms: Area Studies Revisited*. Lincoln: Nebraska University Press, 2003:231–251.

Barazangi, Nimat Hafez. "Muslim Women's Islamic Higher Learning as a Human Right." In Mahnaz Afkhami and Erika Friedle, eds., *Muslim Women and the Politics of Participation: Implementing the Beijing Platform*. Syracuse, NY: Syracuse University Press, 1997:43–57.

Barsh, Russell. "The Fortunate Unmeasurability of Human Rights." Paper presented at the Conference titled "Towards an Indicators System in Human Rights," International Institute for the Sociology of Law, Oñati, Gipuzkoa, Spain, September 16–17, 1999.

Bauer, Joanne R., and Bell, Daniel A., eds. *The East Asian Challenge for Human Rights*. New York: Cambridge University Press, 1999.

Bell, Lynda S., Nathan, Andrew J., and Peleg, Ilan., eds. *Negotiating Culture and Human Rights*. New York: Columbia University Press, 2001.

Bergmann, Frithjof. "Two Critiques of the Traditional Theory of Human Rights." In J. R. Pennock and J. W. Chapman, eds., *Human Rights*. New York: New York University Press, 1981:52–57.

Bobbio, Norberto. *The Age of Rights*, rev. ed. Oxford: Blackwell, 1995.

Charvet, John. "A Critique of Human Rights." In J. R. Pennock and J. W. Chapman, eds., *Human Rights*. New York: New York University Press, 1981:31–51.

Cranston, Maurice. "Human Rights, Real and Supposed," and "Human Rights: A Reply to Professor Raphael." In D. D. Raphael, ed., *Political Theory and the Rights of Man*. Bloomington: Indiana University Press, 1967:43–53 and 95–100.

Diamond, Larry, et al., eds. *Consolidating the Third Way of Democracies: Regional Challenges*. Baltimore: Johns Hopkins University Press, 1997.

Donnelly, Jack. *Universal Human Rights in Theory and Practice*. New York: Cornell University Press, 1989.

Donnelly, Jack. *International Human Rights*, 2nd ed. Boulder, CO: Westview Press, 1998.

Downie, R.S. "Social Equality." In A. S. Rosenbaum, ed., *The Philosophy of Human Rights: International Perspectives*. Westport, CT.: Greenwood Press, 1980:127–176.

Dworkin, Ronald. "Taking Rights Seriously." In Morton E. Winston, ed., *The Philosophy of Human Rights*. Belmont, CA: Wadsworth, 1989:96–113.

Engineer, Asghar Ali. *The Rights of Women in Islam*. New York: St. Martin's Press, 1992.

Falk, Richard. *Human Rights Horizons: The Pursuit of Justice in a Globalizing World*. New York: Routledge, 2000.

Freeman, Michael. *Human Rights: An Interdisciplinary Approach*. Cambridge, UK: Polity Press, 2002.

Gavison, Ruth. "On the Relationship between Civil and Political Rights, and Social and Economic Rights." In Jean-Marc Coicaud, Michael W. Doyle, and Anne-Marie Gardner, eds., *The Globalization of Human Rights*. Tokyo: United Nations University Press, 2003:23–55.

Glendon, Mary Ann. *A World Made New*. New York: Random House, 2001.

Hamm, Brigitte I. "A Human Rights Approach to Development." *Human Rights Quarterly* 23:4 (November 2001): 1005–10031.

Henkin, Louis. *The Age of Rights*. New York: Columbia University Press, 1990.

Holder, Cindy, and Corntassel, Jeff J. "Indigenous Peoples and Multicultural Citizenship: Bridging Collective and Individual Rights." *Human Rights Quarterly* 24:1 (February 2002): 126–151.

Howard, Rhoda. *Human Rights in Commonwealth Africa*. Totowa, NJ: Rowman and Littlefield, 1986.

Howard, Rhoda E., and Donnelly, Jack. "Human Dignity, Human Rights, and Political Regimes." *American Political Science Review* 80 (September 1986): 801–817.

Human Development Report 2000. United Nations Development Programme. New York: Oxford University Press, 2000.

Human Development Report 2002. United Nations Development Programme. New York: Oxford University Press, 2002.

Human Development Report 2004. United Nations Development Programme. New York: Oxford University Press, 2004.

Humphrey, John P. *Human Rights and the United Nations: A Great Adventure*. Dobbs Ferry, NY: Transnational, 1984.

Inoue, Tatsuo. "Human Rights and Asian Values." In Jean-Marc Coicaud, Michael W. Doyle, and Anne-Marie Gardner, eds., *The Global-*

ization of Human Rights. Tokyo: United Nations University Press, 2003:116–133.

Islam and Justice: Debating the Future of Human Rights in the Middle East and North Africa. New York: Lawyers Committee for Human Rights, 1997.

Kamenka, Eugene. "Nationalism: Ambiguous Legacies and Contingent Futures." *Political Studies* 41 (Special Issue, 1993): 78–92.

Korey, William. *NGOs and the Universal Declaration of Human Rights: "A Curious Grapevine."* New York: St. Martin's Press, 1998.

Lakoff, Sanford. "Autonomy and Liberal Democracy." *The Review of Politics* 42 (Summer 1990): 378–396.

Lauren, Paul Gordon. *The Evolution of International Human Rights: Visions Seen.* Philadelphia, University of Pennsylvania Press, 1998.

Lipset, Seymour M. "Some Social Requisites of Democracy: Economic Development and Political Legitimacy." *American Political Science Review* 53 (March 1959): 69–105.

Locke, John. *The Second Treatise of Government.* Edited by Thomas P. Peardon. New York: Macmillan, 1952.

MacMillan, Michael C. "Social versus Political Rights." *Canadian Journal of Political Science* 19:2 (June 1986): 283–304.

Marshall, T. H. *Class, Citizenship and Social Development.* Garden City, NY: Doubleday, 1964.

Mayer, Ann Elizabeth. "Universal versus Islamic Human Rights: A Clash of Cultures or a Clash with a Construct?" *Michigan Journal of International Law* 15:2 (Winter 1994): 307–429.

Mayer, Ann Elizabeth. *Islam and Human Rights: Tradition and Politics,* 3rd ed. Boulder, CO: Westview Press, 1999.

Mayo, Bernard. "What Are Human Rights?" In D. D. Raphael, ed., *Political Theory and the Rights of Man.* Bloomington: Indiana University Press, 1967:68–80.

Mill, John Stuart. *On Liberty.* Middlesex: Penguin Books, 1974.

Morsink, Johannes. *The Universal Declaration of Human Rights: Origins, Drafting, and Intent.* Philadelphia: University of Pennsylvania Press, 1999.

Nickel, James. *Making Sense of Human Rights.* Berkeley: University of California Press, 1987.

Okin, Susan M. "Liberty and Welfare: Some Issues in Human Rights Theory." In J. R. Pennock and J. W. Chapman, eds., *Human Rights.* New York: New York University Press, 1981:240–251.

Okin, Susan M. *Is Multiculturalism Bad for Women?* Princeton, NJ: Princeton University Press, 1999.

Parekh, Bhikhu. "The Cultural Particularity of Liberal Democracy." *Political Studies* 40 (Special Issue, 1992): 160–175.

Peffer, Rodney. "A Defense of Rights to Well-Being." *Philosophy and Public Affairs* 8:1 (Fall 1978): 63–87.

Pollis, Adamantia, and Schwab, Peter. "Human Rights: A Western Construct with Limited Applicability." In Adamantia Pollis and Peter Schwab, eds., *Human Rights: Cultural and Ideological Perspectives.* New York: Praeger, 1980:1–18.

Raphael, D. D. "The Rights of Man and the Rights of the Citizens." In D. D. Raphael, ed., *Political Theory and the Rights of Man.* Bloomington: Indiana University Press, 1967.

Roald, Anne Sofie. " Feminist Reinterpretation of Islamic Sources: Muslim Feminist Theology in the Light of the Christian Tradition of Feminist Thought." In Karin Ask and Marit Tjomsland, eds., *Women and Islamization: Contemporary Dimensions of Discourse on Gender Relations.* Oxford: Berg, 1998.

Sano, Hans-Otto. "Development and Human Rights: The Necessary, but Partial Integration of Human Rights and Development." *Human Rights Quarterly* 22:3 (August 2000): 734–751.

Schneider, Peter. "Social Rights and the Concept of Human Rights." In D. D. Raphael, ed., *Political Theory and the Rights of Man.* Bloomington: Indiana University Press, 1967:81–97.

Sen, Amartya. *Inequality Reexamined.* Cambridge, MA: Harvard University Press, 1992.

Sen, Amartya. *Development as Freedom.* New York: Alfred Knopf, 1999.

Sengupta, Arjun. "On the Theory and Practice of the Right to Development." *Human Rights Quarterly* 24:4 (November 2002): 837–889.

Shue, Henry. *Basic Rights: Subsistence, Affluence, and U.S. Foreign Policy.* Princeton, NJ: Princeton University Press, 1980.

Stowasser, Barbara. "Gender Issues and Contemporary Quran Interpretation." In Yvonne Yazbeck Haddad and John Esposito, eds., *Islam, Gender, and Social Change.* Oxford: Oxford University Press, 1998:30–44.

Taha, Mahmoud Mohamed. *The Second Message of Islam.* Syracuse, NY: Syracuse University Press, 1987.

Tseng, Chien-Yuan. "On People's Human Rights (Part 1)." Association for Asian Reseach. (January 8, 2003). http://www.asianresearch.org/articles/1150.html Visited: February 19, 2005.

Wadud, Amina. *Qur'an and Woman: Rereading the Sacred Text from a Woman's Perspective.* New York: Oxford University Press, 1999.

Waltz, Susan. "Universalizing Human Rights: The Role of Small States in the Construction of Universal Declaration of Human Rights." *Human Rights Quarterly* 23:1 (February 2001): 44–72.

Waltz, Susan. "Reclaiming and Rebuilding the History of the Universal Declaration of Human Rights." *Third World Quarterly* 23:3 (2002): 437–448.

Waltz, Susan. "Universal Human Rights: The Contribution of Muslim States." *Human Rights Quarterly* 26:4 (November 2004): 799–844.

Welch, Claude E., and Meltzer, R. I., eds., *Human Rights and Development in Africa.* Albany, NY: State University of New York Press, 1994.

Wellman, Carl. *The Proliferation of Rights: Moral Progress or Empty Rhetoric?* Boulder, CO: Westview Press, 1999.

Wellman, Carl. "Solidarity, the Individual and Human Rights." *Human Rights Quarterly* 22:3 (August 2000): 639–657.

3

Persistent and Current Human Rights Issues

Human rights are universal, indivisible, interrelated, and interdependent. While they are mutually reinforcing, the violation of one right could lead to the violation of other rights. This interdependency creates nests of interrelated issues that affect the realization of all human rights. Chapter 3, under the following subheadings, examines some of the major areas that have presented challenges to the advancement of human rights and efforts to overcome these challenges:

1. Racism and Ethnic Cleansing
2. Abuse in Custody: Prisoners, Torture, and Police Brutality
3. Armed Conflicts and International Violence: Arms Trade, Child Soldiers, Land Mines, and Terrorism
4. Global Refugee Crisis
5. Economic Crises: Globalization, Poverty, and Debt
6. Labor Rights, Child Labor, and Corporate Accountability
7. Gender Discrimination and Women's Rights
8. Environmental Protection and Rights

Racism and Ethnic Cleansing

One of the most significant challenges to the advancement of human rights or an important catalyst to their violation has been racism. Racism, embedded in sociocultural structures, exists in all societies in various degrees in overt or subtle forms. Racism is a contravention of human rights: while the universalism of human rights calls for nondiscrimination, racism uses mainly biological differences as markers to collapse individuals and people into categories of superiors and inferiors. Although modern genetic sciences have not been able to sort people into racial groups, physical features of people such as skin color or hair texture are continuously employed to construct racial identities and to discriminate against people.

While racism may be as old as human history, it has assumed more severe forms in modern times, parallel to the advancement of capitalism, the racialized trans-Atlantic slave trade, and European colonial enterprises. As Europeans subjugated most of the people in other parts of the world, racism was employed to justify the domination of people who did not necessarily share the lighter skin or other physical features of the prototypical European.

As race is mainly a culturally constructed notion, racism and racial discrimination can be extended to groups that are biologically similar but demonstrate cultural differences (e.g., language or religion). Then, ethnic differences come to the forefront and are used as grounds for discrimination or even genocide, as in the case of the ethnic conflicts observed in the 1990s in what was then Yugoslavia. Racism can take the form of organized hate groups such as the Ku Klux Klan in the United States, discrimination in housing and employment in Great Britain, social and ethnic exclusion in France, xenophobic skinheads and neo-Nazis in Germany, and outright genocide in Bosnia and Rwanda in the 1990s and in the Darfur region of Sudan in 2003.

Numerous theories have attempted to explain the origin of racism and individuals' propensity to hold racist beliefs and attitudes and to demonstrate racist behavior. Economic theories have been particularly well defined and noteworthy in this regard. Some survey studies in the United States found racism to be more common among lower classes. It is argued that poor people who are frustrated and desperate tend to think that other ethnic or racial groups are taking their jobs, but there is also a great deal of prejudice and discrimination among people who have attained a certain level of success and income and who want to protect this by building social and racial barriers to keep others out (Wieviorka, 1996:10–14).

When racism becomes extreme, it can take the form of ethnic cleansing. Andrew Bell-Fialkoff defines population cleansing as the planned, deliberate removal from a certain territory of an undesirable population distinguished by one or more characteristics such as ethnicity, religion, race, class, or sexual preference. These characteristics must serve as the basis for removal for the violence to be termed *ethnic cleansing* (Bell-Fialkoff, 1996:3). Cleansing can involve forced migration, deportation, and extermination, which may be used in different stages of the conflict or simultaneously. Usually, racial pressures increase when there is political instability. Looking to blame some other force, a government losing popularity may incite racism and intolerance that then leads to ethnic violence.

Most of the struggles against racism are geared toward dealing with its consequences. Several humanitarian organizations try to help victims of racism. The United Nations created the High Commissioner for Refugees to assist displaced people, many of whom are escaping racially charged hostilities and ethnic cleansing. The Southern Poverty Law Center in Montgomery, Alabama, maintains a Klanwatch program that keeps tabs on the Ku Klux Klan and other hate groups in the United States, including those established on the Internet. The organization has also developed videos and teaching materials that are distributed at low cost as a part of its Teaching Tolerance program. Among other organizations that work to discourage racism and violence is the Simon Wiesenthal Center; it disseminates information about hate groups and operates the Museum of Tolerance in Los Angeles, which seeks to promote intercultural understanding and information about the Nazi genocide. The UN Subcommittee on Prevention of Discrimination and Protection of Minorities investigates racial issues and uses advocacy and promotion of human rights to help counter racism.

In 1997, the UN General Assembly agreed to hold a World Conference against Racism, Racial Discrimination, Xenophobia and Related Intolerance. The main objectives included reviewing the factors that lead to racism, racial discrimination, and xenophobia; assessing the progress made in fighting against racism as well as the obstacles to preventing racism; increasing the level of awareness about racism and related intolerance; and formulating recommendations. The conference was held in Durban, South Africa, between August 31 and September 7, 2001, and was attended by top government officials from several countries and numerous non-governmental organizations (NGOs). The developing country delegations insisted on reparations for European and American racism that had disturbed the economic and social fabric of their societies during the periods of imperial expansion, trans-Atlantic slave trade, and colonial rule; they also were highly critical of Israel's policies in the occupied territories, condemning Zionism as racism. Developing countries' demands did not compel the powerful industrial countries to elevate the message of the conference, and the conference ended with a widely shared sense of disappointment.

Abuse in Custody: Prisoners, Torture, and Police Brutality

Human rights apply to all human beings; even those who are in custody or imprisoned for committing crimes are entitled to the protection of their rights. Unfortunately, prison conditions worldwide do not meet minimum standards, and security forces in many countries commit abuses and engage in torture. Perhaps the biggest challenge to improving prison conditions is changing the pervasive view that prisoners deserve what they get and that a prison should be a place where offenders are thoroughly punished for their crimes.

The UN Standard Minimum Rules for the Treatment of Prisoners is the most widely known and accepted document regulating prison conditions. Although these standards are known to prison administrators all over the world, they are seldom fully enforced. Human Rights Watch, one of the largest international human rights organizations, reports that millions of prisoners are confined in filth without adequate food or medical care, with little or nothing to do, and in constant threat of violence either from other inmates or from their guards (Human Rights Watch Prison Project, 1993). In addition to the overall low quality of care, many conditions represent more extreme and unusually cruel treatment. Human Rights Watch has documented excessive use of solitary confinement and overemphasis on rules in Japan, often fatal assaults on inmates by guards in South Africa, and sexual abuse of women prisoners in the United States. Children are often abused and shackled in U.S. detention facilities, and super-maximum security prisons, where prisoners face extreme social isolation, enforced idleness, and extraordinarily limited recreational and educational opportunities, are appearing all over the country. Women inmates tend to experience further degrading treatment and abuse, which often take the form of sexual assaults by prison guards and other correction officers (Human Rights Watch, "Women in Custody," 2005).

In addition to the International Covenant on Civil and Political Rights, created to protect the physical integrity of people, the UN Convention against Torture and Other Cruel, Inhuman or Degrading Treatment or Punishment was adopted in 1984 and entered into force on June 26, 1987. As of May 2005, 146 countries were party to this convention. Yet torture continues to be common and documented in many nations around the world. Officials in some countries favor methods that leave little evidence of torture, whereas others are unconcerned about whether the procedure leaves marks. Torture is often part of a larger plan of terror designed to keep people oppressed. It is frequently used in conjunction with disappearances to ensure compliance. Generally torturers view their victims as less than human. When people are dehumanized, they are easier to maltreat. One study found that torturers felt they were serving their countries by performing torture (Crelinsten and Schmid, 1995).

More recently, the ill-treatment and torture of prisoners by U.S. Army personnel in Afghanistan, the photographed and widely publicized abuse of Iraqis held at the Abu Ghraib prison in Iraq, and the various allegations about the conditions and treatment of individuals accused of terrorism by the United States and detained in Guantánamo Bay in Cuba have led to protests invoking various human rights and humanitarian laws (e.g., the Geneva Conventions). (See also Chapter 4.)

The UN Human Rights Commission investigates human rights abuses, including claims of torture. Several human rights organizations, national or international, also work to pressure governments to make changes. Amnesty International is perhaps the most outspoken against cruel punishments, prison conditions, and torture. An organization in Minnesota, the Center for Victims of Torture, helps victims recover from the physical and emotional wounds they have sustained through torture.

Armed Conflicts and International Violence: Arms Trade, Child Soldiers, Land Mines, and Terrorism

The end of the Second World War marked not only the birth of a human rights regime under the auspices of the United Nations but also the beginning of a major conflict. The period, roughly between 1945 and 1990, is referred to as the Cold War. The term refers to the state of conflict between the two superpowers, the United States and the Soviet Union, and their military allies, respectively organized in NATO and the Warsaw Pact, which had military forces that were armed and mobilized but did not actually fight. Although the super powers and their military allies did not attack each other or engaged in direct warfare, the Cold War period was saddled by several military conflicts around the world, most of which were instigated by the superpower conflict and rivalry and thus served as proxy wars between the two superpowers. The collapse of the Berlin Wall in November 1989 and the subsequent disintegration of the Soviet Union ended the Cold War but not the conflicts between the parties that were drawn into proxy wars or supported by rival superpowers (e.g., North and South Korea, India and Pakistan, various internal conflicts in African states such as Angola, Mozambique, and Somalia). In fact, new conflicts emerged afterward (e.g., between Armenia and Azerbaijan, Chechnya and Russia), some of which can be classified as civil wars (e.g., Rwanda, Yugoslavia).

Wars and other forms of armed conflicts create conditions that are definitely unsuitable for the protection of human rights. They cause numerous deaths, disabilities, displacement of people, and economic hardship. Spending money on arms always means channeling resources away from important services that would help meet people's basic needs and human rights, especially in developing countries. However, the arms trade is a big business, in which the industrial countries are the main suppliers. Between 1993 and 2000, arms transfer agreements with developing nations comprised 67.7 percent of all arms purchases worldwide and reached 69 percent in 2000, with a value of over $25.4 billion; the United States, Russia, and France have dominated the arms market, and as the top ranking country, between 1997 and 2000, the United States made $31.5 billion from its arms transfer agreements with developing nations (Grimmett, 2001). Moreover, arms manufacturers enjoy substantial federal subsidies, which have made some critics call the practice "welfare for weapons dealers" (Hartung, 1996).

A problem that has become more apparent in the recent military conflicts is the dependence of rival armies and militias on child soldiers. Arguably, some wars and armed conflicts are sustained by recruiting the young. Although the majority of the child soldiers around the world might have been recruited by private militia or opposition groups (Smolin, 2000:964), several states, including the United States, routinely recruit children in their late teens. Younger ones, sometimes no more than seven or eight years of age, are recruited in times of civil war. After studying recruitment in 180 countries, Human Rights Watch reports that "more than 300,000 children are fighting with governments and armed groups in more than 40 countries. . . . In 87 countries children are recruited into government armed forces, paramilitaries, civil militia and non-state armed groups," and although seventy-three countries uphold the principle that no one under the age of eighteen will be recruited militarily, "the situation remains unclear in 25 countries." The report also notes that child soldiers "receive little or no training before being thrust into the front lines," are subject to brutal treatment and punishment "for their mistakes or desertion," and girls in particular are at risk of rape and sexual slavery (Human Rights Watch, 2001).

In its effort to stop the recruitment and participation of children younger than eighteen in armed conflicts, the UN adopted an optional protocol to the Convention on the Rights of the Child in May 2000. In December 2000, the World Veterans Federation passed a resolution calling for universal ratification of the protocol.

The destruction caused by wars and armed conflicts and their threat to human rights continue even after the actual fighting is over. Land mines have been particularly notorious for having such an impact. Land mines kill or maim over 26,000 people annually. Ninety percent of the casualties are civilians going about normal activities—gathering water, working in fields, and traveling on rural roads. In the 1990s, experts estimated that more than 100 million land mines were dispersed across seventy countries (Marshall, 1998).

Land mines were originally developed as countermeasures against tanks. The tank mines were large and easy to detect, so antipersonnel mines were developed to protect the antitank mines. Armies like land mines because they are simple to use, low-tech, and cheap. Indiscriminate use of antipersonnel mines began with the United States in Indochina during the 1960s and early 1970s, especially during attacks against Laos. The Soviets scattered "butterfly mines" over suspected guerrilla strongholds in Afghanistan after the 1979 intervention. These mines, resembling toys in their appearance, attracted many children to play with them and caused their deaths (International Committee of the Red Cross, 1994:3–35).

Maps of mine fields are seldom made and detection and demining are extremely dangerous and expensive. In Poland, 15 million land mines were cleared after World War II, but by the mid-1970s 4,000 mine-related deaths and 9,000 mine-related injuries had occurred as a result of undetected mines. Newer mines are often equipped with antihandling and antidetection devices that make deactivation even more dangerous. Mercury tilt switches can make mines detonate as soon as they are moved, and mines fitted with microprocessors detect movement and detonate. Metal detectors are often used in mine clearance, but not all mines use metal. Some have cardboard or plastic housings. Specially trained dogs can sniff out the explosives used and then the mine can be destroyed, but it costs as much as $1,000 to remove each mine, and many workers have been killed in the mine-clearing attempts (International Committee of the Red Cross, 1994).

Mines are concentrated in Central America, Africa, the former Yugoslavia, Afghanistan, Iran and Iraq in the Middle East, and Southeast Asia. Most of those affected by them live in rural areas without the medical infrastructure to handle the types of injuries sustained from land-mine explosions. In addition to direct blast injuries, severe infections occur as a result of dirt, clothing, metal, and plastic driven into tissue and bone. Consequently, many victims need to have limbs amputated, yet they often do not have access to trained medical personnel or enough money for prosthetics, rehabilitation treatment, or physical therapy.

The destructive impact of land mines is often felt in a country's economy as well, as these devices limit access to otherwise productive land. Already scarce farmland or traditional grazing lands become inaccessible because of land mines and there is a negative effect on food production, income, and the economic rights of people. Moreover, humanitarian efforts in heavily mined areas are often curtailed because of the danger.

The United Nations has worked hard to get a universal ban on land mines. The United States declared a moratorium on the sale of land mines in 1992. The most effective effort, however, has come from nongovernmental organizations (NGOs) that banded together to form the International Campaign to Ban Land Mines. This unique effort started with six organizations and eventually included over 1,000 NGOs from all over the world. The campaign lobbied governments to sign a treaty banning land mines. For their efforts, the International Campaign to Ban Landmines and its director, Jody Williams, were awarded the Nobel Peace Prize in 1997. In December of the same year, 122 nations signed a global treaty banning land mines, the Convention on the Prohibition of the Use, Stockpiling, Production and Transfer of Anti-Personnel Mines and on Their Destruction (Marshall, 1998). Although the United States pressures other countries to ban mines, it has not signed the treaty and is seeking to have exception clauses for mines used on the North Korea/South Korea border and for "smart mines" that self-destruct over time.

Another issue of violence that concerns human rights is terrorism, domestic or international. International terrorism is not a new issue but began receiving increased attention following the September 11, 2001, attacks in the United States. Dictionary definitions of terrorism relate it to political violence and define it as violence or the threat of violence carried out for political purposes. This is a rather narrow definition that ignores the violence and state of terror inflicted upon people, especially women and children, in their immediate surroundings. Terrorist acts, taking place in the private or public domain, involve a number of human rights violations, ranging from the individual's freedom of movement to the right to life. In the public domain, political terrorism (or terrorism for political purposes) is employed by both states and nonstate actors. Terrorism constitutes a human rights issue as it directly involves human rights violations; further, measures taken to prevent political terrorism may infringe on people's rights. In designing antiterrorism measures, the challenge is to strike a balance between security concerns and the protection of human rights.

International human rights law recognizes state sovereignty and the state's right to address its security concerns. All major global and regional treaties on fundamental freedoms, with the exception of the African Charter on Human and Peoples' Rights, include provisions recognizing that some rights may be derogated in time of public emergency (e.g., Article 4 of the International

Covenant on Civil and Political Rights [ICCPR]; Article 15 of the European Convention for the Protection of Human Rights and Fundamental Freedoms [ECHR]; and Article 27 of the American Convention on Human Rights [ACHR]). These conventions also mandate certain rights that are not subject to suspension under any circumstances, meaning they cannot be derogated. The right to life; freedom of thought, conscience, and religion; freedom from torture and cruel, inhuman, or degrading treatment or punishment; freedom from subjugation of to forced medical or scientific experimentation; freedom from slavery and servitude; the principle of equality before law; and the principle that criminal laws cannot be applied retroactively are specified in the ICCPR as rights that cannot be subject to derogation. Moreover, the conventions stipulate that all emergency measures restricting rights must be strictly limited in time, subject to regular review, consistent with other obligations under international law, and free of discrimination. They further require the state to inform the Secretary-General of the UN or the relevant regional organization about the provisions from which the state has derogated as well as the reasons for such action. In a General Comment issued in 2001, the UN Human Rights Committee introduced additional elements that cannot be subject to lawful derogation. General Comment No. 29, paragraph 11 reads:

> States parties may in no circumstances invoke article 4 of the Covenant as justification for acting in violation of humanitarian law or peremptory norms of international law, for instance by taking hostages, by imposing collective punishments, through arbitrary deprivations of liberty or by deviating from fundamental principles of fair trial, including the presumption of innocence. (OHCHR, 2003, Annex II)

There has been a serious concern within the human rights agencies and organizations, that the counterterrorism measures taken after the September 11 attacks fail the human rights tests. With the aim of assisting "policy makers and other concerned parties in developing a vision of counter-terrorism strategies that are fully respectful of human rights," the United Nations Office of the High Commissioner for Human Rights (OHCHR) issued a "compilation of findings of judicial and quasi-judicial bodies of the United Nations and regional organizations on the issue of the protection of human rights in the struggle against terrorism" (OHCHR, 2003). The UN High Commissioner of Human Rights, the UN Secretary-General, and NGOs have repeatedly warned that the fight against terrorism has been used by states to restrict freedoms of citizens and repress political opponents. Addressing the UN Security Council ministerial meeting on terrorism on January 20, 2003, Secretary-General Kofi Annan raised these issues and noted that "even as many are rightly praising the unity and the resolve of the international community in this crucial struggle, important and urgent questions are being asked about what might be called the 'collateral damage' of the war on terrorism— damage to the presumption of innocence, to precious human rights, to the rule of law, and to the very fabric of democratic governance" (UN press release, 2003).

Global Refugee Crisis

Wars, ethnic conflict, and state terrorism cause many people to flee their homes and seek refuge elsewhere. The number of displaced people globally has now reached the level of crisis. During the 1980s, there were 8 million international refugees worldwide. By the 1990s, there were 15 million. Only in 2004 did the trend begin to reverse; in June 17, 2005, the UN High Commissioner of Refugees (UNHCR) announced that the global number of refugees had fallen 4 percent to 9.2 million, the lowest number in almost a quarter of a century. However, this caveat was immediately added: "the total number of people of concern to UNHCR rose to 19.2 million from 17 million the previous year. This figure includes refugees, asylum seekers, returnees, stateless people and a portion of the world's internally displaced people" (UNHCR, 2005). Another estimate set the number of internally displaced people in 2004 at 25 million (*Human Development Report 2005*:296).

Most of the refugees are women and children—many of whom are fleeing from conflict zones, where rape and sexual abuse have been used as a tool of war by soldiers. In many instances agencies of the United Nations or some governments have set up camps to house the refugees fleeing across their borders. Frequently, life in the camps is not much better than the conditions the refugees fled from. Hundreds of Somali women were raped in these camps between April 1992 and November

1993, mostly by bandits, but some were raped by Kenyan soldiers and police (Barber, 1997:8–10). Moreover, these camps often become bases for opposition guerrilla fighters. The aid that flows from other governments and international humanitarian organizations is sometimes skimmed by militants based in the camps. During the 1978–1991 conflict in Cambodia, the United States and other nations funded refugee camps in Thailand that became bases for three Cambodian guerrilla forces fighting the Vietnamese-backed government. One of these was the notorious Khmer Rouge.

In 1994, 1.5 million Rwandan and 300,000 Burundian refugees who were mostly Hutus fled to Zaire and Tanzania. The refugee camps in Zaire were controlled by Hutu militiamen and former Rwandan army troops who launched attacks across the border against Rwanda's new Tutsi-dominated government. When Tutsis from Zaire smashed the camps in November 1996, more than 500,000 declined to follow the militias deeper into Zaire. They walked home to Rwanda, telling reporters that they had been held hostage for two years. In fact, there is evidence that guerrillas used physical and psychological coercion to keep them in the camps. This included withholding the news that the Rwandan government promised a safe return and spreading propaganda that the Tutsis would slaughter them if they went home. According to the International Rescue Committee, which supplied some of the sanitation and water services at the biggest camp in Zaire, the organizational structure of the camp allowed the militiamen to determine food distribution and access to hospitals, and in the militia-ran camps, the refugees were more like hostages. Pointing to these kinds of abuses, some analysts argue that refugee aid can have the effect of prolonging conflicts and civilian suffering, and they criticize powerful countries for using aid as a substitute for political initiatives that would resolve root causes of emergency migrations including war, ethnic conflict, famine, economic imbalance, and environmental damage (Barber, 1997:8–12).

Another dimension of the refugee crisis is the growing difficulty for individuals to migrate to other countries. Many countries in the West, including the United States, have tightened their immigration laws, severely limiting the numbers of refugees and asylum seekers who are allowed to settle in their borders permanently. Other countries with meager means are already facing problems in addressing the needs of their increasing and impoverished populations and are poorly equipped to accommodate the refugee demands.

In addition to the question of whether people can emigrate is the treatment of people when they arrive from other countries. Many refugees are detained while their cases are processed. In the United States, for example, refugees and asylum seekers are not legally entitled to due process and other protections set out for citizens. Some detainees linger in jails (called detention facilities) for more than a year before their cases are heard. In Britain, refugee organizations estimate that less than one-third of asylum seekers whose applications are denied leave the country or are deported, and in the 1990s, approximately 50,000 people were living in Britain without civil status and with no social or political rights ("Britain's Asylum Shambles," 1998:20).

In 1945, the UN Charter laid out principles of refugee humanitarian aid. In 1951, the UN Office of the High Commissioner for Refugees was established. One of the principal tenets of UN policy is that countries should avoid forcibly returning individuals to countries where their lives or freedom are threatened. This forcible return is called *refoulement*. Although countries have tried to avoid *refoulement*, in many instances it occurs. In the European Union, asylum seekers are often returned to "safe third countries," if they have arrived in Europe by stopping in another country first. Many potential U.S. asylum seekers have been returned under the same policy. There are often no safeguards that the "safe third country" will not return them to their country of origin. Although half of all asylum claims were granted in Europe in 1984, less than one in ten was granted in 1998 ("Britain's Asylum Shambles," 1998:20). This leaves many refugees with no choice but to go home where they fear persecution.

Economic hardship and unemployment in developing countries lead many to seek their fortunes in wealthier states. Due to the tight labor and migration rules of industrial countries, however, they are usually denied entry, and they resort to alternative means. These "economic refugees" have also been increasing in numbers, and while some manage to cross borders illegally, and start working as illegal immigrants, others try to secure entry by seeking asylum and consequently complicate and exacerbate the problems faced by refugee agencies and organizations.

Economic Crisis: Globalization, Poverty, and Debt

Globalization is a politically loaded term; it stirs emotions and divides people into camps of pro- and anti-globalization. The ambiguity of the term constitutes part of the problem, but the essence of the conflict is about the impact of globalization. Does it mean progress? If so, who are the beneficiaries and who pays for it?

The United Nations defines globalization as shrinking space, shrinking time, and disappearing of borders (*Human Development Report 1999*). This rather vague description can be clarified by defining globalization as a *process* that involves (1) increased human mobility and interaction, (2) creation of a single/integrated market, and (3) development of common norms and values. Defined as a process rather than an event, globalization is not new. It has been going on since ancient times, though technological developments, especially in transportation and communication, and sociopolitical changes have speeded up the process at certain junctures. As improvements in navigation technology and the advancement of capitalism served as the technological and social catalysts that accelerated globalization in the fifteenth and eighteenth centuries, respectively, rapid progress in communication and information technologies, as well as the collapse of the Soviet system and the end of the Cold War, has expedited the globalization process during the last two decades. Thus, in addressing the changes during these more recent periods, we can talk about a recent *phase* of globalization rather than a new phenomenon (Arat, 2005).

The impact of globalization has been mixed. Increased exchange of goods and services improved people's access to a wide range of goods and raised the income levels of many. Focusing on the increased income in some countries, certain observers have championed "globalization," which they largely associated with the liberalization of trade (Friedman, 2000). However, the benefits have not been shared equally. The UN Development Programme's Human Development Index, which tracks human welfare measures, including income, education, and various factors affecting life expectancy, show that overall quality of life rose 44 percent from 1980 to 1995. However, this great gain occurred largely in fifteen countries, mostly Asian, that have greatly improved the standard of living for their people. On the other hand, income gaps have been increasing both within and among countries. *Human Development Report 2000* indicates that "the distance between the incomes of the richest and poorest country was about 3 to 1 in 1820, 35 to 1 in 1950, 44 to 1 in 1973 and 72 to 1 in 1992" and "gaps between rich and poor are widening in many countries," both industrial and developing (p. 6). The average annual growth of income per capita for the 1990–1998 period was negative in fifty countries, and only one of them was a developed country (p. 6). The gross domestic product (GDP) per capita has shown a steady decline since the 1970s, especially in South Asian and sub-Saharan African countries. According to the UN data, by the end of 1998, at least 150 million of the world's workers were unemployed, and hunger and food insecurities affected 790 million people (*Human Development Report 2000:* 8). In 1990, the number of people living in extreme poverty had been reduced at least by 130 million, but in 2003 eighteen countries, which would have a combined population of 460 million, had human development index scores lower than the 1990 figures (*Human Development Report 2005:*3).

The gap between the rich and poor is striking: the world's richest 500 individuals have a combined income greater than that of the poorest 416 million. Beyond these extremes the 2.5 billion people living on less than $2 a day—40 percent of the world's population—account for 5 percent of global income. The richest 10 percent, almost all of whom live in high-income countries, account for 54 percent (*Human Development Report 2005:*4).

Moreover, aid from the developed world has shown a steady decline, despite the fact that the economies of donor countries grew after 1992 (*World Development Report 2000/2001*, 2001:190).An upward trend has been noted since 1997, but still only .25 percent of the gross national income of the richest countries is spent on development assistance (*Human Development Report 2005:*7). On the other hand, the net capital transfer through loans, exports, and other means marked a net benefit for the industrial world. While the net transfer of funds from the north to south was $19.1 billion in 1980, by 1990 the direction of the flow had changed and $27.5 billion was transferred from south to north (UNIFEM, 1990:6).This change in the flow of funds that aggravates the already wide economic disparities between the industrial and developing countries was largely a result of the debt crisis that reached its peak in the 1980s but continues to be a problem in many developing countries.

Capital shortage is endemic in the developing world and forces many countries to seek loans for investments to stimulate their economies. They typically turn to the World Bank and the International Monetary Fund (IMF). While the World Bank, as an international development agency, issues aid and loans mostly for development projects in member states, acquiring the approval of the IMF allows the country to borrow not only from the IMF but also from commercial banks. Both of these agencies grant loans on conditions that demand the applicant countries to make "structural adjustments" in their economies. Many analysts hold these structural adjustment policies responsible for the deterioration of the living conditions in the recipient states, perpetuating their dependency on debt and the transfer of wealth from already poor countries to the wealthy ones that house the financial centers. Trying to curb inflation, structural adjustment policies attempt to reduce money supply; they require applicant governments to cut spending, freeze wages, and eliminate subsidies. These policies also demand that the governments privatize state-owned and -run economic enterprises, liberalize economy through deregulation, liberalize trade by eliminating quotas and reducing tariffs on imports, devalue the national currency, open the country to foreign investments, and reform the tax system.

While anti-inflation policies shrink wages and increase the out-of-pocket expenses for the lower classes that rely on government subsidies for staple goods and basic services, opening up the economy to foreign trade and businesses often leaves local producers unable to compete against global producers and forces them out of business. With emphasis placed on exports, farmlands are often converted from supplying local needs to growing "cash crops" for export and often with large foreign investment. Consequently, economies that were once self-sufficient in feeding their populations start importing food items; unemployment and poverty increase; and the recipient country, unable to improve its economic output and wealth, seeks new loans to pay off the old debts. Pointing out that the IMF and the World Bank "often contributed in the past to the social crisis of developing countries by supporting policies that condemned millions of human beings to a life of misery and grave violations of human rights," Pierre de Senarclens states that these financial agencies "continue to propose development strategies that take no account of human rights as proclaimed by the United Nations and the treaties ratified by states on the subject" (de Senarclens, 2003:153). Similarly, UNICEF (the United Nations Children's Fund) observes that "the real cost of [structural] adjustment is being paid disproportionally by the poor and by their children," especially by women and girls (UNICEF, 1997:28). Other studies show a decline in girls' school enrollments and increase in domestic violence in countries that implemented the structural adjustment policies (Vickers, 1991:22–30).

Moreover, the neo-liberal policies, now implemented practically everywhere, reinforce the market-led globalization and erode the state capacity and will with regard to promoting public good, regulating private economic activities, providing services (e.g., education, health care), and investing toward improving the quality of life and human development. The ultimate impact of globalization seems to be increased unemployment, poverty, widened gaps in income and wealth, declines in labor rights and unionization rates, increases in child labor, and growth in global criminal acts such as trafficking in humans, drugs, weapons, and money. Henry Shue provides a succinct summary: "the radical inequality in power existing at the beginning of globalization has enabled globalization to be structured so that it makes the radical inequality in wealth progressively worse" (Shue, 2003:169).

Competing for investments, governments try to make their countries more attractive to investors by cutting down the "cost of labor." Reducing the cost of labor means lowering wages, benefits, and a whole range of labor standards. Willing to sacrifice labor rights, governments discourage or even actively prevent unionization. Declining wages force poor families to take their children out of school and put them to work; it is estimated that 250 million children, at ages ranging from four to fifteen, are working, and many of them in dangerous and unhealthy conditions (Arat, 2002). Unemployment or inadequate wages also make many people victims of international mafias engaged in human and drug trafficking. Trafficked people are then forced into working at sweatshops or in the sex industry. (See next section on labor rights.)

Two of the effects of the resultant grinding poverty are increased malnutrition and poorer health care. In some countries, medicines are no longer subsidized and poor families must make difficult choices in their already stretched budgets. Most of the more than one billion people who live in poverty in the developing world receive no effective biomedical care at all. Polio vaccines are unknown to many people, measles and malaria kill millions each year, childbirth involves mortal risk, and tuberculosis is as lethal as AIDS (Farmer, 1995:14).

To help reverse these trends, various governmental and nongovernmental agencies have developed health and welfare programs. The Carter Center has worked on many health issues—ameliorating the guinea worm and river blindness and helping to increase the world immunization rate from 20 percent to 80 percent (Carter Center, 1998). Oxfam has numerous poverty reduction programs. UNICEF sponsors programs to improve the health, education, and well-being of children. According to UNICEF, most of the development goals that would allow improvements in social and economic rights are not out of reach:

> An additional $40 billion a year could ensure access for all the world's people to basic social services such as health care, education and safe water.
>
> Two thirds of this amount could be found by developing countries if they realigned their own budget priorities. Redirecting just one quarter of the developing world's military expenditure—or $30 billion of $125 billion, for example—could provide enough additional resources to reach most of the goals for the year 2000. A similar shift in the targeting of development aid by donor countries could generate much of the rest.
>
> This premise is set out in the 20/20 initiative, which calls for developing countries to increase government spending on basic social services from the current average of approximately 13 per cent to 20 per cent, and for donor countries to earmark 20 per cent of official development assistance. (ODA) (UNICEF, 1997:14)

Unfortunately, there have been no concrete steps to meet these objectives. Many analysts contend that a new world economic order is necessary to eliminate, or at least reduce, the extreme poverty in the world. Regardless of human rights issues, it is in the best long-term political and security interests of the developed countries to have a developing world that is economically secure. The misery of poverty can often lead to political instability, a greater refugee population, and increasing disease. After the September 11, 2001, attacks, economic factors that feed international terrorism have started to receive some attention as well.

At the UN's Millennium Summit meeting held in September 2000, a global development agenda with time-bound and measurable goals was set. What came to be known as the Millennium Development Goals (MSGs) includes eight goals with eighteen specific targets and forty-eight indicators by which to measure progress. All 191 members of the UN pledged to meet the MDGs by the year 2015. The eight broad goals include (1) reducing the number of people suffering from extreme poverty (living on less than one dollar a day) and hunger by half; (2) achieving universal primary education; (3) empowering women and promoting equality between men and women by eliminating gender disparity in education; (4) reducing child mortality rates by two-thirds; (5) reducing the maternal mortality ratio by three-quarters; (6) stopping the spread of diseases and reversing their increasing trend, particularly HIV/AIDS and malaria; (7) ensuring environmental stability by reversing the loss of environmental resources, reducing the population that has no access to safe drinking water by half, and improving the sanitation and other conditions for slum dwellers; and (8) creating global partnership for development by focusing on the developing countries' need for aid, trade, debt relief, medicine, and technological advancements. The "Millennium Declaration" issued at the summit meeting and adopted by the General Assembly on September 8, 2000 (document no: A/55/L.2), also outlined the member states' commitment to human rights, good governance, and democracy.

The assessment of the progress before the 2005 World Summit, referred to as the Millennium Summit+5, presented a grim picture. *Human Development Report 2005* noted that "if the current trends continue, there will be large gaps between MDG targets and outcomes" (p. 5). The meeting, which was held in September 2005 and attended by the top leaders of 191 countries, failed to produce a consensus and a concerted effort, largely because of the several objections raised by the United States (see Chapter 4). On the positive side, most of the developed countries agreed to cancel the outstanding debt of the poorest countries and pledged to increase their development assistance levels. Moreover, the language of the outcome document is strong on human rights. It reaffirms the member states' commitment to human rights; addresses many issues as directly related to human rights; repeatedly mentions human rights, development, peace, security, and democracy as mutually reinforcing goals; and reiterates the universality, interrelatedness, and interdependence of human rights (document no: A/RES/60/1).

Labor Rights, Child Labor, and Corporate Accountability

Despite the shrinking world, borders have not disappeared and globalization is taking place in an international political structure that is still based on the state system. Within this system borders may be porous for some but have been firm for others. For example, while capital tends to be free and mobile, people/workers cannot move freely. Those who hold "migrant worker status" are subject to mistreatment and exploitation; lacking citizenship, they fall into a particularly vulnerable category (Maher, 2002). On the other hand, seeking cheap labor, many multinational corporations move their production to low-income, low-wage countries. This trend triggers the spiral effects of declining wages and unionization, as well as the problems of child labor and sweat shops, which epitomize unsafe working conditions and labor exploitation.

Forming and joining unions are human rights, and unions are essential to the protection of labor rights. Historically, unionization in a country increases as the country becomes more industrialized; thus, older industrial countries have registered higher levels of unionization. However, according to an International Labour Organization (ILO) survey that included ninety-two countries, trade union membership has been declining rapidly; more than seventy countries experienced a sharp decline between 1985 and 1995, and in only fourteen countries did the union membership rate exceed 50 percent of the national work force (ILO, 1997). In Africa, where only 10 percent of the workforce is in the formal sector, union members are estimated to be only 1–2 percent of the total workforce (*Human Development Report 1993*).

As unionization declines, working conditions and wages decline. Dismal wages increase families' need for more wage earners and elicit the problem of child labor. Since this practice is illegal in most countries, obtaining the exact count of child laborers is impossible. According to an ILO estimate, however, in the late 1990s, 250 million children, 140 million boys and 110 million girls, between the ages of 5 and 14 were working, and 120 million of them worked full time; approximately 95 percent of these child laborers were in developing countries (ILO, 1998). Rich countries are not immune to the problem either. For example, the United Kingdom and the United States are estimated to have 2 million working children each (Arat, 2002). About 15–20 percent of child laborers in developing countries, girls in particular, work without pay, in family farms and businesses, or for their parents' creditors as bound laborers. Bonded child labor is considered to be an acute problem in Asia. Although child laborers tend to be more visible in cities, more of them are in rural areas. Rural children constitute about two-thirds of all child laborers (Arat, 2002). What is underestimated in all child labor statistics is the share of domestic workers because of the "hidden" nature of the work, but the practice is extensive and involves numerous problems, especially in the case of girls (UNICEF, 1997:30–35).

When the findings of various country studies and surveys are combined, it becomes clear that "child labor emanates from poverty and persists with a host of other interrelated problems such as unskilled adult labor force, poor and exploitative work conditions, weak labor laws and unions, inadequate social services, and wrongheaded economic policies formulated by governments and international financial organizations. All of these have been more arresting in developing countries" (Arat, 2002:185–186).

Threats by the governments of industrial countries to ban the import of products that involve child labor, or consumer boycotts, have been ineffective in fighting child labor, because export industries in developing countries employ only a small number of child laborers. Moreover, such bans are counterproductive and harmful to the children, since they result in pushing children to work in even less secure sectors, such as the sex industry (Arat, 2002).

The international community has been concerned about child labor for a long time and attempted to curb it at the first session of the ILO in 1919, by establishing fourteen years as the minimum age for children to be employed in industry (ILO Convention 5). In 1973, the Minimum Age Convention of ILO (Convention 138, or C138) defined child labor as economic activity performed by a person under the age of fifteen and prohibited it for being hazardous to the physical, mental, and moral well-being of the child as well as for preventing effective schooling.

However, since C138 was considered too complex and difficult to implement, in 1999 the ILO adopted a new convention, Worst Forms of Child Labor Convention (C182). (See Chapter 7 on conventions.) The Convention, which entered into force on November 19, 2000, prioritizes the struggle against the *worst forms of child labor* and calls for their elimination for all persons under the age of eighteen. Article 3 defines the *worst forms of child labor* as comprising (a) all forms of slavery or practices similar to slavery, such as the sale and trafficking of children, debt bondage, and serfdom and forced labor or compulsory labor, including forced or compulsory recruitment of children for use in armed conflict; (b) the use, procuring, or offering of a child for prostitution, for the production of pornography, or for pornographic performance; (c) the use, procuring of, or offering of a child for illicit activities, in particular for the production and trafficking of drugs as defined in the relevant international treaties; (d) work which, by its nature or the circumstances in which it is carried out, is likely to harm the health, safety, or morals of children (Arat, 2002).

On November 20, 1989, the UN General Assembly adopted the Convention on the Rights of the Child, which also includes several articles against economic exploitation and abuse of children. Among all UN conventions, the Convention on the Rights of the Child enjoys a special status and popularity; it was ratified by practically all member states of the UN, except the United States and Somalia.

The solution to the problem of child labor has to be a comprehensive one that would target eliminating the poor family's need for child labor and creating educational opportunities for children. In 1992, the ILO launched its International Program on the Elimination of Child Labor (IPEC), which involved educational programs and schools, to help countries in combating child labor. In addition to making education accessible and making schools attractive to the parents by providing school meals and even stipends for parents to compensate for the children's labor, the root cause of the problem, poverty, needs to be tackled. Oded Grajew, the director and president of the Foundation for Children's Rights in Brazil, treats the problems related to educational access and quality of schools as secondary but identifies poor families' need for money as the main explanation for the prevalence of child labor ("Battling Brazil's Child Labor Brutality," 1997). Need is the driving force everywhere. According to the United Nations' Economic and Social Commission for Asia and the Pacific (ESCAP), in Cambodia, a war-torn and impoverished country, "98 per cent of girls in prostitution are found to be the main providers for their families" (BBC News, 2000).

Poverty and deteriorating economic opportunities have become a feature of Eastern European countries and former Soviet Republics after the collapse of the "communist regimes." Political and economic freedom in these societies came at the cost of economic security. In addition to moving away from full employment, access to education, and comprehensive social services, which were guaranteed in the previous planned economies, the transition to market economies and loosened state control and regulations created conditions most opportune for corruption. Organized crime and trafficking of consumer goods, drugs, arms, and human beings have reached a level that has undermined not only human security and rights but also peace (Richard, 2000; United Nations Office for Drug Control and Crime Prevention, 1999).

While desperate situations force desperate people to take risks and participate in illegal trade and immigration voluntarily, many others are lured into trafficking under false pretenses and end up in "modern day slavery" in sweatshops or the sex industry. For the latter, kidnapping of girls and young women has become common in Eastern Europe, as it has been for some time in the Third World. Nepali girls average thirteen years of age when they are trafficked to India. In the Sudan, women and children are kidnapped and sold into slavery. The men are killed or left behind to raise ransom. Girls become concubines, children tend animals, and women become servants. Although there are numerous conventions against slavery in place, some governments have done little to stop it. Thailand, India, Myanmar, Pakistan, and Nepal all have laws against slavery, kidnapping, and child prostitution, but enforcement is minimal. In Brazil, the government has spoken out strongly against forced labor but the Amazon region is vast and few policemen and labor inspectors have been assigned to enforce existing laws and policies ("Flourishing Business of Slavery," 1996:43–45).

The poor labor conditions and increasing trafficking alarmed the UN members and led them to develop a new convention. The International Convention on the Protection of the Rights of All Migrant Workers and Members of Their Families was adopted as General Assembly resolution of 45/158 on December 18, 1990, and entered into force July 1, 2003. The worsening labor conditions in developing countries and highly publicized reports on labor abuses in firms owned or contracted by multinational corporations attracted public attention as well. In order to control the damage caused by bad publicity, in the 1990s certain corporations took some initiatives to improve and promote labor rights. These initiatives were in the form of corporate codes of conduct and involve rules and procedures to which corporations commit themselves to uphold labor rights and environmental protection; they define the company's level of accountability for working conditions in the contracted supplier factories. Being voluntary commitments, they involve no external mechanism of enforcement. Thus, it is not clear whether these agreements will serve any meaningful end other than corporate risk management and image change. To be effective, the codes of conduct should be comprehensive and include clearly set standards, auditing systems that are established and run by agencies independent of corporations, and penalties for noncompliance (Braun and Gearhart, 2006).

However, there is now an increasing interest in addressing the responsibility of nonstate actors, including corporations, with regard to the protection or violation of human rights (Andreopoulos, Arat, and Juviler, 2006). The UN Secretariat and General Assembly have been taking some initiatives and appreciating the crucial role played by nonstate actors and their potential contribution to the promotion of human rights. A resolution of the UN General Assembly (53/114), adopted in March 1999 indicates that "individuals, groups, institutions and non-governmental organizations have an important role to play and a responsibility in . . . promoting human rights and fundamental freedoms" (A/RES/53/144). In addition to the "global compact" initiative of Secretary-General Kofi Annan, the UN effort to revise the state-centered character of the human rights regime is expressed in an annual publication of the UN, which treats the old approach as anachronistic:

> Developed in a state-centered world, the international system of human rights protection is suited to the postwar era, not the era of globalization. New Actors— global corporations, multilateral organizations, global NGOs—wield great influence in social, economic, even political outcomes (*Human Development Report 2000*, 43).

Gender Discrimination and Women's Rights

Despite the common tendency to treat women as a homogenous and unified group, they hardly constitute a monolithic group with identical problems. They live in countries with diverse historical experience and development levels; and within each country, the issues pertaining to women vary according to race, ethnicity, class, religion, residence, educational levels, and other characteristics. Nevertheless, the common denominator of women in all societies, including the industrialized ones, is their subordinate status. Women compose the poorest and the least powerful segment of the population throughout the world; they are denied equal access to education, job training, employment, health care, ownership, and political power (*Human Development Report 2005*, Tables 25–30). The oppression of Third World women is even more intense because of the legacy of Western imperialism, which culminated in economic dependency. Moreover, the economic and political structural changes introduced by colonial powers, and later imposed by international lending and development agencies, have further widened the gender gap in these countries. Women in many developing countries are denied the right to inherit property, and in some places where they have property rights, they cannot control the land to which they have title, or manage the shops they own.

Women usually work in family farms and businesses as unpaid laborers. When employed, they tend to hold lower positions and are paid less than men who do the same or comparable work. In some countries women still cannot enjoy full citizenship rights; they are denied the right to vote or run for office. Where women's political rights are recognized by statute, their *de facto* denial is common. Women are consistently underrepresented in their country's parliament (the average being 10 percent) and cabinet posts (less than 5 percent) (*Human Development Report 2005*). Moreover, the progress in women's participation in decision making has been unsteady.

Discrimination against women becomes most obvious when health indicators are examined. In addition to the health problems they share with men, "since women [also] face such physical changes as menarche, menstruation, pregnancy, childbearing, lactation, and menopause, the crisis in world health is a crisis of women" (Morgan, 1984:2).Yet, women's health receives very little medical attention, they lack equal access to the health care system, and their health suffers from physical hardships and malnutrition. In developing countries 50 percent of all women of childbearing age and 60 percent of pregnant women suffer from nutritional anemia (UNIFEM, 1989:4).

In many countries, the mortality rate of female children is higher than that of males. Due to the preference for males, female infanticide and—more recently, where sonogram technology has become available—the abortion of female fetuses is high; both the nutritional quality and quantity of food for the female tend to be poor; and girls and women are less likely than males to receive preventive health care or curative medicine when they fall ill. In the 1980s, in Bangladesh, malnutrition was about three times more common among young girls than among boys, and in rural Punjab of India, families spend more than twice as much for the care of male infants as for female babies (*Human Development Report 1990*:31). In these countries, as well as others where social biases against women are strong, life expectancy and the child survival rate for males have been higher than those for females. Consequently, despite their natural disadvantages, males outnumber females. The "masculine sex ratios" are particularly high in the oil-rich Gulf states; in 1990 the number of females per 100 males was 48 in the United Arab Emirates, 60 in Qatar, 73 in Bahrain, 76 in Kuwait, 84 in Saudi Arabia, and 91 in Oman (*Human Development Report 1993*).

Female deprivation leads to the deprivation of future generations and feeds the poverty cycle. Children of malnourished and uneducated mothers are more likely to suffer from malnutrition, be more susceptible to diseases, or die.

Women are further overburdened by work, even though their work is usually not compensated (*Human Development Report 2004*, Table 28). According to UNIFEM reports, "Women in developing countries produce, process and market up to 80 percent of the food," and in Africa "88 percent of rural African women work in agriculture . . . [and] 80 percent of the family's food is produced, processed and stored by women"; in order "to transport water, fuel and goods to and from market, women spend 2,000 to 5,000 hours a year or the equivalent of an eight-hour job . . . [and they] run 70 percent of micro-enterprises" (UNIFEM, 1989:5). In agriculture, women's workload does not show much of a decline during the slack seasons, and women have practically no leisure time because they are held responsible for household activities and domestic chores throughout the world. It is estimated that women typically work about 25 percent longer hours than men, and according to a UN survey of 1990, if women's unpaid work in house and family care were counted as productive output in national income accounts, global output value would increase by 20 to 30 percent (*Human Development Report 1990*:32, 45).

Although both the United Nations Charter and the Universal Declaration of Human Rights recognized equality between men and women in the 1940s, these principles of equality and nondiscrimination were not enforced to improve the status of women. Even the UN has failed to promote women to top offices until very recently and is still far from achieving gender equality within its own ranks. However, starting in the 1970s, some significant efforts to address gender disparities have been initiated by various intergovernmental and nongovernmental organizations, as well as by government agencies.

A very important stimulus was the UN General Assembly resolution of December 1972 that declared 1975 as the International Women's Year. The International Women's Year Conference in Mexico City in 1975 was flooded by over 900 proposals and amendments presented by countries and delegates. The Conference led the UN General Assembly to approve its World Plan of Action and to declare the period of 1976–1985 to be the United Nations Decade for Women. These changes initiated within the UN context, the most visible and comprehensive intergovernmental organization, put women on the agenda of other conferences and organizations. The UN itself created specialized agencies to foster the programs and policies developed at these conferences. Seventeen months after the Mexico Conference, the Voluntary Fund for the United Nations Decade for Women was established by the UN General Assembly. The Fund's name was changed to UNIFEM in 1985. Working in association with the United Nations Development Programme (UNDP), UNIFEM "provides direct financial and technical support to low-income women in developing countries, who are striving to raise their living standards. It also funds activities that bring women into mainstream development decision-making" (UNIFEM, 1990).

The flow of new information on the extent of social and economic contributions of women, as well as on their detrimental conditions and subjugation, expedited the preparation and ratification of the Convention on the Elimination of All Forms of Discrimination against Women (CEDAW), which was adopted by the UN General Assembly in 1979. The Convention included a provision on the creation of a committee of experts to oversee the implementation of the CEDAW, through the examination of periodic reports submitted by the states parties and by issuing general recommendations.

A global financial organization, the Women's World Bank, was established, also in 1980. Distinct from the World Bank, the Women's World Bank tries to create credit opportunities for female owners of micro-enterprises. By serving as a guarantor, the Bank encourages commercial banks to lend to women who lack property or collateral, and are thus normally denied credit. Microcredit opportunities for poor women are also created by the Grameen Bank, which was established in Bangladesh in 1983 and became a model emulated in several other countries.

Women's groups have worked closely with UN agencies and other organizations and have pressured their governments to ratify human rights treaties and fulfill their obligations. Major international human rights organizations, such as Amnesty International and Human Rights Watch, started to revise and broaden their missions to address women's rights. In the 1990s, women started to address the male biases in the international human rights law and in its interpretation, and the motto of the international women's movement became "Women's Rights as Human Rights." This approach criticized the artificial separation of the public and private domains of life and the treatment of human rights as applying to the public domain only, where the state is seen as the main violator. Proponents of women's rights pointed out that women face violence and many other forms of human rights violations peculiar to them (e.g., rape, battering, forced marriage, trafficking of women, "honor' crimes, genital mutilation, dowry burning, forced sterilization or pregnancy) on a daily basis and these violations are not addressed in the international human rights discourse or system. In 1992, the CEDAW Committee issued a General Recommendation (no. 19) indicating that although the wording is not explicit, the prohibition of violence against women is indeed covered under the Convention and states should report on measures that they were taking to combat gender-based violence. In 1993, the UN Commission on the Status of Women drafted the Declaration on the Elimination of Violence against women, and the Second World Conference on Human Rights, held in Vienna, recognized women's rights as human rights. The fourth UN Conference on Women, held in Beijing in 1995, identified twelve critical areas in eliminating gender discrimination. They include the persistent and increasing burden of poverty on women; inequalities and inadequacies in and unequal access to education and training; inequalities and inadequacies in and unequal access to health care and related services; violence against women; the effects of armed or other kinds of conflict on women, including those living under foreign occupation; inequality in economic structures and policies, in all forms of productive activities, and in access to resources; inequality between men and women in the sharing of power and decision making at all levels; insufficient mechanisms at all levels to promote the advancement of women; lack of respect for and inadequate promotion and protection of the human rights of women; stereotyping of women and inequality in women's access to and participation in all communication systems, especially in the media; gender inequalities in the management of natural resources and in the safeguarding of the environment; and persistent discrimination against and violation of the rights of the girl child. Another concern that surfaced during the Beijing conference was the marginalization of women's issues by delegating them to separate and underfunded agencies. Thus, the final document, Beijing Declaration and Platform for Action, also called for mainstreaming women's rights.

In 1999, the UN General Assembly adopted an Optional Protocol to the CEDAW. The Optional Protocol is important for permitting individuals to bring their cases of violations to the attention of the CEDAW committee. Another important development for women has been the acknowledgment of the incongruous situation that while women suffer more at times of conflict and war, they are not integrated into peace talks and negotiations. Thus, the UN Security Council unanimously adopted Resolution 1325 on women, peace, and security, on October 31, 2000.

The outcome assessments of the Beijing conference, known as Beijing+5 and Beijing+10, highlighted the negative impact of globalization on women and the spread of HIV. However, some important issues such as discrimination based on sexual orientation and women's reproductive rights have not been articulated in international documents, mainly due to the pressure asserted by the Holy See (the Vatican) and some conservative state governments and groups.

Environmental Protection and Rights

Environmental destruction poses a grave threat to human rights. Often destruction of forests, pollution of streams, and other environmental degradation threaten the ability of people who use traditional methods of hunting, fishing, and farming to get food and drink clean water. One person in five in the world does not have access to clean water (Johnston, 1997:5; *Human Development Report 2005*:243). Additionally, the way that many countries have gone about developing natural resources has involved persecution of people protesting environmental destruction.

In Nigeria in 1996, nine environmental activists, including one Nobel Peace Prize nominee, were executed after protesting against Shell Oil Company's environmental destruction (Hammer, 1996:58–69). In Irian Jaya, Indonesia, a U.S. corporation, Freeport-McMoRan, has been mining copper and gold since 1973. When this largest gold mine in the world, with an estimated value of $50 billion, became a target of criticism by the indigenous people whose lives it threatened, the Indonesian government stationed troops at the mine to protect it. In 1995, the military killed at least sixteen people and tortured others near the mine. The mine has created enormous environmental destruction; billions of tons of acid-producing mine tailings dumped in the local river have contaminated the drinking water (Bryce, 1996:66–70). The Amungme people in the region filed a $6 billion class action lawsuit against the company. They failed in that effort but forced the company to take certain measures to improve its human rights practices (Shari, 2000).

Environmental rights are considered in a new category of human rights, referred to as the "third generation rights." (See Chapter 2.) Neither the Universal Declaration of Human Rights nor the two UN covenants are explicit on environmental rights—although some would argue that the International Covenant on Economic, Social and Cultural Rights contains implicit references to environmental rights in several articles. For example, Article 1 covers the "right of peoples to self-determination and to freely dispose of their natural wealth and resources." Article 11 obliges the state parties to provide "programmes to improve methods of production, conservation and distribution of food; disseminating knowledge of principles of nutrition; measures to achieve the most efficient development and utilization of natural resources; equitable distribution of world food supplies." In addressing the right to health, the Covenant calls for "steps to be taken for the healthy development of the child, improvement of all aspects of environmental and industrial hygiene" (Article 12). However, countries around the world are becoming more concerned about the environment and about overexploitation of resources. The UN and regional organizations issued several treaties that oblige states to uphold certain environmental standards and prevent environmental deterioration under the auspices of global or regional organizations. The first important international document that addresses environmental protection as a human rights issue was the Stockholm Declaration on the Human Environment. Issued at the 1972 UN Conference on Environment, the document reads that "man has the fundamental right to freedom, equality and adequate conditions of life, in an environment of a quality that permits a life of dignity and well-being, and he bears a solemn responsibility to protect and improve the environment for present and future generations" (Principle 1) (UNEP, 1972).

In 1990, the UN Commission on Human Rights adopted a resolution that emphasized the link between the preservation of the environment and the promotion of human rights. In 1994, the UN held a meeting of international experts on human rights and environmental protection in Geneva, where the principles of an environmental rights declaration were drafted. The Draft Declaration of Principles on Human Rights and the Environment states that human rights, an ecologically sound environment, sustainable development, and peace are interdependent and indivisible. It further asserts that all people have a right to a secure, healthy, and ecologically sound environment. Other provisions cover healthy food and water and safe and healthy work environments. Environmental rights are promoted in various international conferences that do not necessarily focus on human rights. Many NGOs, such as the Natural Resources Defense Council, Greenpeace, and the Nature Conservancy, also work hard on environmental issues and protection.

References

Andreopoulos, George, Arat, Zehra F. Kabasakal, and Juviler, Peter, eds. *Non-State Actors in the Human Rights Universe.* New York: Kumarian Press 2006.

Arat, Zehra F. "Analyzing Child Labor as a Human Rights Issue: Its Causes, Aggravating Policies, and Alternative Proposals." *Human Rights Quarterly* 24:1 (February 2002): 177–204.

Arat, Zehra F. Kabasakal. "Human Rights and Globalization: Is the Shrinking World Expanding Rights?" *Human Rights and Human Welfare* 5 (2005): 137–146.

Barber, Ben. "Feeding Refugees or War? The Dilemma of Humanitarian Aid." *Foreign Affairs* 76:4 (July/August, 1997): 8–15.

"Battling Brazil's Child Labor Brutality: An Interview with Oded Grajew." *Multinational Monitor* 18:1–2 (January–February, 1997): 20–23.

BBC News, September 15, 2000. http://news.bbc.co.uk/1/hi/world/asia-pacific/926853.stm (accessed January 4, 2001).

Bell-Fialkoff, Andrew. *Ethnic Cleansing.* New York: St. Martin's Press, 1996.

Braun, Reiner, and Gearhart, Judie. "Realizing Rights in the Workplace: Corporate Codes of Conduct and Empowerment from Below." In George Andreopoulos, Zehra F. Kabasakal Arat, and Peter Juviler, eds., *Non-State Actors in the Human Rights Universe.* New York: Kumarian Press, 2006.

"Britain's Asylum Shambles: Those Fleeing Persecution Deserve Better Treatment." *Economist* (February 14, 1998): 20.

Bryce, Robert. "Spinning Gold." *Mother Jones* (September/October 1996): 66–70.

Carter Center. www.emory.edu/CARTER_CENTER (accessed June 1998).

Crelinsten, Ronald, and Schmid, Alex, eds. *Politics of Pain: Torturers and Their Masters.* Boulder, CO: Westview Press, 1995.

De Senarclens, Pierre. "Human Rights at the International Level: Implementation and Distributive Justice." In Jean-Marc Coicaud, Michael W. Doyle, and Anne-Marie Gardner, eds., *The Globalization of Human Rights.* Tokyo: United Nations University Press, 2003:137–159.

Farmer, Paul. "Medicine and Social Justice." *America* (July 15, 1995): 13–18.

"Flourishing Business of Slavery." *Economist* (September 21, 1996): 43–45.

Friedman, Thomas L. *The Lexus and the Olive Tree: Understanding Globalization.* New York: Anchor Books, 2000.

Grimmett, Richard F. *Conventional Arms Transfers to Developing Nations, 1993–2000. Congressional Research Service to Congress.* Washington, DC: The Library of Congress, August 16, 2001.

Hammer, Joshua. "Nigeria Crude: A Hanged Man and an Oil-Fouled Landscape." *Harper's Magazine* (June, 1996): 58–69.

Hartung, William D. *Welfare for Weapons Dealers: The Hidden Costs of the Arms Trade.* Arms Trade Resource Center Report, 1996. World Policy Institute. http://www.worldpolicy.org/projects/arms/reports/hcrep.html (accessed June 2, 2005).

Human Development Report 1990. United Nations Development Programme. New York: Oxford University Press, 1990.

Human Development Report 1993. United Nations Development Programme. New York: Oxford University Press, 1993.

Human Development Report 1999. United Nations Development Programme. New York: Oxford University Press, 1999.

Human Development Report 2000. United Nations Development Programme. New York: Oxford University Press, 2000.

Human Development Report 2004. United Nations Development Programme. New York: Oxford University Press, 2004.

Human Development Report 2005. United Nations Development Programme. New York: Oxford University Press, 2005.

Human Rights Watch Prison Project. *Human Rights Watch Global Report on Prisons.* New York: Human Rights Watch, 1993.

Human Rights Watch. "Key Findings of the Global Report on Child Soldiers 2001." http://www.hrw.org/campaigns/crp/cs-report2001.htm (accessed June 2, 2005).

Human Rights Watch. "Women in Custody." http://www.hrw.org/women/custody.html (accessed June 2, 2005).

ILO (International Labour Organization). *Child Labor: Targeting the Intolerable.* Report IV of the International Labour Conference, 86th Session, Geneva, 1998.

ILO. *World Labor Report 1997–98: Industrial Relations, Democracy and Social Sstability.* (October 15, 1997). http://www.ilo.org/public/english/dialogue/ifpdial/publ/wlr97/index.htm (accessed September 23, 2005).

International Committee of the Red Cross. *Landmines: Time for Action.* Geneva, Switzerland: ICRC Publications, 1994.

Johnston, Barbara Rose. *Life and Death Matters: Human Rights and the Environment at the End of the Millenium.* Walnut Creek, CA: Alta Mira Press, 1997.

Maher, Kristen Hill. "Who Has a Right to Rights? Citizenship's Exclusion in an Age of Migration." In Alison Brysk, ed., *Globalization and Human Rights*. Berkeley: University of California Press, 2002:19–43.

Marshall, Tyler. "Nobel Prize Sets Off Land Mine." *Los Angeles Times* (February 6, 1998).

Morgan, Robin, ed. *Sisterhood is Global: The International Women's Movement Anthology*. New York: Anchor Books, 1984.

OHCHR (Office of the High Commissioner for Human Rights). Digest of Jurisprudence of the UN and Regional Organizations on the Protection of Human Rights while Countering Terrorism. 2003. http://www.ohchr .org/english/about/publications/docs/digest.doc (accessed June 2, 2005).

Richard, Amy O'Neill. *International Trafficking in Women to the United States: A Contemporary Manifestation of Slavery and Organized Crime*. Washington, DC: Center for the Study of Intelligence, April 2000.

Shari, Michael. "Freeport McMoRan—A Pit of Trouble," *Business Week* (July 31, 2000).

Shue, Henry. "Global Accountability: Transnational Duties Towards Economic Rights." In Jean-Marc Coicaud, Michael W. Doyle, and Anne-Marie Gardner, eds., *The Globalization of Human Rights*. Tokyo: United Nations University Press, 2003:160–177.

Smolin, David M. "Strategic Choices in the International Campaign against Child Labor." *Human Rights Quarterly* 22:4 (November 2000): 942–987.

UNEP (United Nations Environment Programme). Declaration of the United Nations Conference on the Human Environment. http://www .unep.org/Documents.multilingual/Default.asp?DocumentID=97& ArticleID=1503 (accessed February 23, 2006).

UNICEF (United Nations Children's Fund). *The State of the World's Children 1997*. New York: Oxford University Press, 1997:28.

UNIFEM (United Nations Development Fund for Women). 1988–1989. "Strength in Adversity: Women in the Developing World." Report on the United Nations Development Fund for Women. New York: United Nations Development Fund for Women, 1989.

UNIFEM. *Annual Report 1990*. New York: United Nations Development Fund for Women, 1990.

United Nations press release. 20/1/2003 http://www.unhchr.ch/ huricane/huricane.nsf/view01/B3D505E6A8B47C5AC1256CB5002F4 DED?opendocument (accessed June 2, 2005).

United Nations High Commissioner of Refugees (UNHCR). News Stories. http://www.unhcr.ch/cgi-bin/texis/vtx/news/opendoc.htm?tbl=NEWS&id=42b191e82 (accessed June 18, 2005).

United Nations Office for Drug Control and Crime Prevention. *Global Programme against Trafficking in Human Beings. An Outline for Action.* February 1999.

Vickers, Jeanne. *Women and the World Economic Crisis.* London: Zed Books, 1991: 22–30.

Wieviorka, Michel. "The Seeds of Hate." *UNESCO Courier* (March 1996): 10–14.

World Development Report 2000/2001. World Bank. New York: Oxford University Press, 2000.

4

The United States and Human Rights

L ike all other countries, the United States does not have a human rights record free from problems. However, its record deserves closer examination since it involves a relatively long history of human rights discourse, as well as significant contradictions. The United States was a key player in the formation of the international human rights regime under the auspices of the United Nations, which has included the promotion of human rights in its charter and has led the movement to protect such rights globally. Moreover, with its enormous wealth and superpower position in world politics, the United States has had the ability to influence the conditions surrounding human rights in other countries.

Although earlier chapters touched on the U.S. position and impact on some human rights issues, this chapter focuses directly on the country's approach to human rights and examines it under three headings: human rights conditions and practices within the borders of the United States; U.S. participation in the international human rights regime; and the human rights impact of U.S. foreign policy.

Human Rights Conditions and Practices in the United States

The United States was a pioneer nation in the development of representative government, the rule of law, and political rights

(Henkin, 1990). As a wealthy country, it has also provided the basic needs for most of its population and overall has maintained a fairly high standard of living. The Declaration of Independence has been a key document for the advancement of political rights. The Constitution of the United States is even more important not only for bestowing popular will and representative government at a time when absolute monarchy was the norm but also for incorporating a bill of rights that has been an inspiration for people around the world. The presidency of Franklin D. Roosevelt was decisive in broadening the concept of human rights and fostering human rights ethics both at home and abroad. In addition to his 1941 "Four Freedoms" speech that put forward a framework of human rights, in 1944 Roosevelt expounded the content of some of those rights in his less-known proposal for a "second Bill of Rights under which a new basis of security and prosperity can be established for all" and paved the way for the progress of economic and social rights. (See Chapter 1.) His New Deal program had already established an innovative step toward recognizing these rights.

However, the message of these groundbreaking initiatives in political and legal philosophy has been always eclipsed by the restrictions imposed by structural factors. The extensive dependence of the country's economy on slavery and the racism that prevailed even after the abolition of slavery thwarted human rights endeavors to extend these rights to all citizens. Although later amendments to the Constitution gradually expanded suffrage, discrimination against African Americans and other minorities, as well as women, has prevailed. Officially endorsed segregation in schools and public places, and restrictions on voting, most salient in the southern states, were not ended until the 1960s, when the country faced major racial turmoil. Racial profiling by the police continues to be a problem and results in a disproportionate representation of Blacks and Hispanics within the increasing prison population. It is estimated that the number of prison inmates per 100,000 U.S. residents increased from 411 to 486 between 1995 and 2003, and one in approximately every twenty black males was in prison in mid-2004 (Bureau of Justice Statistics, 2005). African Americans are also likely to receive more severe sentences than white individuals for similar crimes. They constitute 42 percent of the prisoners on death row (Bureau of Justice Statistics, 2005).

Among all industrialized countries, the United States has the highest level of poverty, and poverty rates tend to be higher for minority groups (Rodgers, 2006). There has been little effort to reverse the injustices inflicted on the Native American population, which continues to constitute perhaps the poorest segment of the nation. In addition to the major gaps among racial and ethnic groups on all social and economic indicators, an important shortcoming of the U.S. political economy has been its inability to address the economic and social rights of a considerable segment of its population, lagging behind other industrialized countries. Access to health care constitutes a major problem because of the increasing cost of health care and medication. Among the wealthy countries, the United States is the only one that lacks a universal health insurance system; in 2003, 45 million nonelderly Americans (more than one in every six) had no health insurance (*Human Development Report 2005*:58). The lack of affordable housing, particularly acute in urban areas, has reached a crisis level and has made homelessness a major item on municipal agendas since the 1980s.

The booming economy and prosperity of the 1950s gave way to a different trend in the 1970s: real incomes started to decline; unemployment and part-time employment increased; and low-paying service sector jobs replaced industrial employment. The improvements in the economy of the late 1990s did not reach many. Income gaps continued to be wide and growing. The United States has the highest inequality score (Gini Index = 40.8) among the top twenty countries on the human development scale (*Human Development Report 2005*:270).

In the United States, the highly acclaimed "welfare reform" legislation of 1996 revamped the "welfare system as we know it," but it trapped thousands of the most vulnerable children of the country in deteriorating conditions. An impact assessment by the Institute of Women's Policy Research, which compared the 1996 and 2000 figures, yielded disturbing findings: the average income dropped for families living in extreme poverty; the number of uninsured poor children living in single-parent households increased dramatically; and these children experienced a decline in their access to income assistance (TANF), Medicaid, and food stamps. By 1999, in their reports about welfare reform, the U.S. Conference of Mayors agreed that the legislation had had a broad negative impact on hunger and homelessness in U.S. cities (Mittal and Rosset, 1999:87). According to the U.S. Department of Agriculture, in 1999 at least 10 percent of U.S. households, including 12 million children, faced food insecurity, and 3.1 million individuals were actually experiencing hunger; at the same time, only 60 percent of those eligible for food stamps were receiving them. By 2002, the percentage of households experiencing food insecurity and hunger had reached 11.1 percent and 3.5 percent, respectively (Rodgers, 2006:198).

Increasing layoffs and the downward spiral of wages are intertwined with the predicament of unions. Trade union membership in the United States has been falling in recent years (ILO, 1997). While the unionization rate has remained high in some industrialized countries (e.g., in Sweden, 87 percent; Iceland, 93 percent; Denmark, 97 percent; Finland, 100 percent; and Norway, 72 percent), in the United States, where unions have never been as strong, union membership fell from a low 20 percent in 1983 to about 12.5 percent in 2004 (ILO, 2005).

When Alexis de Tocqueville examined the U.S. criminal justice and prison systems over two hundred years ago, he was impressed. Today, however, the system's overreliance on incarceration creates numerous problems. Both the number of prisons built and the amount of money the government spends on prisons have increased over the years. During the last two decades (1982–2001), direct government spending showed a profound increase at all levels—municipal (244 percent), county (373 percent), state (452 percent), and federal (492 percent)—with states ranked at the top, spending nearly $60 billion in 2001 (Bureau of Justice Statistics, 2004). Despite these increases, however, prisons and prisoners suffer from overcrowding, unhealthy and unsafe environments, and violence at the hands of other inmates and guards. The poor are likely to be more affected than the affluent by this situation, since the biases in the system tend to deny them adequate defense (Bright, 2003). Torturous treatment by officers that results in deaths has become common. It was noted that "new generation" tasers—powerful dart-firing electroshock weapons deployed or tried experimentally by more than 5,000 U.S. police and correctional agencies—caused more than forty deaths in 2004, bringing the number of such deaths reported since 2001 to seventy, but the officers involved were cleared of wrongdoing in most of the cases (Amnesty International, 2005).

The death penalty has been another area of concern. Only the United States among the industrialized countries recognizes the death penalty. Since the U.S. Supreme Court lifted a moratorium on executions in 1976, a total of 944 prisoners had been put to death by the end of 2004, including 59 people executed that year (Amnesty International, 2005). Until the recent Supreme Court ruling against the execution of juveniles (March 1, 2005), the United States was one of the six countries that allowed the death penalty for offenders under eighteen, and at that time had seventy juvenile offenders on death row. Prisoners with histories of serious mental illness continue to be sentenced to death and executed—a practice that is not allowed in any other industrialized country. Finally, the United States belongs to a small group of thirteen countries that permit life sentences without parole for young offenders; however, with the exception of Israel, Tanzania, and South Africa (which together had less than a dozen young offenders in prison without parole in 2005, as opposed to 2,222 in the United States), such sentences are never or very rarely used in these other countries (Human Rights Watch/Amnesty International, 2005:106).

Since the September 11 attacks, the number of foreign detainees held by the United States has increased, and their situation has been particularly problematic. At the U.S. naval base in Guantánamo Bay, Cuba, hundreds of detainees have been held on suspicion of possible links to al-Qa'ida or the Afghan Taliban group but without an official charge or trial for years. In June 2004, the U.S. Supreme Court allowed Guantánamo detainees access to federal courts, but the problems persisted. Prolonged detentions, the lack of access to detainees by their lawyers, human rights groups, and the UN, and numerous allegations of torture and cruel treatment led the United Nations to call for closing of the Guantánamo Bay camp in February 2006. However, the Bush administration has been dismissive.

Allegations about the ill-treatment and torture of detainees held elsewhere—in Afghanistan, Iraq, and other countries—have been rampant as well. The widely publicized photographs and reports of the abuse and torture of detainees by U.S. soldiers at the Abu Ghraib prison in Iraq confirmed at least some of these allegations. The American Civil Liberties Union (ACLU) has described acts of torture and other unlawful treatment of detainees such as strangulation, putting lit cigarettes into detainees' ears, depriving them of sleep, beating them, and chaining them in a fetal position for up to twenty-four hours or more (Human Rights Watch, 2004). Amnesty International has charged that U.S.

forces operating some twenty-five detention facilities in Afghanistan and seventeen in Iraq, where detainees are routinely denied access to their lawyers and families. Moreover, a large number of detainees "were alleged to remain in secret detention in undisclosed locations," and allegations have been made "that the U.S. authorities were involved in the secret transfer of detainees between countries, exposing detainees to the risk of torture and ill-treatment" (Amnesty International, 2005). Between 2003 and 2004, up to thirty-one detainees may have died due to torture and ill-treatment in Afghanistan and Iraq. Steps were taken to prosecute some three dozen soldiers for this treatment. Although the Army Criminal Investigation Command recommended charging seventeen U.S. soldiers implicated in prisoners' deaths for murder, conspiracy, and negligent homicide, the Pentagon decided not to try them ("Pentagon Will Not Try 17 G.I.'s," 2005.)

The U.S. government's willingness to undermine the due process rights and anti-torture provisions of numerous human rights treaties, including the Geneva Conventions that protect the rights of foreign combatants in times of war, has alarmed the human rights community. In addition to an FBI document suggesting that President George W. Bush himself might have authorized unlawful interrogation methods (Human Rights Watch, 2004), a memo issued by Alberto R. Gonzales, White House counsel to President Bush, that characterized the Geneva Conventions as "quaint" raised questions about the Bush administration's respect for human rights. Gonzales's nomination for attorney general, the office charged with upholding national and international law, and his ultimate confirmation were perceived as another expression of indifference and exceptionalism by the U.S. government. Moreover, questions about the legality of the war in Iraq and the violations of human rights by U.S. forces and their allies led to the convening of people's tribunals. Partially modeled after the 1967 Russell Tribunal on the Vietnam War, the World Tribunal on Iraq involved "hearings investigating various issues related to the war on Iraq, such as the legality of the war, the role of the United Nations, war crimes and the role of the media, as well as the destruction of cultural sites and the environment" (World Tribunal, 2005). It began with the Jakarta Peace Consensus in May 2003, continued for two years with sessions held in Brussels, Berlin, Barcelona, Copenhagen, New York, London, Rome, Genoa, Mumbai, Stockholm, various cities in Germany, Japan, and Korea, and was concluded in Istanbul in a culminating three-day meeting in June 24–27, 2005. The Jury of Conscience of the World Tribunal established various charges, including crimes of aggression and human rights violations, against the governments of the United States and the United Kingdom, as well as the UN Security Council (World Tribunal, 2005).

The security measures taken after the September 11 attacks have imposed threats to the freedoms of U.S. citizens as well. The Patriot Act of 2001, passed by the Congress just forty-five days after the attacks virtually without any debate and signed by President Bush on October 26, gives broad, unprecedented powers to the attorney general to certify and then detain noncitizens suspected of terrorist activities or of threatening national security for indefinite periods. It does not provide a clear definition of "terrorism" or other key terms; it also does not provide for meaningful judicial review for detainees who would wish to challenge their certifications and subsequent detention. With its vague terminology and open-ended provisions, the law was predestined to encourage abuses, as it undermines the system of checks and balances on law enforcement. It not only dismisses due process safeguards under the law but also expands the government's ability to invade privacy in many ways (American Civil Liberties Union, n.d.). Moreover, the Patriot Act inspired a proliferation of similar laws worldwide, prompting abuses that the United States had for years been pledging to counter. In the United States, President Bush's authorization of the electronic surveillance of U.S. citizens, without a court warrant, became public knowledge in January 2006, and generated criticisms and concerns about the protection of civil liberties.

Finally, the September 11 attacks, which constitute crimes against humanity, triggered public hostility in the United States toward the Muslim population. Hate crimes against Muslims, Sikhs, and people of Middle Eastern and South Asian descent, as well as attacks on their religious or cultural centers, were reported in newspapers all around the country in the days and weeks following September 11, 2001.

Historically, the United States has been willing to undermine the rights of its own citizens whenever there were external threats, real or expected, to the country. Even Woodrow Wilson and Franklin Roosevelt, two presidents known for championing human rights, did not hesitate to impose restrictions on labor rights and several freedoms during the first and second World

Wars, respectively. The Espionage Act (1917) and the Sedition Act (1919) suspended the protective provisions of the Bill of Rights by restricting freedoms and labor rights and imposing severe penalties for anyone criticizing the U.S. form of government, the Constitution, and the flag, and for all acts that would "incite, provoke, or encourage resistance" to the government or "advocate any curtailment of production" (Lauren, 1998: 89). The internment of U.S. citizens of Japanese descent and the branding of more than 600,000 Italian-born and 300,000 German-born United States residents as "enemy aliens"—and thus justifying policies requiring them to carry Certificates of Identification, limiting their travel, and seizing their personal property—took place during Roosevelt's presidency, actually within the same year he delivered his famous "Four Freedoms speech" to Congress (Hummel, 1986).

The red scare of the 1950s, epitomized by the "witch hunt" of Senator Joe McCarthy of Wisconsin, was a major assault on freedoms of thought and association. The blacklisting of suspected Communists cost many people their reputations as well as the means of earning a living, and the efforts taken to avoid being labeled "Communist" or "traitor" depressed the advocacy of social justice and trade unionism. In the 1960s, civil rights activists and opponents of the war in Vietnam, and in the 1970s, members and supporters of the Black Panther Party, were subject to intimidation and interrogation by the FBI, as well as to police brutality and abuse.

The wars in Afghanistan and Iraq were used to restrict the freedom of the press. According to Reporters without Borders, the United States had a good ranking on the world press freedom index in 2003, but came in only 135th out of 166 countries ranked when the U.S. government's attacks on press freedom in Iraq were measured (Reporters without Borders, 2004).

Although there has been some improvement with regard to gay and lesbian rights, intolerance and resistance to equal treatment exist in both society's and the states' approaches. Gender discrimination prevails despite the progressive legislation that followed the women's movement of the 1970s. The gender gap in employment opportunities, income, and political representation has not been closed, and the progress observed in some other areas, such as women's reproductive rights, is threatened by the increasing political influence of conservative and religious groups.

The Convention on the Elimination of All Forms of Discrimination against Women (CEDAW), which was adopted by the UN General Assembly in 1979, was disregarded, if not rejected, in the United States. As of June 2005, 180 countries—over 90 percent of the members of the United Nations—were party to the Convention, but the United States remained the only country that signed but did not ratify it. The U.S. position on this Convention is partially affected by the ideological frictions within its domestic politics; President Carter signed the Convention but the Congressional Foreign Relations Committee, chaired by conservative Senator Jesse Helms, blocked its ratification. However, the reluctance of the United States to be a party to the CEDAW is also in line with the country's overall position toward international treaties and multilateralism. (See the next section.)

Many women in the United States, one of the wealthiest countries in the world, with a gross domestic product per capita of over $37,000, lack access to a decent income, healthy living and work environments, and health care. In 2002, 59 percent of women in the this country, aged fifteen or older, were economically active, mostly in the service sector, but they earned 62 percent of what men earned, and women constituted 63 percent of the unpaid family workers (working on family farms, in family-owned shops, etc.). As in most countries, women in the United States work for more hours daily (in all kinds of activities) than men, and women's workdays in the United States (453 minutes per day) are the second longest among the industrialized countries, trailing only Italy (470 minutes per day) (*Human Development Report 2004*, Tables 24, 27–28).

Women are underrepresented in unions. Lacking comprehensive maternal leave and affordable child care, women in the United States also lag on several indicators behind the women in other industrialized countries, where governments have offered advanced welfare policies and social services that do not carry the stigma that is typically attached to welfare recipients in the United States (Stetson and Mazur, 1995).

Violence is a problem faced by many women on a daily basis. Domestic violence and sexual assaults of various forms, including incest and rape—in custody, by strangers outside the home, and by partners—are common incidents. In 1994, 96.8 cases of rape per 100,000 women aged fifteen or over were officially recorded in the United States—a statistic that ranges between 3.0

and 49.9 for the majority of high-income countries, except for Canada and Australia, where rates were higher at 267.3 and 199.1, respectively (*Human Development Report 2000*:247). (However, crime statistics, especially those for sexual assaults, tend to be unreliable indicators because not all incidents are reported.)

Women are also underrepresented in decision-making posts. Hitting a "glass-ceiling," they can rarely reach the top in the corporate world. Although American women acquired the right to vote and run for public office in the early twentieth century (and earlier in some states), they have never held more than 15 percent of the seats in either the House or the Senate. Noting the slow pace of progress, analysts estimate that it would take 300 years for Congress to have equal representation between men and women. The gender gap in political representation is particularly important because women's participation in decision making would increase the probability that policies would be formulated to address women's issues and advance gender equality. Male dominance in the legislative bodies of the fifty states offers at least a partial explanation for the defeat of the Equal Rights Amendment (ERA) to the Constitution, although the role of conservative women and organizations should not be ignored (Schlafly, 1989). The ERA includes two clauses: "Men and women shall have equal rights throughout the United States and every place subject to its jurisdiction" and "Congress shall have the power to enforce this article by appropriate legislation." Written in 1921 by suffragist Alice Paul, the ERA has been introduced in Congress every session since 1923. It finally passed Congress in 1972 but was ratified by only twenty-five states. By the July 1982 deadline the amendment had not obtained ratification by thirty-eight states, the number required for an amendment to be included in the Constitution, and the ERA initiative failed.

U.S. Participation in the International Human Rights Regime

There is no doubt that the United States played a key role in the establishment of human rights regimes both globally and within the Western hemisphere. Multilateralist presidents, Woodrow Wilson and Franklin D. Roosevelt in particular, were instrumental not only in defining universal human rights but also in helping to establish institutional mechanisms to promote and enforce these rights.

The League of Nations and the human rights references in its constitution were supported by President Woodrow Wilson, whose famous Fourteen Points included peoples' right to self-determination and the necessity for equality of rights across national borders. However, Wilson was unable to convince U.S. lawmakers to join the League of Nations; also, his resistance to condemning racism in the League's constitution tainted his record. Both restricted the U.S. capacity to influence the League's policies in favor of universal human rights. What Wilson failed to do in relation to the League, however, was later compensated for by Franklin D. Roosevelt's leadership in the establishment of the United Nations. While the incorporation of human rights into the UN Charter resulted mainly from persistent efforts by non-governmental organizations, before the emergence of the UN the U.S. government had supported resolutions in defense of human rights at the eighth Conference of American States. Roosevelt's broad vision of human rights, which included not only civil and political freedoms but also social and economic rights, influenced the conception of human rights in the UN's Universal Declaration. Eleanor Roosevelt—whose commitment to social justice, antidiscrimination, and human rights surpassed that of her husband—chaired the Human Rights Commission that was charged with developing international human rights standards and was personally involved in the committee that drafted the Universal Declaration of Human Rights (Glendon, 2001). Her involvement helped shape the content of the document, although the U.S. State Department was not eager about the inclusion of social and economic rights (Lauren, 1998; Morsink, 1999).

The positive influence of the United States was clearer and more conspicuous in the cases of the Genocide Convention and the Nuremberg and Tokyo trials after the Second World War. Immediately after the war the leaders of the Allied Powers leaned toward summary execution of the Nazi leaders but ultimately decided on a treaty that created the Nuremberg tribunal, largely because of the insistence of U.S. officials. In Gary Jonathan Bass's words, U.S. Secretary of War Stimpson made the convincing argument that "to choose anything other than trials was inconsistent with liberal democratic principles—that mass executions would be, in the last analysis, un-American. Nuremberg was the American thing to do" (as quoted in Tucker, 2001:71). However, "the stated objectives were lofty enough, but the taint of victor's justice was pervasive. At Nuremberg (and Tokyo) only the losing leaders were tried, even though allied leaders had engaged in such acts as attacking cities through conventional, incendiary, and atomic bombings, thus failing to distinguish between combatants and civilians—a cardinal principle of international humanitarian law" (Forsythe, 2000:85).

Although the United States tends to criticize other countries for their failure to respect human rights and often pressures them into signing and ratifying international human rights documents, its own rate of ratification has been very poor. The United States is a party to only half of the eight major United Nations human rights conventions. As shown in Table 4.1, even those ratifications came fairly late, three of them taking place during President Clinton's administration. The United States has also declined to sign some optional protocols to these conventions or the International Convention on the Protection of the Rights of All Migrant Workers and Members of Their Families.

TABLE 4.1.
The status of the United States on major human rights treaties

Human Rights Treaty (and date of adoption by the UN General Assembly)	Date Signed by the U.S.	Date Ratified by the U.S.
Convention on the Prevention and Punishment of the Crime of Genocide, December 9, 1948	December 11, 1948	November 25, 1988
International Convention on the Elimination of All Forms of Racial Discrimination, March 7, 1966	September 28, 1966	October 21, 1994
International Covenant on Economic, Social and Cultural Rights, December 16, 1966	October 5, 1977	—
International Covenant on Civil and Political Rights, December 16, 1966	October 5, 1977	June 8, 1992
Convention on the Elimination of All Forms of Discrimination against Women, December 18, 1979	July 17, 1980	—
Convention against Torture and Other Cruel, Inhuman or Degrading Treatment or Punishment, December 10, 1984	April 18, 1988	October 21, 1994
Convention on the Rights of the Child, New York, November 20, 1989	February 16, 1995	—
International Convention on the Protection of the Rights of All Migrant Workers and Members of their Families, December 18, 1990.	—	—

Source: Office of the High Commissioner of Human Rights http://www.ohchr.org/english/countries/ratification/index.htm (accessed June 20, 2005)

This undistinguished rate of treaty ratification is often justified by U.S. officials because of the federal structure of the U.S.
government, claiming that if the federal government brings the
country into international treaties the rights of the fifty states
would be compromised. The incompatibility of international
treaties with the U.S. Constitution and the fear of creating a world
government that would undermine national sovereignty are presented as other reasons. Another argument is that such treaties are
irrelevant to the United States because the laws of the country already include the treaty provisions. The rest of the world sees it
differently, of course, and finds this "American exceptionalism"
problematic as it puts the United States above international law,
setting a precedent for other countries and consequently weakening the implementation and overall effectiveness of the international system in protecting human rights.

U.S. resistance turned into overt objection in the case of the
Rome treaty that created the International Criminal Court (ICC)
to try crimes against humanity. (See Chapter 1.) On July 17, 1998,
when the Rome statute was voted on, the United States voted
against it along with China, Iraq, Israel, Libya, Sudan, and Yemen.
In fact, the United States attempted to block the creation of a permanent criminal court by actively lobbying against it. The U.S.
government has opposed the treaty on two grounds. The first is
the concern that the ICC could be used to make U.S. military personnel, operating in several countries, subject to politically motivated charges. This position was articulated by Ambassador
Scheffer:

> There is a reality, and the reality is that the United States
> is a global military power and presence. Other countries
> are not. We are. Our military forces are often called
> upon to engage overseas in conflict situations, for pur-
> poses of humanitarian intervention, to rescue hostages,
> to bring out American citizens from threatening envi-
> ronments, to deal with terrorists. We have to be ex-
> tremely careful that this proposal [for a standing court]
> does not limit the capacity of the armed forces to legiti-
> mately operate internationally. We have to be careful
> that it does not open up opportunities for endless frivo-
> lous complaints to be lodged against the United States
> as a global military Power. (as quoted in Forsythe,
> 2000:103–104)

However, as the statute includes several measures to pre-
clude politically motivated prosecutions, this claim by U.S. officials is called "a smoke screen argument" (Forsythe, 2000:104).
The other objection of the United States refers to the way investigations leading to prosecution are initiated. According to the
treaty rules, states parties, the UN Security Council, and the Prosecutor of the ICC may all bring matters before the court subject
to the approval of a pretrial panel of judges. The United States
has worried that this procedure would result in circumventing
the authority of the UN Security Council, in which the United
States has considerable control because of its veto power.

Consequently, the U.S. government not only actively lobbied
other nations against ratifying the treaty, but when it failed in its
efforts to prevent the establishment of the ICC, it intensified its
efforts to curtail the power of the Court. It tried to secure bilateral
agreements with individual countries to assure that they will not
use the Court to bring charges against U.S. citizens. These efforts
were intensified after George W. Bush came to power and removed the signature placed by President Clinton on the treaty.
(President Clinton had signed the treaty on December 31, 2000,
not with the intent of having it ratified but only to improve the
U.S. position in engaging other countries in a dialogue that might
result in changes favored by his country.) Finally, the United
States attempted to secure its position by putting pressure on
states parties to the treaty. The pressure spilled into the open in
December 2004, when the U.S. Congress approved a provision in
a government spending bill that mandated withholding some
economic assistance to countries that refuse to grant immunity
for U.S. nationals before the ICC (Amnesty International, 2005).

The U.S. approach and conduct toward the ICC have been
criticized by many countries and human rights organizations for
undermining and weakening the Court. However, the crisis in the
Darfur region of Sudan, which involved genocidal acts against the
Sudanese in the region by a militia that was suspected of having
government support, forced the United States to take a step toward recognizing the ICC. On March 31, 2005, the UN Security
Council passed a resolution referring the Darfur case to the ICC,
thus giving the Court the authority to investigate and prosecute
those who are responsible for the massive human rights violations committed in this region.

Another contentious issue has been the international campaign to ban land mines. The United States was one of the first

countries to call for the total elimination of antipersonnel mines in 1994, and in 2001 it provided $69.2 million for international mine action programs, yet it has refused to join the 1997 Mine Ban Treaty. It is the only NATO country that is not a party to the Treaty. Although President Clinton failed to sign the 1997 Mine Ban Treaty, he had formulated a policy geared toward attaining U.S. ratification of the treaty by 2006. The Bush government, however, rejected any such notion and reversed the ten-year policy to eliminate all antipersonnel land mines. It postponed the destruction of "persistent" land mines until 2010 and asserted the U.S. military's right to use self-deactivating "smart" mines indefinitely. The International Campaign to Ban Land Mines has noted that "these so-called 'smart' mines tend to be scattered by air and are thus difficult to mark and map, pose tremendous challenges and costs for demining teams, and threaten the lives and limbs of innocent civilians and U.S. troops who step on the weapons soon after they've been planted" (International Campaign, n.d.). With 11.2 million antipersonnel mines, the United States has the third largest stockpile in the world, after China and Russia (International Campaign, 2004).

Over the years, in relation to other international treaties, the United States has displayed similar postures and policies that have had significant negative repercussions on human rights. Withdrawing from the 1972 Anti-Ballistic Missile Treaty, the country pursued the Star Wars project in the 1980s. While the U.S. government has been campaigning against the proliferation of nuclear weapons and actively trying to prevent other countries from developing nuclear capabilities, it refused to join the Comprehensive Test Ban Treaty in order to maintain its own ability to test new generations of nuclear weapons. The Bush administration has also withdrawn the U.S. signature from the 1997 Kyoto Protocol, which aims at minimizing global warming by reducing the "greenhouse" gas emissions of thirty-five industrialized countries, by claiming that the implementation of the Protocol would hinder the growth of the U.S. economy and that the exemptions granted to the developing countries will render the treaty ineffective anyway.

The U.S. position on international efforts to promote economic and social rights has been equally disturbing. At the Habitat Conference, held in Istanbul in 1996, the U.S. government stood alone in rejecting the right to housing; the same year, when the World Food Summit met in Rome, the head of the U.S. government delegation indicated that the country could not support language in the final document concerning the right to food, because doing so would place the new U.S. welfare reform law in violation of international law; and in December 1998, the United States was the only country that cast a negative vote on the UN General Assembly resolution that urged all countries to eliminate obstacles to development and the protection of economic, social, and cultural rights along with civil and political rights (Mittal and Rosset, 1999:xii–xiii). Finally, at the Millennium Summit meeting, held in New York on September 14–16, 2005—five years after adoption of the Millennium Declaration and the Millennium Development Goals (MDGs)—the U.S. delegation, led by its new UN Ambassador John Bolton, demanded hundreds of changes in the draft of the outcome document. The United States objected to pledging an increase in its current development aid, which was approximately .16 percent of the country's gross national product at the time, to .7 percent by 2015—a millennium goal set in 2000 for all developed countries, and all other developed countries have pledged to meet this goal. The U.S. attempt to remove all human rights references to the MDGs in the document and to address the development and poverty reduction goals in vague language was blocked by the firm resistance of the other members of the UN, but they could not prevent the final document from turning into a rather diluted version of the original draft. The United States also reiterated its objections to several global human rights related initiatives that it had been opposing in other forums, including disarmament, the Kyoto Protocol, the Comprehensive Test Ban Treaty, and the International Criminal Court.

The United States has been delinquent in paying dues to the United Nations and its various agencies as well. When the UN does not receive funds from its major contributor, the work of many of its agencies is hampered, including the agencies that have programs in the human rights area or that provide humanitarian aid. Some charge that "the United States can pick and choose the international conventions and laws that serve its purpose and reject those that do not," and criticize this practice by labeling it "international law á la carte" (Spiro, 2000:9).

U.S. Foreign Policy and Human Rights

The U.S. government, along with many other governments, has a proclaimed policy of promoting human rights in the conduct of its world affairs. The Foreign Assistance Act of 1961 (as amended in 1975), noting that a "principal goal of the foreign policy of the United States is to promote the increased observance of internationally recognized human rights," charges the State Department with the task of preparing and submitting country reports on human rights practices of foreign states (Section 502B). Two relevant sections of the Act also specify its focus and criteria as internationally recognized human rights: "The Secretary of the State shall transmit to the Speaker of the House of Representatives and the Committee on Foreign Relations of the Senate, . . . a full and complete report regarding . . . the status of *internationally recognized* human rights" (Section 116 [d] [1]); and "The Secretary of State shall transmit to the Congress, as a part of the presentation materials for security assistance programs proposed for each fiscal year, a full and complete report, prepared with the assistance of the Assistant Secretary of Human Rights and Humanitarian Affairs, with respect to practices regarding the observance of and respect for *internationally recognized* human rights in each country proposed as a recipient of security assistance" (Section 502B [b], emphasis mine).

However, the issue of human rights is only one of the factors, and not always the dominant one, that go into the formulation of foreign policy, and the U.S. government's priorities and understanding of human rights have not been always conducive to influencing human rights practices in other countries for the better. Nevertheless, the enormous economic and political power of the United States allows it to use human rights as a bargaining chip, and it has been able to improve human conditions in various countries through negotiation. For example, in the late 1990s the U.S. government was able to convince China to release several dissidents and agree to sign the International Covenant on Civil and Political Rights. Similarly, during the global anti-apartheid movement, the United States, by employing sanctions against the apartheid regime in South Africa, was instrumental in bringing about the release of Nelson Mandela from prison and ultimately changing the country's system of government.

The U.S. commitment to international human rights, however, is considered more forceful in rhetoric than in practice, and critics find the gap hypocritical. In addition to "the U.S. exceptionalism" discussed earlier in the chapter, other aspects of U.S. foreign policy over the years have been subject to numerous criticisms for undermining or violating human rights in other parts of the world.

They include: the narrow definition of human rights that excludes social and economic rights; double standards and inconsistent implementation of criticisms and sanctions on different countries; support for repressive regimes that serve U.S. national interests; and promotion/imposition of neo-liberal economic policies that undermine social and economic rights.

The Universal Declaration of Human Rights embodies a long list of rights, and the subsequent declarations, covenants, and protocols developed within the United Nations and various regional organizations have expanded the scope of these rights, emphasizing their equality and interdependency. However, there has been resistance to this trend and some prioritization has taken place among the nations. For the United States, social and economic rights have never been equal to civil and political rights; they are referred to as desirable "goals" or "aspirations," not classified as "human rights'" (Alston, 1993:61).

The Carter administration, known for emphasizing the importance of human rights in foreign policy formulation, pushed social and economic rights aside by referring to them as "aspects of life" that are not quite qualified to be included among human rights. Although Carter's secretary of state, Cyrus Vance, incorporated "the right to the fulfillment of such vital needs as food, shelter, health care, and education" into his definition of human rights and included their promotion as a foreign policy objective, he hinted at their secondary position by saying that their fulfillment would "depend upon the stage of a nation's economic development" and their promotion by the United States would be a "broader challenge" (Vance, 1989:343–348). Similarly, the Country Reports on human rights practices, annually published by the U.S. State Department, included some reference to these rights under Carter's presidency but without labeling them "rights." The language employed was this: "Government Policies Relating to the Fulfillment of Such Vital Needs as Food, Shelter, Health Care and Education."

In preparing these reports, in its first year of reporting, the Reagan administration eliminated the category and addressed some issues that would fall into this category under a subheading of "social, economic and cultural conditions"; it then eliminated the topic completely. The succeeding Bush administration maintained this approach but more aggressively. Addressing the United Nations Commission on Human Rights in Geneva in 1992, U.S. Vice President Dan Quayle criticized the UN Commission for trying to make employment, health care, or literacy human rights issues while they belonged to other agencies and committees of the UN (MacShane, 1993).

Although the Reagan and first Bush administrations openly rejected social and economic rights, other administrations, including Carter's, had not been any different in ignoring them in practice. Whenever the United States has protested human rights violations, the government has followed a narrow interpretation of the Lockean notion of human rights and the state's role in pursuing them. Human rights have been reduced to basic civil rights (e.g., freedom of speech; freedom from torture, arbitrary arrest, imprisonment, etc.) and considered violated only if the infringement is seen as the direct result of state action.

On April 26, 1993, Warren Christopher, Secretary of State in the Clinton administration, articulated the United States' position at the Fourth World Conference of the National Endowment of Democracy. His speech employed the term "human rights" to mean exclusively civil and political rights; he defined those rights, democracy, and market reforms as three forces that feed each other, and justified the involvement of the United States in these areas by their close ties as well as on moral grounds (Christopher, May 3, 1993:312–313). A few months later, on June 14, at the World Conference on Human Rights in Vienna, he announced the human rights agenda of the United States for the post–Cold War era:

> In this post–Cold War era, we are at a new moment. Our agenda for freedom must embrace every prisoner of conscience, every victim of torture, every individual denied basic human rights. It must also encompass the democratic movements that have changed the political map of our globe.
>
> The great focus of our agenda for freedom is this: expanding, consolidating and defending democratic progress around the world. It is democracy that establishes the civil institutions that replace the power of oppressive regimes. Democracy is the best means not just to gain—but to guarantee—human rights. (Christopher, June 21, 1993:441)

Treating human rights and democracy as symbiotic and interchangeable concepts, as evident in Christopher's words, has been another component of U.S. foreign policy followed over the years. Democracy and human rights are related concepts, but there is no one-to-one correspondence. The U.S. governments have taken the position of supporting procedural democracies as a way of supporting human rights. However, the right to vote is only one human right, and regimes that permit periodic elections in which candidates from different parties compete may repress several other civil and political rights and can be completely indifferent to social and economic rights (Arat, 1999). Fareed Zakaria uses the term "illiberal democracies" to refer to the "half of the 'democratizing' countries in the world today," which function as procedural democracies with periodic, multiparty, and competitive elections but fall short of guaranteeing basic liberties and protecting the constitutional rights of their citizens (Zakaria, 1997:23–24).

When the United States included the protection of human rights among its foreign policy objectives, it did so mainly as a part of its "anticommunist" agenda (Moynihan, 1989). The rhetoric of human rights was reduced in scope to cover only those rights that were believed to be violated in the Soviet Union and other "Communist" regimes. On March 25, 1977, Jimmy Carter implicitly acknowledged the role and compartmentalization of human rights in the ideological struggles of the Cold War in the following sentences: "Mr. Brezhnev and his predecessors have never refrained from expressing their view when they disagreed with some aspects of social and political life in the free world. And I think we have a right to speak out openly when we have a concern about human rights wherever those abuses occur" (quoted in Moynihan, 1989:25). The anti-Soviet rhetoric was also strong during the Reagan years. The introduction of the country reports for 1981 states that "it is a significant service to the cause of human rights to limit the influence the USSR (together with its clients and proxies) can exert" (p. 9). The staunch anti-Communist disposition and a human rights orientation that is partial to civil and political liberties, demonstrated by U.S. governments, were reinforced by some U.S.-based human rights organizations that employed a similar human rights discourse in the 1970s and 1980s (e.g., Human Rights Watch under the leadership of Aryeh Neier).

Yet even civil and political rights have been ignored during the formulation and implementation of policies concerning specific countries, or they have been overridden by other policy concerns such as security and trade. During the Cold War years, the violations of civil and political rights by anticommunist authoritarian regimes were ignored for "security" reasons, although the economic gains from collaboration with repressive regimes were often substantial. Similarly, President Clinton largely ignored the gross human rights violations in China, which came under public scrutiny as China has become more open, for the sake of both countries' commercial interests.

An element of international contention, seen as displaying both the hypocritical posture of the United States and its double standards, has been its leniency toward Israel's aggression and violation of Palestinians' rights in the occupied territories. The United States has not only been silent but has also played an enabling role by feeding Israel's repressive machinery through direct aid and arms sales and by blocking international efforts to impose sanctions on Israel through the use of its veto power in the UN Security Council.

U.S. foreign policy has been ambiguous also with regard to women's rights. On one hand, the country began to pay more attention to the impact of development aid on women. The Percy Amendment of 1973 required the inclusion of women in all projects of the United States Agency for International Development USAID, and the agency developed several training sessions and manuals to meet these requirement. In the early 1990s, the State Department's annual country reports on human rights practices began monitoring women's condition and supplying information on the violations of women's rights or progress toward improving women's status. On the other hand, a presidential policy, commonly known as "the global gag rule," impinged on the reproductive rights and health of women in developing countries. Originally instituted by President Reagan in 1984, the rule prevents organizations that receive U.S. aid from providing abortion services, counseling on abortion, participating in political debates on abortion or lobbying for it in their own country, or even mentioning abortion in their consultation and education programs. It prohibits funding for any foreign organization that goes against these restrictions, even if the organization carries out such activities through funds obtained from other sources.

This policy was repealed by President Clinton in 1993 but reinstituted in 1999, when the conservative Republican members of Congress threatened him with further withholding of the nearly $1 billion of unpaid dues to the United Nations. The policy was meant to be limited only to fiscal year 2000, but George W. Bush reactivated the policy as one of his first official acts, when he became president. The full impact of this ban could not be measured, but it is agreed that it not only restricted women's access to safe abortion and increased unintended pregnancies, maternal mortality, and child deaths, but also, due to the reduction in their funding, limited the services of those agencies that refused to follow the rule in many areas, including educational programs geared toward preventing the spread of HIV and AIDS (Baird, 2004).

U.S. foreign policy has been subject to criticism not only for being lenient on authoritarian governments and repressive regimes that serve the geopolitical and economic interests of the United States but also for the U.S. involvement in toppling democratic governments, installing coercive rulers in their place, and being instrumental in the implementation of brutal policies. A number of coups d'état that ousted the elected governments in Latin American countries from the 1950s through the 1980s are cases in point. U.S. participation in the military coups of Guatemala in 1954 and Chile in 1973, in particular, is well documented and confirmed by CIA documents released in the 1990s. In addition to sponsored coups, personnel of the repressive machinery of these states were trained and maintained by "Operation Condor" and the U.S. Army School of Americas. Operation Condor was a Latin American military network created in the 1970s whose key members were Argentina, Brazil, Bolivia, Chile, Paraguay, and Uruguay, later joined by Ecuador and Peru in less central roles. It was a Cold War–era configuration backed by the United States in its effort to "contain Communism," but as a covert intelligence and operations system, it was used by the Latin American military states, which defied international law to hunt down, seize, and execute political opponents across borders. The military leaders and officers who ordered and carried out the atrocities against union leaders, student activists, and other left-wing critics were trained at the School of the Americas (SOA), run by the U.S. Army. The SOA was initially established in Panama in 1946 but was moved to Fort Benning, Georgia, in 1984 under the terms of the Panama Canal Treaty; its purpose was to train Latin American security personnel in combat, counterinsurgency, and counternarcotics. The SOA trained approximately 60,000 Latin American officers, using the infamous torture manuals released by the Pentagon and the CIA in the mid-1990s. Dubbed the "School of Assassins" by its critics, the SOA has been a base for destabilizing Latin American democracies and enabling massive human rights violations in the "dirty wars" of the military (Gill, 2004; McSherry, 2005).

The U.S. Army School of the Americas officially closed its doors on December 15, 2000. On January 17, 2001, it was replaced by the Western Hemisphere Institute for Security Cooperation. Section 911 of the 2001 National Defense Authorization Act (H.R. 5408) added a new section 2166 to Title 10, U.S. Code (the part of U.S. law that governs the military) and specified certain changes, including these: (1) defining the purpose of the renamed institute as "to provide professional education and training to eligible personnel of nations of the Western Hemisphere within the context of the democratic principles set forth in the Charter of the Organization of American States . . . while fostering mutual knowledge, transparency, confidence, and cooperation among the participating nations and promoting democratic values, respect for human rights, and knowledge and understanding of United States customs and traditions"; and (2) requiring each student to receive at least eight hours of instruction in "human rights, the rule of law, due process, civilian control of the military, and the role of the military in a democratic society."

Another counterproductive aspect of the foreign policy of the United States is its promotion of U.S. economic interests at the expense of human rights in the developing world and its dogmatic commitment to a market economy. Some of the above mentioned regime changes were supported by the United States in an effort to protect U.S. companies against those governments' efforts to nationalize their countries' natural resources (e.g., the copper industry in Chile) and secure the unregulated operation of the multinational companies in those countries (e.g., United Fruit Company in Guatemala).

Some of the economic policy goals have been pursued through multilateral organizations such as the IMF and the World Bank. Since the governance of these international financial agencies follows a weighted voting system—the wealthier countries that pay a higher membership fee have votes in proportion to their national wealth—the U.S. has asserted considerable control over the agencies' policies, including the content of the structural adjustment requirements. In fact, the close cooperation between the U.S. Treasury Department, the IMF, and the World Bank has led many of their critics to label the formula solutions of the trio as "the Washington Consensus," referring to Washington, D.C., the city that houses all three agencies. Even Joseph Stiglitz, who served as an economic consultant to the Clinton administration as well as Chief Economist at the World Bank, criticized the U.S.

Treasury Department for pursuing "market fundamentalism" and imposing on the borrowing states a senseless neo-liberal philosophy, which offers little help for the financial problems of these countries (Stiglitz, 2003).

This approach of the United States became a subject of criticism among many, including United Nations officials who worked in the human rights area. They accused the U.S. government of "preaching a new determinism, a kind of inverted Marxism, which claims that market freedom and economic freedom are both the necessary and the sufficient condition of all freedom and of the enjoyment of human rights," pointing out that "the experience of some of the world's regions and countries shows how misguided these doctrines are" (Lalumiere, 1993:10). Nevertheless, such policies have continued to be promoted by successive U.S. governments at an increasing rate. In fact, a global economic liberalization program was launched by the North American Free Trade Agreement (NAFTA) initiative, which included Canada, Mexico, and the United States. Even as NAFTA was being criticized for violating economic rights and catering to the interest of big businesses and corporations at the expense of small farm owners and wage earners, similar free trade agreements were being pushed in Central and South America, as well as in Africa. The promotion of neo-liberal economic policies gained new momentum under the leadership of President George W. Bush. The human rights record of the Bush administration has been particularly problematic because it not only promoted corporate expansion and economic liberalization but also allowed the states that have been supportive of Bush's antiterrorism policies to restrict the freedoms of their own citizens under the guise of fighting terrorism.

Tony Evans, insisting that the assessment of human rights should involve the analysis of interests and power, notes that the United States not only formulated "an American conception of rights," based on ideas of individualism, freedom, and *laissez-faire* economics, but also used human rights as a justification for projecting this particular conception of rights across the globe to assert its hegemony and gain access to world markets (Evans, 1998:6–7). He claimed that concerns over preserving its hegemonic status and self-interest led the United States to take a position on human rights that preserved its status quo:

> There is obvious tension between promoting universal values and the exercise of state hegemony. Constraints

on state power designed to protect universal human rights are constraints on all states, even the hegemon. To avoid this difficulty, the hegemon must sustain a view of human rights that demands little change to the existing social practices. (Evans, 1998:7)

Nevertheless, as countries move toward privatization and free trade under United States' leadership and pressure from funding agencies such as the IMF and the World Bank, the U.S. view of democracy and the Lockean notion of human rights have become more widespread and have gained a stronghold. As the U.S. preoccupation with economic liberalization and anti-terrorism intensifies, the future of all human rights looks grimmer.

References

Alston, Philip. "The Importance of the Inter-play between Economic, Social and Cultural Rights, and Civil and Political Rights." In *Human Rights at the Dawn of the 21st Century.* Proceedings of the Interregional Meeting organized by the Council of Europe in advance of the World Conference on Human Rights, palais de l'Europe, Strasbourg, January 28–30, 1993. Strasbourg: Council of Europe Press, 1993:59–74.

American Civil Liberties Union. "The Sun Also Sets: Understanding the Patriot Act 'Sunsets'" n.d. http://action.aclu.org/reformthepatriotact/sunsets.html (accessed June 20, 2005).

Amnesty International. *Amnesty International Report 2005.* "United States of America." http://web.amnesty.org/report2005/usa-summary-eng (accessed June 22, 2005).

Arat, Zehra F. "Human Rights and Democracy: Expanding or Contracting." *Polity* 32:1 (Fall 1999): 119–144.

Baird, Karen. "Globalizing Reproductive Control: Consequences of the 'Global Gag Rule.'" In Rosemai Tong, Anne Donchin, and Susan Dodds, eds., *Linking Visions: Feminist Bioethics, Human Rights, and the Developing World.* Boulder, CO: Rowman & Littlefield, 2004:133–145.

Bright, Stephen B. "The Right to Counsel: Gideon V. Wainwright at 40: Overviews and Perspectives: Turning Celebrated Principles into Reality." *The Champion* 27 (January/February 2003): 6–11.

Bureau of Justice Statistics. "Correction Statistics," 2005. http://www.ojp.usdoj.gov/bjs/correct.htm (accessed June 18, 2005).

Christopher, Warren. "Democracy and Human Rights: Where America Stands." *U.S. Department of State Dispatch* (June 21, 1993): 441–446.

Christopher, Warren. "Support for Global Human Rights Strengthens Democracy at Home." *U.S. Department of State Dispatch* (May 3, 1993): 312–313.

Evans, Tony. "Introduction: Power, Hegemony and the Universalization of Human Rights." In Tony Evans, ed., *Human Rights Fifty Years On: A Reappraisal.* Manchester: Manchester University Press, 1998:1–23.

Forsythe, David P. *Human Rights in International Relations.* Cambridge: Cambridge University Press, 2000.

Gill, Lesley. *The School of the Americas: Military Training and Political Violence in the Americas.* Durham, NC: Duke University Press, 2004.

Gillies, David. *Between Principle and Practice: Human Rights in North-South Relations.* Glendon, Mary Ann. *A World Made New.* New York: Random House, 2001.

Henkin, Louis. *The Age of Rights.* New York: Columbia University Press, 1990.

Human Development Report 2000. United Nations Development Programme. New York: Oxford University Press, 2000.

Human Development Report 2004. United Nations Development Programme. New York: Oxford University Press, 2004.

Human Development Report 2005. United Nations Development Programme. New York: Oxford University Press, 2005.

Human Rights Watch. "U.S.: Did President Bush Order Torture?" News. December 21, 2004. http://hrw.org/english/docs/2004/12/21/usint 9925.htm (accessed June 2, 2005).

Human Rights Watch/Amnesty International. *The Rest of Their Lives: Life without Parole for Child Offenders in the United States.* New York: Human Rights Watch, 2005.

Hummel, Jeffrey. "Not Just Japanese Americans: The Untold Story of U.S. Repression During 'The Good War.'" *Journal for Historical Review* 7:3 (Fall 1986): 285–318.

International Campaign to Ban Land Mines. "U.S.A Retains Mines, Abandons Mine Ban Treaty in New Policy." 2004. http://www.icbl.org/problem/country/usa (accessed June 18, 2005).

International Campaign to Ban Land Mines. n.d. http://www.banminesusa.org (accessed June 18, 2005).

ILO (International Labour Organization). *World Labor Report 1997–98: Industrial Relations, Democracy and Social Stability* (October 15, 1997). http://www.ilo.org/public/english/dialogue/ifpdial/publ/wlr97/index.htm (accessed September 23, 2005).

ILO (International Labour Organization). "Trade Union Membership." Excel data file provided by the ILO office upon request. October 11, 2005.

Lalumiere, Catherine. "Opening Statement." In *Human Rights at the Dawn of the 21st Century.* Proceedings of the Interregional Meeting organized by the Council of Europe in advance of the World Conference on Human Rights, palais de l'Europe, Strasbourg, January 28–30, 1993. Strasbourg: Council of Europe Press, 1993:1–20.

Lauren, Paul Gordon. *The Evolution of International Human Rights: Visions Seen.* Philadelphia: University of Pennsylvania Press, 1998.

MacShane, Denis. "Labor Standards and Double Standards in the New World Order." In Jeremy Brecher, John Brown Childs, and Jill Cutler, eds., *Global Visions: Beyond the New World Order.* Boston: South End Press, 1993:197–206.

McSherry, J. Patrice. *Predatory States: Operation Condor and Covert War in Latin America.* Boulder, CO: Rowman & Littlefield, 2005.

Mittal, Anuradha, and Rosset, Peter, eds. *America Needs Human Rights.* Oakland, CA: Food First Books, 1999.

Morsink, Johannes. *The Universal Declaration of Human Rights: Origins, Drafting, and Intent.* Philadelphia: University of Pennsylvania Press, 1999.

Moynihan, Daniel P. "The Politics of Human Rights." In Walter Laqueur and Barry Rubin, eds., *The Human Rights Reader.* New York: Meridian, 1989:25–40.

"Pentagon Will Not Try 17 G.I.'s Implicated in Prisoners' Deaths." *New York Times* (March 26, 2005).

Reporters Without Borders. *United States—Annual Report 2004.* http://www.rsf.org (accessed February 5, 2005).

Rodgers, Harrell R., Jr. *American Poverty in a New Era of Reform,* 2nd ed. Armonk, NY: M.E. Sharpe, 2006.

Schlafly, Phyllis. "A Short History of E.R.A.," The Phyllis Schlafly Report, September 1986. http://www.eagleforum.org/psr/1986/sept86/psrsep86.html (accessed February 23, 2006).

Spiro, Peter J. "The New Sovereigntist: American Exceptionalism and Its False Prophets." *Foreign Affairs* 79:6 (November/December 2000): 9–15.

Stetson, Dorothy McBridge, and Mazur, Amy G., eds. *Comparative State Feminism.* Thousand Oaks, CA: Sage, 1995.

Stiglitz, Joseph. *Globalization and Its Discontents.* New York: W.W. Norton, 2003.

Tucker, Robert W. "The International Criminal Court Controversy." *World Policy Journal* 18:2 (Summer 2001): 71–81.

Vance, Cyrus. "Law Day Speech on Human Rights and Foreign Policy." In Walter Laqueur and Barry Rubin, eds., *The Human Rights Reader.* New York: Meridian, 1989:343–348.

World Tribunal on Iraq. http://www.worldtribunal.org/main/?b=1 (accessed June 23, 2005).

Zakaria, Fareed. "The Rise of Illiberal Democracy." *Foreign Affairs* 76 (November/December 1997): 23–43.

5

Chronology of
Human Rights Events

lthough a notion of human rights has existed in all cultures and societies, the terminology of human rights is relatively new. "Universal human rights" is a modern concept and became a part of international discourse especially after the First World War. However, the most significant event for the advancement of human rights has been arguably the establishment of the United Nations (UN) in 1945. Starting with its Charter, the UN assumed the mission of promoting human rights. The first important human rights–related product of the UN was the Universal Declaration of Human Rights in 1948. Since then, the UN's major human rights events have been, for the most part, issuing declarations and covenants to which nations of the world subscribe. It should be noted that declarations and resolutions are documents that include general statements and principles on which nations agree, but they do not bind the signatory states; covenants, conventions, and treaties, used somewhat interchangeably, have binding power for the states that ratify them and become international law upon their ratification by a specific number of nations. The following is a chronology of the major human rights events.

1919   The International Labour Organization (ILO) is founded by the Treaty of Versailles to formulate international labor standards through conventions and recommendations setting minimum standards of basic labor rights: freedom of association, the right to organize, collective bargaining, abolition of forced labor, equality of opportunity and

123

1919   treatment, and other standards regulating conditions
(*cont.*) across the entire spectrum of work-related issues. After
         the Second World War, it becomes the first specialized
         agency of the United Nations in 1946.

1926   The League of Nations adopts the Slavery Convention,
         which intends (a) to prevent and suppress the slave
         trade, and (b) to bring about, progressively and as soon
         as possible, the complete abolition of slavery in all its
         forms, and enters into force on March 9, 1927.

1930   The ILO adopts the Forced Labor Convention (which en-
         ters into force on January 5, 1932). The Forced Labor
         Convention firmly establishes the intention of the ILO to
         explicitly target slavery through the institution of formal
         procedures and legal instructions to monitor violations.

1941   U.S. president Franklin Roosevelt delivers the State of
         the Union message, which includes one of the first refer-
         ences to the "Four Freedoms"—freedom of speech, free-
         dom of religion, freedom from want, and freedom from
         fear—freedoms that, he states, should prevail every-
         where in the world.

1944   Declaration of Philadelphia. Two famous passages are
         incorporated into the constitution of the ILO: "All
         human beings, irrespective of race, creed, or sex, have
         the right to pursue both their material well-being and
         their spiritual development in conditions of freedom and
         dignity, of economic security, and equal opportunity";
         and "Freedom of expression and association are essential
         to sustained progress."

1945   Establishment of the United Nations. The Preamble to
         the UN Charter includes the phrase "to reaffirm faith in
         fundamental human rights, in the dignity and worth of
         the human person, in the equal rights of men and
         women, and of nations large and small." Among its pur-
         poses are to achieve international cooperation "in pro-
         moting and encouraging respect for human rights and
         for fundamental freedoms for all without distinction as
         to race, sex, language, or religion" (Article 1.3).

1946 The UN General Assembly approves and ratifies the Nuremberg Principles, which establish the right and authority of nations to punish violations of human rights and specify that soldiers may not be acquitted on the grounds of following orders of superiors when they violate the rules of war.

1948 The Convention on the Prevention and Punishment of the Crime of Genocide is adopted by the UN General Assembly (and enters into force on January 12, 1951). The convention recognizes genocide as a crime under international law and states that those accused of it, in wartime or peace, can be tried by the country where the crime is committed or by such international tribunals as have jurisdiction.

The UN General Assembly adopts the Universal Declaration of Human Rights, which prescribes that all human beings are entitled to all human rights and fundamental freedoms set forth in the declaration. This is the most fundamental of all UN instruments; most subsequent human rights statements are based on its tenets.

The ILO adopts the Freedom of Association and Protection of the Right to Organise Convention (which enters into force on July 4, 1950).

The American Declaration of the Rights and Duties of Man, based on the Universal Declaration of Human Rights, is approved by the Ninth International Conference of American States, in Bogotá, Colombia.

1949 The Council of Europe is established. Its statutes include the statement, "Every member of the Council of Europe must accept the principles of the rule of law and of the enjoyment by all persons within its jurisdiction of human rights and fundamental freedoms." The Council also proposes the establishment of an internal organization to ensure the collective guarantee of human rights.

The Geneva Conventions are adopted by the UN. The four conventions represent a significant attempt to protect war

1949
(*cont.*)
victims. They attempt to protect wounded and sick armed forces in the field or on the sea from cruel treatment, assure decent treatment for prisoners of war, and protect civilians. They expressly prohibit the use of violence—in particular, torture, mutilation, or cruel treatment, the taking of hostages, or any degrading treatment. The conventions also oblige each party to search for those who have committed such abuses.

The ILO adopts the Right to Organise and Collective Bargaining Convention (which enters into force on July 18, 1951). The Convention prescribes adequate protection for workers against anti-union discrimination in employment.

The Convention for the Suppression of the Traffic in Persons and of the Exploitation of the Prostitution of Others is adopted by the UN General Assembly (and enters into force on July 25, 1951). The convention parties agree to punish any person who, to gratify another, procures, entices, or leads away, for the purpose of prostitution, another person, even with that person's consent, or exploits the prostitution of another person, even with the person's consent.

1950
The European Convention for the Protection of Human Rights and Fundamental Freedoms opens for signatures by the Council of Europe on November 4 (and enters into force on September 3, 1953). The Convention establishes the inalienable rights and freedoms of each citizen, obliging all states parties to guarantee these rights, and sets up a mechanism for the enforcement of the obligations entered into by states parties. Three institutions are entrusted with this responsibility: the European Commission of Human Rights (set up in 1954), the European Court of Human Rights (set up in 1959), and the Committee of Ministers of the Council of Europe, composed of the Ministers of Foreign Affairs of the member states or their representatives.

1951
The UN adopts the Convention Relating to the Status of Refugees. Parties to the Convention agree to give refugees "national treatment"—that is, treatment at least as favor-

able as that accorded their own nationals with regard to such rights as freedom of religion, access to courts, elementary education, and public relief. (The convention covers only persons who become refugees as a result of events occurring before January 1, 1951.)

The ILO adopts the Equal Remuneration Convention (which enters into force on May 23, 1953). The Convention institutes the "principle of equal remuneration for men and women workers for equal value."

1952   The UN adopts the Convention on the International Right of Correction. It provides that when a state party finds a news report filed between countries or disseminated abroad that is capable of damaging its foreign relations or national prestige, that state may submit its version of the facts to any other states where the report was publicized, and that these other states are obliged to release such a communiqué to news media within their territories.

1955   The Standard Minimum Rules for the Treatment of Prisoners are adopted by the UN. These seek to set standards for acceptable treatment of prisoners and management of penal institutions.

1956   The UN adopts the Supplementary Convention on the Abolition of Slavery, the Slave Trade, and Institutions and Practices Similar to Slavery. It requires parties to expedite, through legislative and other measures, the complete abolition of such practices as debt bondage, serfdom, and the use of a woman, without the right to refuse, as an object of barter in marriage.

1957   The UN approves the Convention on the Nationality of Married Women. Contracting states agree that neither celebration nor dissolution of marriage between a national and an alien can automatically affect the nationality of the wife.

The ILO adopts the Abolition of Forced Labor Convention (which enters into force on January 17, 1959). Parties to the Convention agree not to use any form of forced or

1957   compulsory labor as a means of political coercion or ed-
(*cont.*)   ucation or as punishment for holding political views ide-
ologically opposed to the established system.

1958   The General Conference of the International Labour Organization adopts the Discrimination (Employment and
Occupation) Convention (which enters into force on June
15, 1960). Each ratifying member agrees to declare and
pursue a national policy promoting equal opportunity
and treatment in employment and occupation with a
view to eliminating any discrimination in respect thereof.

1959   The Organization of American States (OAS) creates the
Inter-American Commission on Human Rights to promote respect for human rights. The commission asserts
its authority to study the human rights situations of
member states.

The Declaration of the Rights of the Child is adopted by
the UN General Assembly. It maintains that children
shall enjoy special protection and be given opportunities
and facilities, by law and other means, to enable them to
develop physically, mentally, morally, spiritually, and so-
cially in a healthy and normal manner in conditions of
freedom and dignity.

1960   The Convention against Discrimination in Education is
adopted by the General Conference of the United Nations Educational, Scientific, and Cultural Organization
(UNESCO). Parties agree to ensure by legislation where
necessary that there is no discrimination in the admission of pupils to educational institutions; to make primary education free and compulsory; to make secondary
education generally available and accessible to all, and
higher education equally accessible to all on the basis of
individual capacity; and to make certain the factors relating to the quality of education provided are equivalent
in all public education.

The Declaration on the Granting of Independence to
Colonial Countries and Peoples is adopted by General
Assembly.

1961   The UN adopts the Convention on the Reduction of Statelessness. It specifies grounds on which a state may not deprive a person of nationality; these include racial, ethnic, religious, or political reasons.

The Council of Europe adopts the European Social Charter (which enters into force on February 26, 1965.) Including provisions on the protection of social and economic rights, the Charter complements the European Convention for the Protection of Human Rights and Fundamental Freedoms.

Amnesty International is established in United Kingdom and in time becomes the largest international human rights organization.

1962   The Convention on Consent to Marriage, Minimum Age for Marriage, and Registration of Marriages is approved by the UN General Assembly. States must take legislative action to specify a minimum age for marriage and to provide for the registration of marriages by an appropriate official. Marriages may not be legally entered into without the full and free consent of both parties.

1963   The UN adopts the Declaration on the Elimination of All Forms of Racial Discrimination. Discrimination against human beings on the grounds of race, color, or ethnic origin is an offense to humanity and shall be condemned as a denial of the principles of the Charter of the United Nations, as a violation of the fundamental freedoms proclaimed in the Universal Declaration of Human Rights, and as an obstacle to friendly and peaceful relations among nations. Special measures shall be taken in appropriate circumstances to secure adequate protection of individuals belonging to certain racial groups, but these measures may not include the maintenance of unequal or separate rights for different racial groups.

1964   The ILO adopts the Employment Policy Convention. Parties to the convention must declare and pursue as a major goal an active policy designed to promote full, productive, and freely chosen employment.

1964 The Civil Rights Act of 1964 is signed by U.S. president
(*cont.*) Lyndon B. Johnson. The act is a landmark in the development of full human rights for all citizens in the United States.

1965 The United Nations General Assembly adopts the International Convention on the Elimination of All Forms of Racial Discrimination, and it enters into force on January 4, 1969. The convention condemns racial discrimination and undertakes to pursue by all appropriate means and without delay a policy of eliminating racial discrimination in all its forms, to promote understanding among the races, and to discourage anything that tends to strengthen racial division.

1966 The UN General Assembly adopts the International Covenant on Economic, Social, and Cultural Rights (which enters into force on January 3, 1976). States parties to the Covenant recognize rights to which all people are entitled, including the right to work, to just and favorable conditions of work, to social security, to an adequate standard of living, to the highest attainable standard of physical and mental health, to education, to take part in cultural life, and to enjoy the benefits of scientific progress.

The UN General Assembly adopts the International Covenant on Civil and Political Rights (which enters into force on March 23, 1976). The Covenant establishes a legal obligation of states to protect the civil and political rights of every individual without discrimination as to race, sex, language, or religion. It ensures the right to life, liberty, security, individual privacy, and protection from torture and other cruel, inhuman, or degrading treatment. The Covenant also guarantees a fair trial and protection against arbitrary arrest or detention and grants freedom of thought, conscience, and religion; freedom of opinion and expression; and freedom of association.

An Optional Protocol to the International Covenant on Civil and Political Rights is adopted by the UN (and enters into force on March 23, 1976). States parties to the Optional Protocol recognize the competence of the Human Rights Committee to receive and consider communications from individuals subject to its jurisdiction who claim to be victims of violation by a state party of any of the rights set forth in the covenant.

The General Conference of UNESCO proclaims the Declaration of the Principles of International Cultural Cooperation. It aims at spreading knowledge, enabling everyone to have access to knowledge, and developing peaceful relations and friendship among peoples.

The General Conference of the International Labor Organization adopts the Employment Policy Convention (no. 122), which enters into force July 15, 1966.

1967 The UN General Assembly adopts the Declaration on the Elimination of Discrimination against Women, which calls for all appropriate measures to be taken to abolish existing laws, customs, regulations, and practices that discriminate against women and to establish adequate legal protection for equal rights of men and women.

The UN General Assembly adopts the Declaration on Territorial Asylum. According to the Declaration, asylum granted by a state to persons seeking asylum from political persecution shall be respected by all other states. No such person shall be subjected to such measures as rejection at the border, expulsion, or compulsory return to any state where he or she may be subjected to persecution except for overriding reasons of national security or to safeguard the population.

1968 The International Conference on Human Rights at Teheran issues the Proclamation of Teheran on May 13. Reviewing the progress made in the twenty years since the adoption of the Universal Declaration of Human Rights, the signatories affirm their faith in the principles of the Declaration and emphasize the interdependency and indivisibility of human rights articulated in the two separate covenants: "Since human rights and fundamental freedoms are indivisible, the full realization of civil

1968
(*cont.*) and political rights without the enjoyment of economic, social and cultural rights is impossible" (Article 13).

The UN General Assembly adopts the Convention on the Non-Applicability of Statutory Limitations to War Crimes and Crimes against Humanity (and enters into force on November 11, 1970). The Convention states principles regarding international cooperation in the detention, arrest, extradition, and punishment of those accused of war crimes and crimes against humanity; for example, there is no statutory limitation on crimes such as genocide, eviction by armed attack, or inhuman acts resulting from the policy of apartheid.

1969 The American Convention on Human Rights is signed in San José, Costa Rica (which enters into force on July 18, 1978). This is one of the most ambitious and far-reaching documents on human rights issued by any international body. Among other features, it bans the death penalty and authorizes compensation for victims of human rights abuses in certain cases.

The ILO receives the Nobel Peace Prize for its work on behalf of human rights.

1971 The UN General Assembly adopts the Declaration of the Rights of Mentally Retarded Persons. The mentally retarded person has, to the maximum degree of feasibility, the same rights as other human beings, including the right to proper medical care, to education and training, to economic security, and to a decent standard of living.

The ILO adopts the Workers' Representatives Convention. Workers' representatives shall enjoy effective protection against any act prejudicial to them, including dismissal, based on their participation in union activities, insofar as they act in conformity with existing laws or other jointly agreed-upon arrangements.

1973 The International Convention on the Suppression and Punishment of the Crime of Apartheid is adopted by the UN General Assembly (and enters into force on July 18,

1976). Inhuman acts resulting from the policies and practices of apartheid and similar policies of racial segregation and discrimination are crimes that violate the principles of international law and constitute a serious threat to international peace and security.

The ILO adopts the Minimum Age Convention (which enters into force on June 19, 1976). The convention mandates declaration of "a minimum age for admission to employment" by each member state but specifies that the minimum age "shall not be less than the age of completion of compulsory schooling . . . and shall not be less than 15 years."

1974   The World Health Conference adopts the Universal Declaration on the Eradication of Hunger and Malnutrition. All men, women, and children have the inalienable right to be free from hunger and malnutrition in order to develop fully and maintain their physical and mental faculties. The eradication of hunger is a common objective of all countries, especially of those in a position to help in its eradication.

The Declaration on the Protection of Women and Children in Emergency and Armed Conflict is adopted by the UN. All states involved in armed conflict or in military operations either in a foreign country or in territories still under colonial domination must make special efforts to spare women and children from the ravages of war.

1975   The Helsinki Agreement or the Final Act of the Conference on Security and Cooperation in Europe is signed in Helsinki by thirty-three nations and the two superpowers—the United States and the Soviet Union. The Helsinki Accords, as they came to be called, reaffirm equal rights and self-determination, and pledge respect for human rights and fundamental freedoms, including freedom of thought, conscience, religion, or belief for all people without distinctions as to race, sex, language, or religion. The signatories agree to promote universal and effective respect for human rights, jointly and separately, including cooperation with the United Nations.

1975 The Declaration on the Use of Scientific and Technologi-
(*cont.*) cal Progress in the Interest of Peace and for the Benefit of
Mankind is adopted by the UN. It states that the results
of scientific and technological developments are to be
used in the interests of strengthening international peace
and security and for the economic and social development of peoples in accordance with the Charter of the
United Nations.

The Declaration on the Rights of Disabled Persons is
adopted by the UN. According to the Declaration, states
shall protect disabled persons against all exploitation, all
regulations, and all treatment of a discriminatory, abusive, or degrading nature.

The Declaration on the Protection of All Persons from
Being Subjected to Torture and Other Cruel, Inhuman, or
Degrading Treatment or Punishment is adopted by the
UN. No state may permit or tolerate torture or other
cruel, inhuman, or degrading treatment or punishment.
Exceptional circumstances such as a state of war, internal
political instability, or other public emergency may not
be used as a justification for such treatment.

1975 is the International Women's Year, as proclaimed by
the UN General Assembly in 1972. Also, the First World
Conference on Women is held in Mexico City. The Conference proclaims the years 1976–1985 to be the UN
Decade for Women. This initiative marks the beginning
of the most profound consideration of women's rights on
a worldwide basis that has ever taken place.

1977 In his inaugural address, President Jimmy Carter makes
it clear that human rights will be an important factor in
U.S. foreign policy. In a speech to the United Nations two
months later, he states that he will recommend the ratification of the major human rights treaties.

1978 The Declaration on Race and Racial Prejudice is proclaimed by the General Conference of UNESCO. All individuals and groups have the right to be different, but

this right and the diversity in lifestyles may not, in any circumstances, be used as a pretext for racial prejudice and may not either in law or in fact justify discriminatory practices.

The Declaration on Fundamental Principles concerning the Contribution of the Mass Media to Strengthening Peace and International Understanding, to the Promotion of Human Rights, and to Countering Racism, Apartheid, and Incitement to War is proclaimed by the General Conference of UNESCO. Journalists must have access to public information for reporting so that individuals may have a diversity of sources from which to check the accuracy of facts and appraise events objectively.

1979   The Code of Conduct for Law Enforcement Officials is approved by the United Nations. In the performance of their duties, law enforcement officials shall respect and protect human dignity and maintain and uphold the human rights of all persons. They may use force only when strictly necessary and to the extent required for the performance of their duty. They may never inflict, instigate, or tolerate any act of torture or other cruel, inhuman, or degrading treatment, nor invoke superior orders or exceptional circumstances as a justification for such treatment.

The UN General Assembly adopts the Convention on the Elimination of All Forms of Discrimination against Women (which enters into force on September 3, 1981). Parties shall take all appropriate measures, including legislation, to ensure the full development and advancement of women, for the purpose of guaranteeing them the exercise of human rights on a basis of equality with men.

The Organization of American States adopts the Statute of the Inter-American Court of Human Rights (which enters into force on January 1, 1980). Seated in San José, Costa Rica, the Court is an autonomous judicial institution, which has the purposes of applying and interpreting the American Convention on Human Rights.

1980   The Second World Conference for the Decade for Women
        is held in Copenhagen to assess the progress made in im-
        plementing the plan of action developed at the 1975
        Mexico City conference; the second purpose is to adopt
        guidelines for international, regional, and national ef-
        forts to assist women in attaining equality in all spheres
        of life as part of a plan of action for the second half of the
        decade.

        The Principles of Medical Ethics is adopted by the Amer-
        ican Medical Association. Health personnel, particularly
        physicians, charged with the medical care of prisoners
        and detainees, have a duty to provide for them the same
        standard and quality of physical and mental health care
        afforded by others. It is a gross violation of medical
        ethics to engage actively or passively in acts that consti-
        tute participation in or complicity with torture or other
        cruel, inhuman, or degrading treatment or punishment.
        The document is replaced by *Revised Principles of Medical
        Ethics,* on June 17, 2001.

1981   UNESCO holds a meeting of experts, in Freetown, Sierra
        Leone, to analyze the forms of individual and collective
        action by which human rights violations can be combated.

        The African Charter on Human and Peoples' Rights is
        adopted on June 27, 1981, by fifty-one member states of
        the Organization of African Unity (OAU) and enters into
        force on October 21, 1986. The charter reiterates the basic
        principles of human rights and stresses decolonization
        and the elimination of apartheid as top priorities. It seeks
        to preserve the traditional African social concept that the
        individual is not considered independent from society.

        The Declaration on the Elimination of All Forms of Intol-
        erance and of Discrimination Based on Religion or Belief
        is proclaimed by the UN General Assembly. All persons
        shall have the right to have a religion or belief of their
        choice and shall have the freedom, either individually or
        in community with others and in public or private, to
        manifest their religion or belief in worship, observance,
        practice, and teaching.

The Universal Islamic Declaration of Human Rights is issued by the Islamic Council of Europe, a non-governmental organization of Muslim scholars. Many of the provisions of this declaration are similar to those in other major human rights instruments; the declaration contains references to the right to life, to freedom under the law, to equality before the law, to fair trial, and to freedom from torture. Its basis is religious rather than regional and draws justification from reference to the Qur'an and the *sunna*.

The Convention (No. 154) concerning the Promotion of Collective Bargaining is adopted by the General Conference of the International Labor Organization and enters into force on August 11, 1983.

1984   The United Nations adopts the Convention against Torture and Other Cruel, Inhuman, or Degrading Treatment or Punishment. The Convention defines torture as any act by which severe physical or mental pain or suffering is intentionally inflicted by, at the instigation of, or with the acquiescence of someone acting in an official capacity, whether to obtain information or confession; to punish, intimidate, or coerce; or for reasons based on discrimination.

The Declaration on the Right of Peoples to Peace is approved by the UN General Assembly.

1985   The Third World Conference for the Decade for Women is held in Nairobi in July to assess the progress achieved and obstacles encountered during the past decade and to formulate strategies for the advancement of women to be implemented through the year 2000 and beyond. International peace and security will be advanced by the elimination of inequality between men and women and the integration of women into the development process.

The Declaration on the Human Rights of Individuals Who Are Not Nationals of the Country in Which They Live is adopted by the UN General Assembly, with the purpose of protecting basic rights and freedoms of "aliens" in a country.

1985 The Inter-American Convention to Prevent and Punish
(*cont.*) Torture is adopted by the General Assembly of the Organization of American States on December 9 in Cartagena
de Indias, Colombia, and enters into force on February
28, 1987.

1986 The UN adopts the Declaration on the Right to Development. It takes individuals to be the center of all economic
activity and affirms that development efforts must improve the well-being of the entire population, not just increase economic indicators.

The UN General Assembly adopts the Declaration on So-
cial and Legal Principles Relating to the Protection and
Welfare of Children, with special reference to Foster
Placement and Adoption Nationally and Internationally.

1987 The European Convention for the Prevention of Torture
and Inhuman or Degrading Treatment or Punishment is
adopted by the Council of Europe (and enters into force
on February 1, 1989).

1988 Almost forty years after the United Nations approves the
Genocide Convention, U.S. president Ronald Reagan
signs the legislation that enables the United States to be-
come the ninety-eighth nation to ratify the agreement.
The legislation amends the Criminal Code of the United
States to make genocide a federal offense.

The Convention (No. 168) concerning Employment Promotion and Protection against Unemployment is adopted
by the General Conference of the ILO and enters into
force on October 17, 1991.

The General Assembly of the Organization of American
States adopts an Additional Protocol to the American
Convention on Human Rights in the Area of Economic,
Social, and Cultural Rights on November 17. Also
known as "Protocol of San Salvador," the Treaty stipulates provisions for the protection of social, economic,
and cultural rights. It enters into force on November 16,
1999.

1989 The Convention on the Rights of the Child is adopted by the UN General Assembly (and enters into force on September 2, 1990). It declares the responsibility of all nations to provide adequate nutrition, education, and health care for the world's children. Other provisions govern child labor, juvenile justice, and child participation in warfare.

The Second Optional Protocol to the International Covenant on Civil and Political Rights, aiming at the abolition of the death penalty, is adopted by the UN General Assembly.

The Convention (No. 169) concerning Indigenous and Tribal Peoples in Independent Countries is adopted by the General Conference of the ILO and enters into force on September 5, 1991.

1990 The General Assembly of the United Nations adopts the International Convention on the Protection of the Rights of All Migrant Workers and Members of Their Families. It enters into force on July 1, 2003.

The Cairo Declaration on Human Rights in Islam is adopted by the Organization of Islamic Conference (OIC) at the Nineteenth Conference of Foreign Ministers, held in Cairo, Arab Republic of Egypt, in August 1990. The Declaration is presented "in contribution to the efforts of mankind to assert human rights, to protect man from exploitation and persecution, and to affirm his freedom and right to a dignified life in accordance with the Islamic Shari'ah."

The African Charter on the Rights and Welfare of the Child is adopted by the Organization of African Unity (OAU) and enters into force on November 29, 1999.

The Organization of American States adopts the Protocol to the American Convention on Human Rights to Abolish the Death Penalty.

1992 The General Assembly of the United Nations adopts the Declaration on the Rights of Persons Belonging to

1992 National, Ethnic, Religious, and Linguistic Minorities.
(*cont.*) The Declaration calls on states to protect the existence
and the national, ethnic, cultural, religious, or linguistic
identities of minorities living in their territories.

The UN General Assembly adopts the Declaration on the
Protection of All Persons from Enforced Disappearance.

The United Nations holds an Earth Summit in Rio de
Janeiro to address the issues of environmental and eco-
logical degradation, environmental rights, and sustainable development. The international community adopts
Agenda 21, a comprehensive global plan of action for
sustainable development.

1993 The World Conference on Human Rights takes place in
Vienna in December. At this conference the United Nations responds to human rights violations throughout
the world by adopting the Vienna Declaration and Programme of Action at the UN World Conference on
Human Rights, which reaffirms its commitment to pre-
viously recognized human rights, with special recognition of the right to development and to economic, social,
and cultural rights. It reiterates the universality, interdependence, and indivisibility of human rights. It also calls
for an end to discrimination, violence, and poverty, and
reiterates the universality, interdependency, and indivisibility of human rights. It declares that the human rights
of women and girl children are an inalienable, integral,
and indivisible part of universal human rights.

The UN General Assembly adopts the Declaration on Violence against Women. The Declaration calls on governments to exercise diligence to prevent, investigate, and
punish acts of violence against women.

The UN Security Council officially names Srebrenica the
world's first UN-protected civilian safe area (though, the
lack of sufficient UN troops in the area results in over
7,000 Muslims to be slain).

International Decade of the World's Indigenous People (1995–2004) is proclaimed by the UN General Assembly in a resolution (RES.48.163) on December 21, with the main objective of strengthening international cooperation for the solution of problems faced by indigenous people in such areas as human rights, the environment, development, education, and health.

1994   The United Nations drafts the Declaration on Human Rights and the Environment. This document focuses on the right to benefit from nature, to consume safe and healthy food, and the right to a healthy environment.

The United Nations proclaims the ten-year period (1995–2004), beginning January 1, 1995, the United Nations Decade for Human Rights Education. The purpose of this proclamation is to broaden awareness of human rights and to make human rights education a part of the curriculum.

The UN Security Council adopts a resolution reemphasizing that "ethnic cleansing" constitutes a clear violation of international law. This echoes a 1992 Security Council resolution condemning "ethnic cleansing" in Bosnia and Herzegovina.

The UN Security Council establishes an International Tribunal for Rwanda. Eight hundred thousand people were killed in Rwanda in one of the worst genocides since the Nazi Holocaust.

The United Nations drafts the Declaration on the Rights of Indigenous Peoples. The document acknowledges that indigenous peoples have the right of self-determination and the right to maintain and strengthen their distinct political, economic, social and cultural characteristics, as well as their legal systems.

The Inter-American Convention on the Forced Disappearance of Persons is adopted by the General Assembly of the Organization of American on June 9, Belem Do Para, Brazil, and enters into force on March 28, 1996.

1994   The Inter-American Convention on the Prevention, Pun-
(*cont.*)   ishment, and Eradication of Violence against Women,
       "Convention of Belem Do Para," is adopted by the Gen-
       eral Assembly of the Organization of American States on
       June 9.

1995   The fourth UN World Conference on Women takes place
       in Beijing in September. The conference focuses on the
       economic empowerment of women and addresses con-
       tinuing inequalities in the areas of health care, education,
       and political participation. The final document of the
       conference identifies twelve critical areas and calls for
       "mainstreaming" women's issues.

       South Africa establishes the Truth and Reconciliation
       Commission to investigate human rights abuses that
       took place under the apartheid government. Archbishop
       Desmond Tutu is appointed head of the commission by
       President Nelson Mandela.

1996   The Council of Europe adopts the revised version of the
       European Social Charter. The revisions are undertaken to
       preserve the indivisible nature of all human rights, up-
       date and adapt the substantive contents of the Charter in
       order to take into account the fundamental social changes
       that have occurred since the text was adopted in 1961.
       The revised Charter enters into force on July 1, 1999.

1997   An international treaty is negotiated among eighty-nine
       countries in Oslo, Norway, to ban antipersonnel land
       mines. The Convention on the Prohibition of the Use,
       Stockpiling, Production and Transfer of Anti-Personnel
       Mines and on Their Destruction, also known as the Ottawa
       Convention in reference to where it was open to signature,
       enters into force on March 1, 1999.

       The Treaty of Amsterdam, adopted by the European
       Union (EU), amends Article 6 of the European Treaty,
       making explicit that the EU is founded on the principles
       of liberty, democracy, human rights, fundamental free-
       doms, and the rule of law. The treaty enters into force on
       May 1, 1999.

1998 The International Criminal Court (ICC) is established by the Rome Statute of the International Criminal Court on July 17, 1998. It enters into force on July 1, 2002, upon its ratification by 60 states. This is the first ever permanent, treaty-based, international criminal court established to promote the rule of law and ensure that the gravest international crimes, meaning crimes against humanity such as a genocide and ethnic cleansing, do not go unpunished.

The Member States of the Organization of African Unity issue the Protocol to the African Charter on Human and Peoples' Rights on the Establishment of an African Court on Human and Peoples' Rights. The Protocol enters into force on January 15, 2004, upon its ratification by fifteen member states.

The Declaration on the Right and Responsibility of Individuals, Groups, and Organs of Society to Promote and Protect Universally Recognized Human Rights and Fundamental Freedoms, known as "The Declaration on Human Rights Defenders," is adopted by the General Assembly of the United Nations. The Declaration provides for the support and protection of human rights defenders in the context of their work.

1999 The ILO adopts the Worst Forms of Child Labor Convention (which enters into force on November 10, 2000). The Convention defines the "child" as "all persons under the age of 18" and mandates the elimination of exploitive and abusive child labor.

Optional Protocol to the Convention on the Elimination of Discrimination against Women (CEDAW) is adopted by the UN (and enters into force on December 22, 2000). It allows individuals and groups to apply to the monitoring Committee about human rights violations in a state that is party to the convention.

The Inter-American Convention on the Elimination of All Forms of Discrimination against Persons with Disabilities is adopted by the General Assembly of the Organization of American States on June 7.

2000   The Optional Protocol to the Convention on the Rights of the Child on the involvement of children in armed conflicts is adopted by the UN General Assembly (and enters into force on February 12, 2002).

The Optional Protocol to the Convention on the Rights of the Child on the sale of children, child prostitution, and child pornography is adopted by the UN General Assembly (and enters into force on January 18, 2002).

The UN General Assembly approves the "Millennium Declaration," which reaffirms the UN mission and its commitment to advance human rights and women's rights, and eradicate poverty.

The Charter of Fundamental Rights of the European Union, which consolidates all fundamental rights into a single document, is proclaimed.

2001   The UN holds the World Conference against Racism, Racial Discrimination, Xenophobia, and Related Intolerance in Durban, South Africa. The Conference attempts to identify the sources, forms, and victims of contemporary racism and take measures to prevent all acts of racism and related intolerance through the cooperation of the international community.

Inter-American Democratic Charter is adopted by the General Assembly of the Organization of American States at a special session held in Lima, Peru, on September 11. In its preamble and several articles, the charter emphasizes the close link between democracy and human rights and the commitment of the member states to both; it acknowledges the "universality, indivisibility and interdependence" of human rights; and specifies that "the suspended member state shall continue to fulfill its obligations to the Organization, in particular its human rights obligations."

2002   On July 1, the Rome Statute that created the International Criminal Court enters into force sixty days after sixty states ratified it. The seat of the Court is the Hague in the

Netherlands, and anyone who commits the crime of genocide, crimes against humanity, war crimes, or the crime of aggression will be liable for prosecution by the Court.

The United Nations holds the World Summit on Sustainable Development in Johannesburg. The meeting brings heads of state, national delegates, and leaders of nongovernmental organizations (NGOs), businesses, and other major groups to focus the world's attention and direct action toward meeting difficult challenges, including improving people's lives and conserving natural resources in the face of a growing population, with ever-increasing demands for food, water, shelter, sanitation, energy, health services, and economic security.

The UN Secretary General initiates the UN Millennium Project to meet the eight Millennium Development Goals, including eradicating extreme poverty and hunger; achieving universal primary education; promoting gender equality and empowerment of women; reducing child mortality; improving maternal health; combating HIV/AIDS, malaria and other diseases; ensuring environmental sustainability; and developing global partnerships for development.

2003 The Commission on Human Rights recommends that the United Nations hold in Geneva an annual intersessional forum on economic, social, and cultural rights to be known as the Social Forum. Bearing in mind that the fight against poverty is an overarching goal for the international community, the theme for the first Social Forum, held on July 22–23, 2004, is defined as "poverty, rural poverty, and human rights."

The Member States of the African Union (formerly Organization of African Unity) issue the Protocol to the African Charter on Human and Peoples' Rights on the Rights of Women in Africa.

2004 The Organization of Islamic Conference adopts the Covenant on the Rights of the Child in Islam.

Amnesty International launches a global campaign to stop violence against women.

2005   The World Summit is held in New York in September, and the UN General Assembly adopts an outcome document. It reaffirms the UN member states' commitment to human rights; underscores the mutually reinforcing effects of human rights, democracy, peace, security, and development; and reiterates the universality, interrelatedness, and interdependence of all human rights. It also seeks the creation of a Human Rights Council.

6

Biographical Sketches

Progress in human rights is cumulative and involves years of hard and dedicated work by people from all parts of the world. The articulation of human rights; dissemination of ideas; struggle for their recognition; acceptance of norms at local, national, and international levels; and incorporation of human rights into domestic and international law involve advocates who are philosophers, scholars, diplomats, political leaders, but most important, activists who risk their own lives and well-being in order to save or improve the lives of others and uphold human dignity. It is impossible to provide a comprehensive list of all the individuals who have participated in this process; many of them are "unknown soldiers," whose important work is not likely to be known or acknowledged beyond their immediate circles.

This section provides short biographies of a few of the advocates who have been fortunate enough to see the impact of their efforts and to enjoy international recognition. The reader will notice that the list includes several Nobel Peace Laureates. This is quite natural, since the constituents of peace are closely related to issues of human rights and those who struggle for peace tend to work also against discrimination, injustice, and human rights violations. Nevertheless, there is no automatic link between the Nobel Prize and human rights advocacy, as some recipients of the prize (e.g., Henry Kissinger) have been criticized and accused of human rights violations by human rights groups.

Hanan Ashrawi (1946–)

Born on October 8, 1946, in Ramallah, on the West Bank in Palestine, Hanan Ashrawi became a political and peace activist early. She has continuously articulated the suffering of the Palestinian people in international platforms and argued for their right to live in peace and tranquility. She earned her bachelor's and master's degrees in literature from the department of English at the American University of Beirut. She pursued her doctoral studies in the United States and obtained her Ph.D. in medieval and comparative literature from the University of Virginia.

Ashrawi returned to the West Bank in 1973 and established the department of English at Birzeit University; later she became the chair of the department. Between 1986 and 1990 she served as Dean of the Faculty of Arts and remained as a faculty member of the university until 1995. Her publications include numerous articles, poems, and short stories on Palestinian culture, literature, and politics, as well as a memoir, *This Side of Peace: A Personal Account*, published in 1995.

As a response to the intermittent closures of the university by the Israeli military, Ashrawi founded the Birzeit University Legal Aid Committee/Human Rights Action Project. During the first Intifada uprising in 1988, she joined the Intifada Political Committee. Following the peace agreements with Israel and its recognition of Palestinian self-rule, she founded the Preparatory Committee of the Palestinian Independent Commission for Citizens' Rights in Jerusalem and was Commissioner General of the committee until 1995.

In 1991, Yasser Arafat, chairman of the Palestinian Liberation Organization (PLO), appointed her the official spokeswoman of the Palestinian delegation at the Middle East Peace Conference in Madrid, where her eloquence and lucidity won international admiration. In 1996, she was elected a member of the Palestinian Legislative Council. The same year, she became Minister of Higher Education and Research of the Palestinian Authority, but she resigned the post in 1998 in protest of political corruption and Arafat's handling of peace talks. In August 1998, she founded the Palestinian Initiative for the Promotion of Global Dialogue and Democracy (MIFTAH), with the objective of assuring respect for human rights, democracy, and peace. Her work for human rights and peace was recognized by the Sydney Peace Prize, awarded to her in 2003 by the Australian government.

In addition to serving as Secretary General of the MIFTAH, Ashrawi is a member of the Independent International Commission on Kosovo and of numerous international advisory boards including the Council on Foreign Relations, the World Bank Middle East and North Africa Region, and the United Nations Research Institute for Social Development. She is also Minister of Information and spokesperson for the Arab League.

Roger Baldwin (1884–1981)

Roger Baldwin was born on January 21, 1884, in Wellesley, Massachusetts, to a wealthy and intellectual family. However, he embraced a leftist ideology, which led him to pursue the rights of the most unfortunate segments of the society and gained the reputation of "the underdog's best friend." He studied at Harvard University, and after his graduation in 1905, he was involved in social work and taught sociology at Washington University in St. Louis.

At the outbreak of World War I, Baldwin became a founding member of the Fellowship of Reconciliation (FOR), and as the direct involvement of the United States in the war was becoming clear, he joined forces with pacifists who shared his views on war and established the American Union against Militarism (AUAM). The organization campaigned against U.S. involvement in the war, conscription, and the arms trade and openly criticized the U.S. imperialist ventures in the Caribbean and Latin America. In 1917, he founded the National Civil Liberties Bureau (NCLB), and within a year he was imprisoned for his public support of conscientious objectors. Further radicalization in prison led him to join the Industrial Workers of the World (IWW) after his release in 1919. The following year he established the American Civil Liberties Union (ACLU) and served as its executive director until 1950. He then become the ACLU's international adviser and headed the International League for the Rights of Man for fifteen years.

In the 1930s, the ACLU was criticized for its left-wing leanings. Concerned about these criticisms as well as the Nazi-Soviet Non-Aggression Pact, which was announced in August 1939, Baldwin launched a campaign to amend the ACLU charter to bar those who were affiliated with "totalitarian organizations" from serving on the ACLU board. In addition to ousting the Communist

Party member Elizabeth Gurley Flynn, the organization carried out anticommunist programs and policies throughout the Cold War years. Nevertheless, Baldwin's concern about the violation of civil liberties led him to oppose the prosecution of U.S. citizens for their Fascist or Communist ideology. He led the ACLU in opposing the internment of Japanese and Japanese-Americans but also maintained a good relationship with the U.S. government. After the War, in 1947, at the request of General MacArthur, he went to Japan to serve as a civil liberties consultant and founded the Japanese Civil Liberties Union. The following year, he was invited by General Lucius D. Clay to Germany and Austria to perform similar services. He continued to be involved in campaigns against various repressive and discriminatory actions and practices, such as the Palmer Raids, the Espionage Act, the Tennessee Anti-Evolution Law, Jim Crow, McCarthyism, and Racial Segregation, until his death on August 26, 1981.

Peter Benenson (1921–2005)

Peter Benenson is best known as the founder of the international human rights organization Amnesty International (AI), but his advocacy work was not limited to the AI. He was born in London as Peter James Henry Solomon on July 31, 1921. On his maternal grandfather's death in 1939, he assumed his grandfather's name, Benenson. Educated in Eton and Oxford, his outrage and activism against political repression and oppression were displayed in his school years. He launched campaigns and mobilized his schoolmates first to support the Spanish Relief Committee, which was formed to help the Republican orphans of the Spanish Civil War, and later to raise funds to bring to Britain two German Jews who had escaped Nazi Germany.

After his graduation from Oxford with a degree in history, he joined the British army. When World War II ended, he returned to school to study law and became a practicing lawyer. In 1946, he also joined the Labor Party, and as a leading figure in the Society of Labour Lawyers, he helped the establishment of the Labor Party's Spanish Democrats Defense Committee. In the 1950s, as a human rights lawyer, Benenson was involved in several international trials: he observed and helped with the trials of Basque nationalists and trade unionists in Spain; advised Greek Cypriot lawyers in defending their clients who were prosecuted under

British colonial law; mobilized British lawyers with different political persuasions to observe the trials in Hungary, which followed the failed uprising against Soviet interference, as well as the "Treason Trial" of Nelson Mandela, Oliver Tambo, Walter Sisulu, and 153 others in South Africa. In 1957, with other legal professionals, including the chief British prosecutor at Nuremburg Hartley Shawcross, he established Justice—an organization of human rights and "rule of law" based in the United Kingdom, and served in the British section of the International Commission of Jurists.

Outraged by the Somoza government's imprisonment of two Portuguese university students for drinking to freedom, on May 28, 1961, Benenson published an article in *The Observer* and called for a one-year Appeal for Amnesty to obtain the release of "prisoners of conscience." Generating thousands of supporters, Benenson's call led to an international meeting in July, in which the participants decided to establish an international movement in defense of freedom of opinion and religion that would be enduring and steady. This marked the birth of Amnesty International. Benenson became its Secretary General, but in 1964 he stepped down because of ill health and assumed an advisory position.

In 1966, a major international controversy arose over an Amnesty report on the torture of guerilla suspects from Aden by the British forces. (Aden had been incorporated into the Federation of South Arabia, in February 1963, against the wishes of the majority of its people but to ensure the protection of British oil interests.) Alleging that the organization was being infiltrated by the British intelligence, Benenson suggested moving AI headquarters to a neutral country. However, an independent investigation did not support his claim of infiltration, and he retired from the organization. After a decade of private life dedicated to writing and prayer—he had become a devout convert to Catholicism—Benenson eventually returned to his active role in AI. His involvement was crucial in various campaigns that took place in the 1980s and 1990s. He also assumed the leadership of a new organization, the Association of Christians against Torture. He died of pneumonia on February 25, 2005, in an Oxford hospital.

Jimmy Carter (1924–)

James Earl "Jimmy" Carter was born on October 1, 1924, in Plains, Georgia, and served as the thirty-ninth president of the

United States. In 1946 Jimmy Carter received his B.S. degree from the United States Naval Academy.

Carter had a successful political career, serving two terms in the Georgia Senate, a term as governor of Georgia from 1971 to 1975, and a term as United States president between 1976 and 1980. As governor, he opened up government positions in Georgia for women and blacks and set in motion several humanitarian programs. During his primary campaign for the presidency, Carter focused on human rights in many of his foreign policy statements and made them an issue in the debates during the general election campaign.

As president of the United States, Carter emphasized human rights in foreign policy formulations. Although he showed the tendency to overlook human rights criteria for other reasons such as security and to persistently undermine social and economic rights, his rhetorical approach was still a favorable change, and the International League for Human Rights in its report cited President Carter's policies as being responsible for significant improvement in human rights around the world. Among his most notable accomplishments was the development of the Camp David accords, which initiated peace between Egypt and Israel.

Carter has remained active in the public policy arena, focusing on the resolution of international discord and promotion of human rights. In addition, he is involved in other issues such as fighting hunger and disease throughout the world as well as constructing homes for the poor through Habitat for Humanity, an organization with which he has had close ties for years. He served on its board of directors between 1984 and 1987. He and his wife Rosalynn continue to participate in Habitat programs and are referred to in the Habitat literature as "our most famous volunteers." The majority of his public involvement is administered through the Carter Library, which is regularly involved in the monitoring of international electoral processes, and the Carter Center, which works on eradication of various diseases in poor regions of the world through preventive medicine and public health measures. As a private citizen, Carter has made significant contributions toward peace in Haiti, Nicaragua, Bosnia, and Korea. He received the Nobel Peace Prize in 2002 for his work in the areas of conflict resolution and human rights.

René Samuel Cassin (1887–1976)

René Cassin is internationally recognized as one of the world's most ardent promoters of human rights. He was born in Bayonne, France, on October 5, 1887. He received his doctorate in judicial, economic, and political science from the University of Aix-en-Provence in 1914. He served as a distinguished professor of law from 1920 until his retirement in 1960. As a jurist, professor, and scholar, with numerous scholarly contributions, Cassin had a significant influence on the moral and legal interpretation of human rights internationally.

Cassin has held many notable judicial positions, including vice president of the French Council of State (1944–1960), membership in the Constitutional Council, and president of the Court of Arbitration at the Hague (1950–1960). He also served as president of the European Court of Human Rights from 1965 to 1968. Between 1924 and 1938, he was a French delegate to the League of Nations, and later he served in the same capacity at the General Assembly of the United Nations on five different junctures.

He was a member of the United Nations Commission on Human Rights beginning with its creation in 1946, served as its vice chairman from 1946 to 1955, chaired it from 1955 to 1957, and was the vice chairman again in 1959. As an expert in international law and with a passionate interest in human rights, he became one of the core and most influential members of the committee of the Commission that drafted the Universal Declaration of Human Rights. In fact, Cassin composed the first full draft of the Universal Declaration.

He received the Nobel Peace Prize in 1968 as a testament to his commitment to improving the lives of others. The same year he was also awarded one of the United Nation's Human Rights Prizes. He died on February 20, 1976.

Shirin Ebadi (1947–)

Shirin Ebadi was born in Hamedan, a city located in northwestern Iran, on June 21, 1947. She grew up and was educated in Tehran, acquiring a degree in law from Tehran University in 1968. In 1969, she became the first female judge in Iran, and while serving as a judge, she worked toward a doctoral degree in law in Tehran University and obtained it in 1971.

In 1975, she became the president of Bench 24 of the [Tehran] City Court, but following the revolution in 1979 and establishment of the Islamic Republic, she was forced to resign under the new policy based on a notion that Islam forbids women from serving as judges. Protesting her demotion to a law clerk, Ebadi applied for early retirement and entered private practice. Turned down by the Bar Association, which was close to the revolutionary government, Ebadi remained "unemployed" for years. She used the time to focus on scholarship. In 1992, she obtained a license to set up her own private practice in law.

As a lawyer, she began taking politically sensitive cases, which put her at odds with the government. Representing the families of serial murder victims, who were killed during an attack on a university dormitory in 1998, enhanced her anti-establishment reputation. In 2000, she received a suspended jail sentence and a professional ban, on the grounds that she had distributed a videotape of confessions by a hard-liner, whose disclosures included claims that some prominent conservative leaders had instigated physical attacks on reformist figures, groups, and their meetings. She was also briefly detained after she attended a Berlin conference on Iran's reforms. Nevertheless, she continued with her pro-reform activities and advocacy of human rights. In 2001, she co-founded the Human Rights Defense Centre, with four other defense lawyers, and became its president.

Ebadi also advocated children's and women's rights and defended women's rights activists in the courts. She was co-founder of the Association for Support of Children's Rights, established in 1995; she served as its president until 2000 and afterward remained involved as a legal adviser. She was a driving force behind the ratification of laws prohibiting all forms of violence against children and reforming family laws in Iran, which curbed discrimination against women in divorce and inheritance legislation.

When her work came to the attention of the international community, she was recognized with awards. Two years after receiving a human rights prize in Norway, she was awarded the Nobel Peace Prize in 2003 for promoting human rights and democracy in her country.

Adolfo Pérez Esquivel (1931–)

Adolfo Pérez Esquivel was born in Buenos Aires, Argentina, on November 26, 1931. After graduation from the National School of Fine Arts in Buenos Aires in 1956, he married and pursued a career as a sculptor and professor of fine arts. He risked his life by advocating human rights at a time when violence and terror were rampant in his country and other Latin American countries.

In the 1960s, Pérez Esquivel began working with popularly based Latin American Christian pacifist groups, and in 1974 he resigned from his academic post to work full-time on coordinating a network of Latin America–based communities that advocated improvement for conditions of the poor through nonviolent means. This effort led to the establishment of El Servicio de Paz y Justicia (Service, Peace, and Justice Foundation). In addition to pointing out political repression, he called attention to the violation of peasants' social and economic rights, noting that this group, denied food and land, also suffered grave human rights abuses. Under his leadership, Servicio Paz y Justicia sought to break the cycle of poverty that caused this type of abuse by championing the rights of workers.

In response to the systematic repression after the Argentine military coup of 1976, he also championed the cause of the 6,000 *desaparecidos*—those who simply disappeared from their homes or off the streets of Argentine cities during the brute rule of the military junta under Pinochet. He was more than instrumental in coordinating the efforts of popularly based organizations to defend human rights and support victims' families throughout the region. Although Pérez Esquivel was a devout Roman Catholic, the organization he founded was ecumenical and not under the auspices of the Roman Catholic hierarchy, which was reluctant to take a strong stand against the government's repression and grave human rights abuses. His vocal protest in such causes made Pérez Esquivel a target of governments in many Latin American countries during the 1970s. He was detained by the Brazilian military police in 1975, jailed in Ecuador in 1976 (along with Latin American and North American bishops), and in 1977, he was arrested in Buenos Aires by the Policía Federal, tortured, and held without a legal charge or trial for fourteen months. He was released in May 1978, but with the obligation to report to the police; he also was subject to various other restrictions. His efforts toward advancing peace and human rights throughout Latin America during the 1970s were recognized by the Nobel Committee which awarded him the Nobel Peace Prize in 1980.

Pérez Esquivel continues with his work as president of the Honorary Council of Paz y Justicia, a member of the Permanent People's Tribunal, and president of the International League for the Rights and Liberation of Peoples based in Milan. Using his status as a Nobel Laureate, he lends his name to peace and human rights efforts all over the globe from appealing to the United Nations in behalf of the people of Sri Lanka to working to ban nuclear testing. He has also been an ardent opponent of the U.S.-led free trade agreement initiatives in Latin America.

Václav Havel (1936–)

Born in Prague on October 5, 1936, Vaclav Havel witnessed the Second World War and the regime change in Czechoslovakia, which brought the Communist Party to power in 1948. After attending a technical college for a while, he graduated from the Prague Academy of the Arts. Upon completing his compulsory military service in the late 1950s, Havel worked as a stagehand, electrician, secretary, and manuscript reader before becoming a playwright in the early 1960s. In his many plays, he has tried to show the dehumanizing effects of mechanization on society and the individual spirit and used his dramatic skills to further the cause of human rights.

When the Soviet Union and other Warsaw Pact armies invaded Czechoslovakia in 1968, Havel addressed groups of Czech artists and writers from an underground radio station, urging them to unite in the cause of human rights. He was able to convince a small group to commit themselves to use whatever means they could to protest repression by the government. Havel's plays and writings were subsequently banned and he was twice imprisoned for his human rights advocacy. In 1977, Havel signed Charter 77, a document protesting the failure of the Czechoslovakian Socialist Republic to abide by the Helsinki Final Act on civil and political rights. The government's response was to arrest large numbers of those who had signed the document, among them Havel, who had been one of the three elected spokespersons for the protest. He was jailed for four months and later brought to trial for sending copies of his banned writings out of the country for publication. He was given a suspended sentence, and he later founded a movement known as the Committee for the Defense of the Unjustly Persecuted; for this, along with six others, he was sentenced to four-and-one-half years at hard labor.

After the collapse of the Berlin Wall, in December 1989, Václav Havel became president of Czechoslovakia. Ethnic tensions between the Czechs and Slovaks led to the collapse of the federal system and in 1992, after the Slovaks issued their Declaration of Independence, he resigned as president. However, in 1993, when the Czech Republic was created, he stood for election as president and won; he held this position for ten years until 2003. During his presidency he continued to work for human rights. He has worked to improve the rights of the Roma people, who were subject to over 1,200 attacks in the Czech Republic in the 1990s. In addition to his efforts to improve human rights conditions in his country, Havel has sought to bring peace to the region, especially to end the conflicts in Bosnia and Kosovo.

Dorothy Height (1912–)

Dorothy Height was born in Richmond, Virginia, on March 24, 1912, when Jim Crow ruled and lynchings were frequent. Thus, she campaigned for equal rights for African Americans and women and became a prominent leader of the civil rights movement in the United States. Her own life has been a continuous struggle against discrimination. When she was refused admission to Barnard College, which had filled its "two Negroes" quota, Height pursued her college education at New York University and graduated in three years. She earned a master of arts in educational psychology and became a social worker. Currently she holds more than twenty honorary doctoral degrees.

At the age of twenty-five, in her quest for women's full and equal employment and educational advancement, Height joined the National Council of Negro Women. In 1944, she joined the staff of the YWCA, where she emphasized the importance of leadership training and interracial and ecumenical education programs. Her work in the YWCA involved many new initiatives, including the inauguration of the Center for Racial Justice in 1965. In 1957, she was appointed president of the National Council of

Negro Women, and she served as president of this organization, one of the oldest civil rights movement associations, for forty-one years, until 1998. As a civil rights activist, she fought against lynching, for desegregation of the armed forces, and for the reformation of the criminal justice system. In the 1960s, Height organized "Wednesdays in Mississippi," which brought together black and white women from the North and South to facilitate dialogue and collaboration.

In her recent memoir *Open Wide Freedom's Gates*, Dorothy Height recalls her active involvement in various civil rights rallies and anxious White House meetings; she tells of standing on stage while Dr. Martin Luther King Jr. delivered his famous "I Have a Dream" speech. Throughout the years, her commitment to equality and human rights has been recognized by numerous organizations. She has been the recipient of the Presidential Medal of Freedom, the Franklin Delano Roosevelt Freedom From Want Award, and the NAACP Springarn Medal. In addition, she has been inducted into the National Women's Hall of Fame and in 2004, she was awarded the Congressional Gold Medal.

Martin Luther King Jr. (1929–1968)

Dr. Martin Luther King Jr., an American national hero and civil rights leader, was born in Atlanta, Georgia, on January 15, 1929. He was an eloquent Baptist minister and leader of the American civil rights movement. He promoted nonviolence as a means of achieving social and political transformation for the oppressed blacks of the United States.

He earned his bachelor of divinity degree from Crozier Theological Seminary in 1951, and his Ph.D. from Boston University in 1955. Dr. King implemented Mohandas Gandhi's philosophy of nonviolent social protest in the civil rights struggle in the United States. In 1957, he co-founded the Southern Christian Leadership Conference (SCLC) and was elected the organization's first president. He was also elected president of the Montgomery Improvement Association, and he gained national prominence with the mobilization of the African American community during a 382-day bus boycott in Montgomery, Alabama, in 1963. Participation in the boycott resulted in his arrest and the bombing of his home. While in prison, he issued the famous "Letter from Birmingham Jail," which played a vital role in mobilizing the national civil rights movement. The same year, he led a massive march on Washington, D.C., where he delivered the celebrated "I Have a Dream" speech, one of the most passionate addresses of his career. King's popularity continued to intensify, as he became *Time* magazine's "Man of the Year" in 1963.

Through his philosophy of nonviolent civil action, King inspired significant national social transformation throughout the United States. He was also a vocal opponent of the war in Vietnam. In recognition of his nonviolent resistance and remarkable leadership of the civil rights movement, he was granted numerous honorary degrees and awards, including the 1964 Nobel Peace Prize— at age 35 he was the youngest recipient of this award—and the Presidential Medal of Freedom. He was assassinated at the Lorraine Motel in Memphis, Tennessee, on April 4, 1968.

Bernard Kouchner (1939–)

Bernard Kouchner was born in 1939 in Avignon, France, grew up in a suburb of Paris, and became an activist as a teenager demonstrating support for Algerian independence and the demands of striking workers. He earned his medical degree in 1964 but demonstrated his interest in world affairs by writing articles and pamphlets on political topics. He traveled to Cuba to meet Argentine guerrilla leader Ernesto (Che) Guevara and interviewed Fidel Castro for *Clarte,* a magazine for young Communists.

In 1968, Kouchner volunteered to help the Red Cross in Biafra, where a bloody civil war had claimed many lives and he became sensitized to human rights abuses. He was frustrated by the Red Cross policy of neutrality that prevented it from taking a stand against human rights abuses. He helped found Médicins sans Frontières (MSF, or Doctors without Borders) in 1971 to bring medical help to populations in dangerous areas, to help heal the wounded, and to speak out against human rights abuses, serving as the organization's founding president until 1977. MSF has grown into the world's largest medical relief organization, with over 2,000 doctors of forty-five nationalities active in over eighty countries.

After a dispute with some of the leadership of MSF on the issue of maintaining neutrality in conflict areas where the organization was active, in 1980 Kouchner founded Médicins du Monde (MDM, or Doctors of the World). Under his presidency,

MDM organized relief efforts in the 1980s in Afghanistan, Armenia, Ethiopia, Brazil, Chile, Colombia, Guatemala, El Salvador, Mexico, Poland, Burma, and Mozambique.

Starting in 1988, Kouchner held many humanitarian posts in the French government, mainly during the Socialist Party rule. These posts allowed him to be active and influential in the European Union and the United Nations. In 1988, the United Nations adopted his proposal that set forth guidelines for providing humanitarian assistance to victims of natural disasters and other emergency situations. In 1990, the General Assembly of the United Nations passed a resolution requiring "access corridors" along which humanitarian relief organizations could travel to provide assistance to the needy. Because of these resolutions, Kouchner was able to push through the passage of Security Council Resolution 688 requiring Iraq to permit relief organizations and governmental units access to Kurdistan to bring supplies in 1991. In 1997, Kouchner left France to run a hospital in southern Sudan; he is credited for coining the term "humanitarian intervention." Kouchner has been recognized with numerous awards, including the 1979 Dag Hammarskjöld prize for human rights and the 1984 Prix Europa for his human rights activities.

Charles Malik (1906–1987)

Charles Malik was born in the Koura district of North Lebanon in 1906. He graduated from the American University of Beirut in 1927 and earned his Ph.D. from Harvard University in 1937. He established the philosophy department and cultural studies program at the American University of Beirut and taught there from 1937 to 1945. In 1945, Malik represented Lebanon at the San Francisco conference at which the United Nations was founded, and he became the Lebanese ambassador to both the United Nations (1945–1955 and 1957–1959) and the United States (1945–1955). He was also elected to the Lebanese National Assembly in 1957 and served for three years, during which he held cabinet posts—first as Minister of National Education and Fine Arts and then as Minister of Foreign Affairs. In 1960, he returned to the academic world.

His work at the United Nations was remarkable and important for human rights. He was one of the original and most influential members of the United Nations Commission on Human Rights, which drafted the Universal Declaration of Human

Rights. In addition to the significant role that he played during the drafting of the Declaration, as chairman of the United Nations Economic and Social Council Malik later played a vital role in the adoption of the Universal Declaration of Human Rights by the General Assembly of the United Nations. He also served as the Rapporteur of the Commission on Human Rights, and in 1951, he chaired the Commission.

In addition to his dedication to the advocacy and promotion of human rights, being a sophisticated intellectual and scholar he published several books and articles on the topic. Following the outbreak of the Lebanese Civil War in 1975, Malik became a founder of the Front for Freedom and Man in Lebanon, which later became known as the Lebanese Front. He died in Beirut on December 28, 1987.

Nelson Mandela (1918–)

Nelson Mandela was born on July 18, 1918, in Transkei, South Africa. In 1939, he attended Fort Hare University College but was later expelled for organizing a student boycott. In 1940, he enrolled at the University of Witwatersrand in Johannesburg, where he received his law degree.

In 1942, Mandela joined the African National Congress (ANC) and, together with Anton Lembede, William Nkomo, Walter Sisulu, Oliver Tambo, and Ashby Mda, he transformed the ANC into a mass movement characterized by boycotts, strikes, and civil disobedience. In 1944, he founded the African National Congress Youth League (ANCYL), with the main objective of attaining for all South Africans full citizenship, direct parliamentary representation, the redistribution of land, trade union rights, and public education.

In 1952, when the ANC introduced a campaign for the Defiance of Unjust Laws, Nelson Mandela was elected National Volunteer-in-Chief with the responsibility of organizing resistance to inequitable legislation. As a result of his participation in the defiance campaign, Mandela was convicted of contravening the Suppression of Communism Act and received a nine-month suspended prison sentence. He continued to be the target of various modes of suppression. In 1956, he was tried for treason and the trial ended in 1961 with his acquittal. In 1960, the ANC was outlawed and Mandela was detained. On June 12, 1964, he received a life sentence for plotting to overthrow the government. From 1964 to 1982, he was incarcerated at Robben Island Prison of Cape Town. Then he was moved to Pollsmoor Prison, where he remained until his release on February 18, 1990.

After his release, Mandela was elected president of the ANC, and in 1994, in South Africa's first democratic and free elections, he was elected president of the country. He served in that capacity for one term, until 1999, and then he retired from politics to assume the role of an international leader who works toward peace and reconciliation in Africa and beyond. In acknowledgment of his persistent struggle against apartheid, remarkable resilience, and advocacy of justice, human dignity, and rights, Mandela has received over one hundred international awards including the 1993 Nobel Peace Prize, which he shared with Frederik Willem de Klerk for ending the apartheid in South Africa.

Rigoberta Menchú (1959–)

Rigoberta Menchú was born on January 9, 1959, as a member of the indigenous Quiché Maya community in Guatemala. She and her family experienced extreme discrimination and ill-treatment from the landowning classes. During the harvest season, Menchú and her family worked fourteen-hour days on the coffee and cotton plantations for subsistence wages. Two of Menchú's brothers died on the plantations—one from inhaling pesticides and one from malnutrition. Her family was not allowed to bury the child who succumbed to malnutrition and was evicted without being paid for fifteen days' work. Life in the city was not much better. Menchú worked in Guatemala City for a short time as a maid. There she endured backbreaking work and slept on a mat next to the family dog.

Menchú learned Spanish, in order to be able to exercise her legal rights, and three other Mayan dialects, so that she could communicate with other tribal groups that suffered similar oppression. Rigoberta Menchú, like her father Vincente Menchú, joined the Committee of the Peasant Union (CUC), and in 1980, she played a significant role in a strike organized by CUC in an effort to obtain improved working conditions for the farmworkers in the Pacific coast region. She later joined the radical 31st of January Popular Front and persuaded the Indian peasant populace to defy repression from the descendants of European immigrants. In 1981 she became wanted by the police for her alleged subversive activities. Guatemala became too dangerous for her so she fled to Mexico, where she continued to work for human rights for the indigenous peoples of Guatemala. Determined to continue her struggle for social justice, she co-founded the United Representation of the Guatemalan Opposition (RUOG).

Her testimony was compiled by an anthropologist in the form of an autobiography, though the factual elements in *I, Rigoberta Menchú* were disputed by some, and the book generated some controversy. In 1992, when she won the Nobel Peace Prize, Menchú used the $1.2 million in prize money to set up a foundation in memory of her father. The Vincente Menchú Foundation works for human rights and education of indigenous peoples in Guatemala and the Americas. Partly due to her efforts, a peace accord was signed between the guerrilla groups and the Guatemalan government in December 1996. In the thirty-five years that the civil war lasted, over 100,000 Guatemalans were killed and at least 40,000 were "disappeared" and are presumed dead, 440 villages were burned to the ground, 100,000 people were wounded, and 200,000 fled to other countries. In 1999, she also played a significant role in the failed attempt to bring the Guatemalan political and military establishment, including ex-military dictator Efraín Ríos Montt, to Spanish courts for committing crimes against Spanish citizens and genocide against the Maya people of Guatemala.

Her work has heightened awareness of the rights of indigenous peoples worldwide, and in 1991, she participated in the UN effort to prepare a declaration of the rights of indigenous people. More recently, she has started to challenge the Mexican pharmaceutical industry and the corporate world for their discriminatory and exploitative practices.

Juan E. Mendez (1944–)

Juan Mendez was born December 11, 1944, in Argentina. He received his education at Stella Maris Catholic University and the Provincial University in Mar del Plata and later from the American University in Washington, D.C. A lawyer and educator, he was in private law practice in Argentina from 1970 to 1975 and was acting dean of the school of economics at Provincial University for the year 1973.

During Argentina's "dirty war," Mendez was imprisoned by the military government without charges for eighteen months. Adopted as a "prisoner of conscience" by Amnesty International in 1976, he was exiled in 1977. He became director of Centro Christo Rey, a Catholic Center for Hispanics in Aurora, Illinois, and then accepted a position with the Alien Rights Law Project under the sponsorship of the Lawyers' Committee for Civil Rights under Law in Washington, D.C. In 1982, Mendez became director of the Washington, D.C., office of Americas Watch (now Human Rights Watch/Americas), a position that allowed him to participate in many of the Americas Watch investigations of human rights violations, particularly in Latin American countries. He has been responsible for several of the Americas Watch reports and other publications on human rights in Latin American countries.

Mendez left Human Rights Watch in the 1990s to become the executive director of the Inter-American Institute for Human Rights based in Costa Rica. The institute has implemented several education programs to make people aware of their rights to humane treatment. He also served as a member of the Inter-American Commission on Human Rights of the Organization of American States between 2000 and 2003, and as its president in 2002.

He has taught law at various universities in the United States and is currently president of the International Centre for Transitional Justice, a nongovernmental organization (NGO) that helps countries emerging from conflict or repression to make human rights violators accountable for their crimes. In July 2004, UN Secretary-General Kofi Annan appointed Méndez the first Special Adviser on the Prevention of Genocide. The office of Special Adviser acts as an early warning mechanism to the Secretary-General and the Security Council about potential situations that could develop into genocide, and to make recommendations to the Security Council about how the UN can prevent these events.

Gertrude Mongella (1955–)

Gertrude Mongella, a feminist, activist, teacher, and politician, was born in 1945 on the island of Ukewere in Lake Victoria, Tanzania (then Tanganyika). She attended the University College of Dar-es-Salaam and earned a bachelor's degree in education.

Since 1975 Gertrude Mongella has held various ministerial positions as a member of the East African Legislative Assembly. In addition, she has represented Tanzania in an official capacity at numerous international conferences and meetings, primarily on issues relating to women and development. She represented Tanzania on the Commission on the Status of Women in 1989 and presented her country's report to the Committee on the Elimination of All Forms of Discrimination against Women in 1990.

Committed to the international struggle for women's rights, Mongella has also been active in international forums in behalf of the world's women. She was the UN Under-Secretary and special envoy of the UN Secretary-General on Women's Issues and Development between 1996 and 1997. She served as the chairperson of the Fourth UN World Conference on Women, held in Beijing in 1995, which earned her the title of "Mama Beijing"; she chaired the Women's Leadership Forum on Peace in Johannesburg in 1996 and participated in the Pan-African Conference on Peace, Gender, and Development, held in Kigali, in 1997. She has been a member of the board of trustees of the UN International Research and Training Institute for the Advancement of Women (IN-STRAW) and has served on the African Committee for Peace and Development; in March 2004, she was elected president of the Pan-African Parliament.

Mary Robinson (1944–)

Mary Robinson was born on May 21, 1944, in County Mayo, Ireland. She was educated at Trinity College and obtained law degrees from the King's Inns in Dublin and Harvard University. She was called to the Bar in 1967, and with her appointment as Reid Professor of Constitutional Law at Trinity College in 1969, at the age of twenty-five she became Ireland's youngest professor of law. That same year, she became a member of the Irish Upper House of Parliament, a position she retained for two decades. In 1988, with her husband Nicholas Robinson, she co-founded the Irish Centre for European Law at Trinity College. Ten years later she was elected chancellor of the university.

In 1990, she became the seventh president of Ireland and the first woman to occupy this position. In her presidential post, which she held for seven years, and throughout her political career she fought for a variety of human rights issues such as the legalization of contraceptives and divorce as well as the decriminalization of homosexuality in Ireland. Eventually both bills were signed into law during her presidency. As president of Ireland, she also focused on the needs of developing countries. She was actually the first head of state to go to Rwanda in the aftermath of the genocide and among the earliest to visit Somalia during the height of the famine there. These endeavors earned her the CARE Humanitarian Award.

In 1997, eleven weeks prior to the end of her term as President of Ireland, she was appointed United Nations High Commissioner for Human Rights. In this position, her responsibilities included strengthening and restructuring human rights mechanisms, providing advisory services and technical assistance to governments, and global monitoring of human rights violations. She became one of the most internationally visible UN officials, exhibiting an uncompromising vocal stance toward governments that engaged in human rights violations. She repeatedly queried the human rights record of many powerful countries, including the United States.

In March 2001, Mary Robinson announced her decision to resign the position of High Commissioner of Human Rights, a decision that became official in September 2002. Since then, she has been honorary president of Oxfam International. She is also a founding member and chair of the Council of Women World Leaders and serves on many boards including the Vaccine Fund.

Now based in New York, she is leading the Ethical Globalization Initiative (EGI), which maintains the goal of incorporating the norms and standards of international human rights into the economic globalization process, which has been undermining the economic, social, and labor rights of many (see Chapter 3), and to assist developing countries to improve their governing capacity and accountability. Since spring 2004, she has also been professor of practice in international affairs at Columbia University, where she teaches international human rights.

Eleanor Roosevelt (1884–1962)

Eleanor Roosevelt was born in New York City on October 11, 1884. She married Franklin Delano Roosevelt on March 17, 1905, and they parented six children. Eleanor Roosevelt's exceptional career in public service was greatly enhanced when her husband was elected president of the United States in 1933. She excelled as an advocate for human rights and the needs of the underprivileged.

During World War I, Eleanor Roosevelt became active in the American Red Cross and regularly volunteered in navy hospitals. She became involved in the Women's Trade Union League, the League of Women's Voters, and the Women's Division of the New York State Democratic Committee. Her numerous humanitarian efforts and anti-racist stance generated national and international respect and admiration. She became one of the best known and most admired public figures of her time.

Soon after President Roosevelt's death and the establishment of the United Nations in 1945, Eleanor Roosevelt was appointed a member of the United States Delegation to the first meeting of the United Nations General Assembly. She continued to serve in that capacity until 1953. A fervent promoter of equal rights, she served as chair of the Commission on Human Rights and provided significant contributions to the drafting of the Universal Declaration of Human Rights, which was eventually adopted by the General Assembly on December 10, 1948.

As a passionate advocate of human rights, Eleanor Roosevelt also became intensely engaged in the creation of the United Nations Children's Fund (UNICEF). In 1953, she became a volunteer member of the American Association for the United Nations. She also served as an American representative to the World Federation of the United Nations Associations. In 1961, President Kennedy again appointed Mrs. Roosevelt to the United States Delegation to the United Nations. She received numerous humanitarian awards during her lifetime, as a testament to her dedicated public service and commitment to equal justice. She died in New York City in November 1962.

Nawal El-Saadawi (1931–)

As a feminist, medical doctor, and writer, Nawal Saadawi has been a major influence on the lives of women in the Arab world and internationally. She was born October 27, 1931, in the Egyptian village of Kafir Tahla. She attended the University of Cairo and graduated in 1955 with a degree in psychiatry. She researched women and neurosis in the Ain Shams University Faculty of Medicine from 1973 to 1976. The injustices and suffering faced by her female patients led El-Saadawi to speak against the repression and plight of women.

Also a talented and prolific writer, El-Saadawi articulates issues of women and their human rights in her novels, essays, and other writings. Her books dealing with the restricted topics of women's sexuality, politics, and religion, however, have enraged Egypt's political and cultural elite. The publication of *Women and Sex*, in 1972, led to her dismissal as Egypt's Director of Public Health. Since then El-Saadawi has written a collection of nonfiction works that address women's oppression under social norms and rules based on a misogynist, male interpretation of Islam, the nature of cultural identity, and problems facing the international women's movement.

Between 1979 and 1980, El-Saadawi served as the United Nations Adviser for the Women's Program in Africa (ECA) and the Middle East (ECWA).In spite of international literary acclaim and admiration for her effective articulation of the women's cause, El-Saadawi has continuously received threats and prosecution in her own country. Her candid support for women's rights has led to her arrest by the Egyptian government on more than one occasion. In 1981 she was imprisoned under Anwar Sadat's presidency and finally released in 1982, a month after his assassination. That same year in 1982, she founded the Arab Women's Solidarity Association (AWSA), a feminist organization, but the Egyptian government banned it in 1991. Undaunted, El-Saadawi continues to fight vehemently against the oppressive Egyptian regime, to criticize Western hypocrisy and imperialist ventures in the Middle East, and to remain an outspoken advocate of women's rights.

Andrei Sakharov (1921–1989)

Born in Moscow on May 21, 1921, Andrei Sakharov graduated from Moscow State University with an honors degree in physics in 1942. Then he joined the P. N. Lebedev Physics Institute in Moscow, where he obtained his doctorate in physical and mathematical sciences in 1947. Between 1947 and 1956, he worked in nuclear physics on a team of scientists developing nuclear arms.

In the late 1950s, Sakharov became increasingly uneasy about the "moral problem inherent in this work." He became politically active during the 1960s and voiced his opposition to nuclear proliferation. His advocacy of putting an end to atmospheric tests was important in the development of the Partial Test Ban Treaty, signed in Moscow in 1963. In addition to his opposition to the arms race, Sakharov also spoke against political discrimination and tried to bring about open discussion of these problems.

In May 1968, he expressed his views in an essay titled "Progress, Peaceful Coexistence, and Intellectual Freedom," in which he claimed that the anti-ballistic missile defense posed a major threat of nuclear war. When the essay was published outside the Soviet Union, Sakharov was dismissed from his position at the Institute and banned from all military-related research. In 1970, he formed the Moscow Human Rights Committee, with friends and fellow scientists who dedicated themselves to changing the repressive measures frequently taken by the Soviet government. For his work on peace and human rights issues he was awarded the Nobel Peace Prize in 1975. He took the opportunity of his Nobel lecture, which was read by his wife Yelena Bonner, because he was not allowed to travel abroad, to speak about the repression in the Soviet Union and to plead for the restoration of human rights. In January 1980, he was arrested for his public protest of the Soviet invasion of Afghanistan in 1979 and was sent to Nizhny Novgorod, a "closed city" not accessible to outsiders, as an internal exile. He remained under tight police surveillance until 1986, when Soviet leader Mikhail Gorbachev initiated new policies of *glasnost* (openness) and allowed him to return to Moscow as a free person. He used his freedom to initiate the first independent legal political organization, and he was elected to the new parliament, the All-Union Congress of People's Deputies, in April 1989. He died of a heart attack on December 14, 1989.

Aung San Suu Kyi (1945–)

Born June 19, 1945, in Rangoon, capital of Burma (since 1989 renamed Myanmar), Aung San Suu Kyi is the daughter of Aung San, a Burmese general who was involved in the nationalist movement that helped the Burmese people liberate themselves from the British and Japanese in 1948. Aung San was assassinated in 1947 when Aung San Suu Kyi was not yet two years old. She continued to live in Burma until 1960, when her mother was appointed Burmese ambassador to India.

While in India, Aung San Suu Kyi became familiar with the teachings of Mohandas Gandhi. At St. Hughes College, Oxford University, she read politics, philosophy, and economics and received her bachelor of arts degree in 1967. Aung San Suu Kyi married, had two sons, and pursued her academic interests in England, Japan, and India until 1988 when she returned to Rangoon to care for her dying mother.

Things had changed dramatically in the time she had been away from Burma. In 1962 a military coup was staged and a junta took over the government. She arrived home in 1988 at a time of great civil unrest. When as many as 3,000 people were killed at a public demonstration as a result of government forces' indiscriminate shooting into the protesting crowds, she decided that the time had come to take an active role in shaping Burmese politics. Her first major public appearance took place on August 26, 1988, before 500,000 people at Shwedagon Pagoda, Burma's most sacred shrine. Aung San Suu Kyi introduced the idea of basic human rights as a political objective for the people of Burma. Even though she envisioned a democratic country that included a strong military, the Burmese government introduced tighter controls to discourage her and others from speaking out.

Aung San Suu Kyi helped found the National League for Democracy in September 1988. She continued to hold rallies despite laws banning political gatherings. All through her campaign for government reform, she stressed nonviolence, but on April 5, 1989, she was nearly gunned down by six soldiers who had been ordered to kill her.

In June 1989, when the junta gave the army the right to shoot political protesters without trial, Aung San Suu Kyi spoke out again and commented that the government was showing its "true fascist colors." On July 20, 1989, she was placed under house arrest and at times was not permitted to see even her husband and two sons. Aung San Suu Kyi was awarded the Nobel Peace Prize in 1991 but her house arrest continued until July of 1995. She continues to be confined to house arrest on and off and experiences considerable restriction in moving within the country. She and her supporters encounter other forms of harassment from the Myanmar government: advisers have been beaten with sticks and chains upon leaving her house; her phone is tapped; and her house has been barricaded. She has encouraged the United States and other governments to implement sanctions against Myanmar in an effort to end the government's repressive policies.

Mother Theresa (1910–1997)

As a humanitarian, Mother Theresa has been a major influence on the lives of countless individuals internationally. She obtained worldwide acclaim with her untiring efforts in search of world peace and on behalf of the poor, which attracted public attention to economic rights. Born Agnes Gonxha Bojaxhiu on August 26, 1910, in Skopje, Macedonia, she chose the name Theresa after Saint Therese of Lisieux.

Mother Theresa joined the Sisters of Loretto and took her initial vows as a nun in 1931. She taught at St. Mary's High School in Calcutta from 1931 until 1948, when she began devoting her time to working with the poor in the slums of Calcutta. She received permission from the Holy See on October 7, 1950, to start her own order, the Missionaries of Charity, which has been expanded to many countries all over the world.

As a humanitarian, Mother Theresa performed a lifetime of service to the poor around the globe. Through piety and charm she transcended politics as an advocate of the poor. Her simplicity and selfless contributions demonstrate the extraordinary passion and energy that characterized her life. Her dedicated work brought her numerous humanitarian awards including the Pope John XXIII Peace Prize (1971), the Nehru Prize (1979) for her advancement of international peace and understanding, and the Nobel Peace Prize in 1979. She died in 1997.

Desmond Tutu (1931–)

Archbishop Desmond Mpilo Tutu has been recognized internationally as one of the principal civil rights activists engaged in nonviolent resistance against the oppressive apartheid system in South Africa. He was born on October 7, 1931, in Klerksdorp, Transvaal. He graduated from the University of South Africa in 1954 and became a teacher, but he resigned his teaching position in 1957 and was ordained an Anglican priest in 1961. In 1966 he obtained his master of theology degree from Kings College in London and returned to South Africa, where he lectured at a theological seminary in Johannesburg from 1967 to 1972.

In 1975, he was appointed "Dean" to Saint Mary's Cathedral in Johannesburg. He was the first black South African to occupy the position. He was later appointed Bishop of Lesotho from 1976 to 1978. In 1978, he was appointed the first black General Secretary of the South African Council of Churches and became internationally recognized as a leading representative for the anti-apartheid movement. From this visible position, Tutu emphasized nonviolent methods of protest and promoted the application of economic pressure by countries engaged in commerce with South Africa. In 1985, he was appointed Johannesburg's first black Anglican bishop, and in 1986 he was elected the first black Archbishop of Cape Town.

Recognized as one of the principal voices in anti-apartheid protest, Archbishop Tutu is the recipient of numerous honorary degrees. In 1984, he received the Nobel Peace Prize in recognition for his role in the nonviolent opposition to apartheid in South Africa. When he received this prize, he used the occasion to describe the plight of black people in South Africa. He was also quick to point out that in reality South Africa is a microcosm of the world and that injustice exists in many other countries. As on many occasions, he pleaded with the international community, and particularly the United States, to exert pressure on the South African government to end what had become a brutal system depriving thousands of their basic human rights.

Since the end of apartheid, Tutu has played a major role in helping South Africa recover from the wounds inflicted by apartheid. Tutu believes that if the crimes and human rights violations that took place under apartheid are acknowledged, the victims will be able to forgive the perpetrators. In 1995, Nelson Mandela appointed Tutu to head the Truth and Reconciliation Commission, which sought to document the crimes committed during apartheid while granting the perpetrators amnesty. Among many of his awards is the 1999 Sydney Peace Prize. In addition to speaking against poverty and repression in Africa, Tutu has criticized the Israeli government's treatment of Palestinians, describing it as a form of apartheid; advocated the right of gay men to be ordained priests; and criticized the Catholic Church's opposition to the use of condoms as a devastating policy in the midst of HIV/AIDS epidemic.

Simon Wiesenthal (1908–2005)

Simon Wiesenthal, a prolific writer and documenter of the atrocities of the Holocaust, was born December 31, 1908, in an Austro-

Hungarian town that is now part of Ukraine. He received a degree in architectural engineering from the Technical University of Prague in 1932 and did further studies at the University of Lemberg. He was a practicing architect in Lemberg from 1939 until he was arrested in 1941. Although he escaped execution by the Nazis through the help of a former employee, he and his wife were assigned to a forced labor camp. She was later helped to escape by the underground, but Wiesenthal had to endure life in a series of concentration camps, finally being liberated by the U.S. troops from the camp at Mauthausen.

For a time he was employed by the U.S. War Crimes Commission to help prepare evidence of Nazi atrocities, but when the position ended, he and several volunteers established the Jewish Historical Documentation Center in Linz, Austria, to continue the work of gathering and preparing evidence against Nazi war criminals. Through his efforts and those of the many volunteers who assisted him, Wiesenthal was responsible for finding and bringing to court almost 1,000 war criminals, including Adolf Eichmann.

In addition to his work of gathering evidence that would stand up in a court of law, Wiesenthal wrote many books and articles. The long list of his honorary degrees and various awards from all over the world attests to the esteem in which Wiesenthal was held. However, his character and work have not been free from controversy. Some analysts and other "Nazi-hunters" criticized Wiesenthal for exaggerating the numbers of victims and other facts, distorting stories, mishandling some cases, showing egotism, and seeking self-glorification. Nevertheless, his unflagging efforts to make the world aware of one of the most massive and systematic violations of human rights in modern times seem particularly important today, when ethnic conflicts and violence are recurring in the form of "ethnic cleansing," "war on terror," and "clash of civilizations."

Wiesenthal spent his last years in Vienna, where he died in his sleep on September 20, 2005; he was buried in the city of Herzliya in Israel on September 23.

7

Major Human
Rights Documents

A major area of accomplishment in the international advancement of human rights has been the creation of declarations
and treaties that define and clarify human rights norms and
establish monitoring bodies. This section introduces some major
human rights documents under three subheadings: (1) documents
issued by the United Nations (UN); (2) conventions adopted by the
International Labour Organization (ILO); and (3) documents
adopted by regional organizations. Two tables at the end of the
chapter list the countries and their status on the major UN and ILO
conventions, respectively.

Major Human Rights Documents
by the United Nations

Universal Declaration of Human Rights

The most important international human rights document produced in the modern age is the Universal Declaration of Human
Rights. Drafted by the Human Rights Commission of the United
Nations, which was headed by Eleanor Roosevelt, the document
articulates a comprehensive list of human rights. The Committee had international membership and was aided by the United
Nations Secretariat and the United Nations Education and Cultural Organization, both of which conducted studies that sur-
veyed human rights–related cultural norms and values upheld

175

in different societies. Three members of the drafting committee, P. C. Chang (China), Charles Malik (Lebanon), and René Cassin (France), were particularly effective intellectual forces in shaping the draft declaration.

The Declaration was adopted and proclaimed by the General Assembly of the United Nations on December 10, 1948. In thirty articles, the Declaration identifies the fundamental rights and freedoms, which are later to be incorporated and elaborated on in other human rights documents. The Declaration, along with two covenants adopted in 1966—"International Covenant of Economic, Social and Cultural Rights" and "International Covenant of Civil and Political Rights"—constitutes the International Bill of Rights. (For the full text of the Universal Declaration of Human Rights, see the appendix at the end of the chapter.)

Convention on the Prevention and Punishment of the Crime of Genocide

The Genocide Convention is the first human rights convention of the United Nations. It was approved and proposed for signature and ratification by the General Assembly on December 9, 1948, and entered into force on January 12, 1951.

Including only nineteen articles, this brief treaty is very important for recognizing genocide, committed in time of war or peace, as an international crime that has to be prevented and punished. Article 2 provides a working definition of genocide:

> In the present Convention, genocide means any of the following acts committed with intent to destroy, in whole or in part, a national, ethnical, racial or religious group, as such:
>
> (a) Killing members of the group;
> (b) Causing serious bodily or mental harm to members of the group;
> (c) Deliberately inflicting on the group conditions of life calculated to bring about its physical destruction in whole or in part;
> (d) Imposing measures intended to prevent births within the group;
> (e) Forcibly transferring children of the group to another group.

Article 3 lists the punishable acts as genocide, conspiracy to commit genocide, direct and public incitement to commit genocide, attempt to commit genocide, and complicity in genocide. The Convention also requires that persons charged with genocide be "tried by a competent tribunal of the State in the territory of which the act was committed, or by such international penal tribunal as may have jurisdiction with respect to those Contracting Parties which shall have accepted its jurisdiction" (Article 6).

Full text of the Convention is available at http://www .ohchr.org/english/law/genocide.htm.

International Convention on the Elimination of All Forms of Racial Discrimination

The International Convention on the Elimination of All Forms of Racial Discrimination was adopted by the United Nations General Assembly on December 21, 1965, and entered into force on January 4, 1969.

The Convention establishes a commitment to eradicating discrimination based on race, color, descent, and national or ethnic origin. Racial discrimination is defined as "any distinction, exclusion, restriction or preference based on race, colour, descent, or national or ethnic origin which has the purpose or effect of nullifying or impairing the recognition, enjoyment, or exercise on an equal footing, of human rights and fundamental freedoms in the political, economic, social, cultural or any other field of public life" (Article 1). States that are parties to the Convention are obliged to implement specific measures aimed at eliminating racial discrimination such as ensuring that all public authorities and institutions act in conformity with that basic obligation; not sponsoring, defending or supporting racial discrimination by any persons or organizations; and reviewing governmental policies and amending, rescinding, or nullifying discriminatory laws and regulations at all levels of political organization. By ratifying the Convention, states agree to guarantee: the right of everyone without distinction to equal treatment before the courts; the security of person; protection against violence and bodily harm; political rights, including universal equal suffrage; freedom of movement and residence; freedoms of peaceful assembly, association, thought, conscience, religion, opinion, and expression; the rights to nationality, education, and cultural activities. In addition, states parties are obliged to assure everyone within their jurisdiction effectual safeguards and remedies against actions of discrimination, including the right to seek just and adequate reparation or satisfaction for any damage suffered as a result of such discrimination. Furthermore, the Convention obliges participating states to prohibit and eradicate racial discrimination in all its forms and "to ensure the adequate development and protection of certain racial groups or individuals belonging to them, for the purpose of guaranteeing them the full and equal enjoyment of human rights and fundamental freedoms" (Article 2–2).

The Convention establishes a Committee on the Elimination of Racial Discrimination composed of eighteen experts of high moral standing, who are elected for four-year terms, to supervise the implementation of the Convention.

Full text of the document can be accessed at http://www .ohchr.org/english/law/cerd.htm.

International Covenant on Economic, Social, and Cultural Rights

The International Covenant on Economic, Social and Cultural Rights is one of the most significant United Nations treaties. The Covenant was adopted by the General Assembly on December 16, 1966, and entered into force on January 3, 1976.

The Covenant identifies basic social, economic, and cultural rights; asserts specific legal provisions; and obliges states parties to fulfill these provisions and realize the enjoyment of the rights "progressively." The Covenant also recognizes the right of all peoples to self-determination by virtue of which "they freely determine their political status and freely pursue their economic, social and cultural development" (Article 1). Subsequent to ratification, states parties commit themselves to assuring women and men of equal entitlement to enjoy economic, social, and cultural rights. Broader substantive obligations acknowledged by the Covenant require affirmative action by participating states to recognize people's rights to an adequate standard of living, including food, clothing, and housing; physical and mental health; education; and participation in cultural life. States parties must recognize the right of people to enjoy the benefits of scientific progress and its application; impartial and favorable conditions of work; rest and leisure; and social security. They must ensure the right of people to form and join trade unions and to strike, and must safeguard the protection of the family, mothers, and children. The overall goal of the Covenant is to create economic, social, and cultural rights, which enable all individuals to develop a valuable independent life in civil society.

The Committee on Economic, Social and Cultural Rights monitors the implementation of the Covenant. Its eighteen members are elected for four-year terms. Member states undertake to submit a first report to the committee within two years of the entry into force of the Covenant and thereafter, once every five years.

Full text of the document can be accessed at http://www.ohchr.org/english/law/cescr.htm.

International Covenant on Civil and Political Rights

The International Covenant on the Civil and Political Rights was adopted by the General Assembly of the United Nations on December 16, 1966, and opened for signatures. The instrument entered into force on March 23, 1976.

The basic premise underlying the International Covenant on the Civil and Political Rights exists in Article 10, which states: "All persons deprived of their liberty shall be treated with humanity and with respect for the inherent dignity of the human person." Hence, the Covenant requires respect for the right to life and forbids torture and cruel, inhumane, or degrading treatment; it asserts the respect for liberty and security of the person and forbids arbitrary and unlawful detention. The Covenant proclaims the right of all peoples to self-determination, and it also asserts that enjoyment of the rights included in the document be guaranteed to all persons without discrimination of any kind as to race, color, sex, language, religion, political or other opinion, national or social origin, property, birth, or other status. However, it allows participating states the right to limit or suspend the enjoyment of certain rights in cases officially "proclaimed public emergencies which threaten the life of a nation" (Article 4). The Covenant includes substantive provisions as well as procedural requirements in relation to arrest, treatment of prisoners, the trial process, the death penalty, national and international freedom of movement, freedom of the press, and the right to political participation and organization.

The International Covenant on Civil and Political Rights also provides for a system of state-to-state complaints. States that consent to be bound by this system agree that the United Nations may receive complaints from other states (which have also agreed to this system) and investigate the complaints. Compliance with the provisions of the Covenant is monitored by the Human Rights Committee, composed of eighteen members elected by the participating states for a four-year term. The committee examines periodic reports submitted by states and considers interstate complaints. The first report of a participating state is due to the committee within one year after it becomes a party to the Covenant, and subsequent reports are due every five years.

Full text of the document can be accessed at http://www .ohchr.org/english/law/cescr.htm.

Convention on the Elimination of All Forms of Discrimination against Women

The Convention on the Elimination of All Forms of Discrimination against Women was adopted by the General Assembly of the United Nations on December 18, 1979, and entered into force on September 3, 1981.

According to the Convention, the term "discrimination against women" refers to "any distinction, exclusion or nullifying the recognition, enforcement or exercise by women, irrespective of their functional freedoms in the political, economic, social, cultural, civil or any other field" (Article 1). States parties are required to take measures including legislation to overcome discrimination in economic and social areas such as employment, education, and health care. The Convention actively goes beyond formal equality and encompasses substantive equality through special measures like affirmative action programs and protection against indirect discrimination. The goal of equality and equal treatment of men and women is reiterated throughout the Convention with the repeated phrase of "on a basis of equality of men and women."

The Convention includes the establishment of the Committee on the Elimination of Discrimination against Women. The committee consists of twenty-three expert members who act in an individual capacity and are elected by the participating states for four-year terms; it reviews the state reports and guides states in effective implementation of the provisions of the Convention.

Full text of the document can be accessed at http://www .ohchr.org/english/law/cedaw.htm.

Convention against Torture and Other Cruel, Inhuman or Degrading Treatment or Punishment

The Convention against Torture and Other Cruel, Inhuman or Degrading Treatment or Punishment was adopted by the General Assembly of the United Nations on December 10, 1984, following several years of preparatory effort. It entered into force on June 26, 1987.

The Convention defines torture and contains provisions to prevent torture and ill treatment, prosecute torturers, and compensate victims of torture. Torture is defined as "any act by which severe pain or suffering, whether physical or mental, is inherently inflicted on a person for such purposes as obtaining from him or a third person information or a confession, punishing him for an act he or a third person has committed or is suspected of having committed, or intimidating or coercing him or a third person . . . when such pain or suffering is inflicted by or at the instigation of or with the consent or acquiescence of a public official or other person acting in an official capacity" (Article 1). Torture is also defined as a crime of "grave nature" and declared as an extraditable offense, and the treaty includes a provision that prevents the extradition or expulsion of people to another state where they may face torture. Further provisions contained in the Convention include the obligation of states parties to systematically review "interrogation rules, instructions, methods and practices as well as arrangements for the custody and treatment of detainees and to investigate allegations of torture" (Article 11). In addition, victims of torture are entitled to compensation, while statements obtained by torture are inadmissible as evidence in proceedings against the victim. The Convention obligates states parties to undertake measures to prevent acts of ill treatment that do not fall within the definition of torture.

The Convention provides for a committee to implement its norms, namely, the Committee against Torture. The Committee includes ten experts who serve in their personal capacity; it is empowered to examine states parties' reports and to receive interstate complaints and individual communications.

Full text of the document can be accessed at http://www .ohchr.org/english/law/cat.htm.

Convention on the Rights of the Child

The Convention on the Rights of the Child was adopted by the United Nations General Assembly on November 20, 1989, and entered into force on September 2, 1990.

Among the rights of the child the Convention includes freedom from discrimination on the basis of race, color, language, religion, political opinion, ethnic origin, and other status. The Convention also includes rights to identity, protection of life, survival, and development; and with permissible conditions of separation from parents. Moreover, freedoms of expression, association, assembly, thought, conscience, and religion as well as the rights of privacy, correspondence, and access to information are addressed by the Convention. Protection from all forms of physical and mental violence and other forms of abuse is mandated. Protective steps, including foster placement and other types of substitute care, are stipulated. Rights and firm procedures for adoption are prescribed. Also mentioned are children's entitlement to quality health care, education, and standards of living necessary for full physical, mental, and moral development. Responsibilities toward disabled and handicapped children are enumerated, alongside the rights of the children of indigenous as well as ethnic or religious minority groups. The Convention ensures protection from economic exploitation, abusive child labor practices, illegal sale or trafficking of children, sexual abuse, and illicit drug use. In addition, torture and other cruel and degrading treatments are prohibited, as well as arbitrary arrest and detention. Restrictions on military recruitment and participation in armed hostilities are imposed for children younger than fifteen (Article 38).

To examine the progress made by participating states in achieving the obligations set by the Convention, a Committee on the Rights of the Child, consisting of eighteen experts of high moral standing and recognized competence in the field covered in the Convention, is elected by state parties from among their nationals and serve in their personal capacity. The Convention on the Rights of the Child has been the most popular international human rights treaty; 190 countries, all UN member states with the exception of Somalia and the United States, have ratified the Convention.

Full text of the document can be accessed at http://www .ohchr.org/english/law/crc.htm.

International Convention on the Protection of the Rights of All Migrant Workers and Members of Their Families

The newest among the all major human rights conventions, the International Convention on the Protection of the Rights of All Migrant Workers and Members of Their Families was adopted by the UN General Assembly on December 18, 1990. It entered into force on July 1, 2003.

The treaty was a response to the increasing rate of migration and the vulnerability of migrant workers and members of their families. The preamble notes that the document stems from a desire "to establish norms which may contribute to the harmonization of the attitudes of States through the acceptance of basic principles concerning the treatment of migrant workers and members of their families." Article 2 defines "migrant worker" as "a person who is to be engaged, is engaged or has been engaged in a remunerated activity in a State of which he or she is not a national," and lists different types of status that such a worker may hold. In addition to reiterating that all fundamental rights and freedoms apply to migrant workers and their families, Article 54 of the treaty specifies some work-related rights:

> ... migrant workers shall enjoy equality of treatment with nationals of the State of employment in respect of:
> (a) Protection against dismissal;
> (b) Unemployment benefits;
> (c) Access to public work schemes intended to combat unemployment;
> (d) Access to alternative employment in the event of loss of work or termination of other remunerated activity, subject to article 52 of the present Convention.

Like all major human rights treaties, this convention also creates a monitoring body. The Convention sets the original membership of the Committee on the Protection of the Rights of

All Migrant Workers and Members of Their Families as ten experts of high moral standing, impartiality, and recognized competence, but increases to fourteen for the period after the Convention enters into force—upon its ratification by the forty-first
state party (Article 72). The committee held its first session in
March 2004.

For the full text of the Convention, see http://www
.ohchr.org/english/law/cmw.htm.

Major Conventions Adopted by the International Labour Organization

Freedom of Association and Protection of the Right to Organise Convention (no. 87)

The Freedom of Association and Protection of the Right to Organise Convention was adopted by the ILO on July 9, 1948, and
entered into force on July 4, 1950.

This Convention represents an important international
agreement concerning workers' freedom of association and protection of the right to organize. The term "organisation" is defined as "any organisation of workers or employers for furthering and defending the interests of workers or of employers"
(Article 10). The treaty guarantees workers and employers the
right to establish and join organizations "of their own choosing
without previous authorization." These organizations, in addition, have the right to self-government devoid of public authorities' interference. The Convention also stipulates that "the law of
the land shall not be such as to impair, nor shall it be so applied
as to impair, the guarantees provided for" in the treaty (Article 8).

Full text of the document can be accessed at http://www.ilo
.org/ilolex/english/convdisp1.htm.

Right to Organise and Collective Bargaining Convention (no. 98)

The Right to Organise and Collective Bargaining Convention was
adopted by the ILO on July 1, 1949, and entered into force on July
18, 1951.

The Convention emphasizes workers' right to "enjoy adequate protection against acts of anti-union discrimination" (Article 1). Employment of a worker cannot be "subject to the condition that he shall not join a union or shall relinquish trade union membership" and no worker can be dismissed or otherwise prejudiced "by reason of union membership or because of participation in union activities outside working hours or, with the consent of the employer, within working hours" (Article 2). The Convention also includes provisions that protect workers' right to collective bargaining.

Full text of the document can be accessed at http://www.ilo.org/ilolex/english/convdisp1.htm.

Forced Labour Convention (no. 29)

The Forced Labour Convention was adopted by the ILO on June 28, 1930, and entered into force on January 5, 1932.

The Forced Labour Convention firmly establishes the intention of the International Labour Organization (ILO) to explicitly target slavery and eliminate all forms of forced labor through the institution of formal procedures and legal mechanism to monitor violations. The Convention specifies that "the illegal exaction of forced or compulsory labour" is a punishable offense (Article 10), and it institutes penalties that member states are obliged to enforce. Furthermore, the Convention stipulates that each ratifying member "undertakes to suppress the use of forced compulsory labour" (Article 1) that "is exacted from any person under the menace of any penalty and for which the said person has not offered himself voluntarily" (Article 2). In addition, ratification of the Convention mandates suppression and eradication of all forms of forced or compulsory labor that is extracted "as a means of political coercion or education or as a punishment for holding or expressing political views," or "as a method of mobilizing and using labour for purposes or economic development, or "as a means of labour discipline." The Convention also describes exceptional circumstances that may call for compulsory labor, but specifies that "only adult able-bodied males who are of an apparent age of not less than 18 and not more than 45 years may be called upon for forced or compulsory labour" (Article 11).

Full text of the document can be accessed at http://www.ilo.org/ilolex/english/convdisp1.htm.

Abolition of Forced Labour Convention (no. 105)

The Abolition of Forced Labour Convention was adopted by the ILO on June 25, 1957. It entered into force on January 17, 1959.

The Convention represents further determination by the ILO to substantially condemn the practice of slavery, totally prohibiting forced labor in all its forms by specifying time tables. It mandates all member states to undertake "effective measures to secure the immediate and complete abolition of forced or compulsory labour" within twelve months after the ratification of the Convention. Most important, participating states are compelled "to suppress and not to make use of any form of forced or compulsory labour whether as means of political coercion or as punishment for striking or other infringements of labour disciplines" (Article 1).

Full text of the document can be accessed at http://www.ilo .org/ilolex/english/convdisp1.htm.

Equal Remuneration Convention (no. 100)

The Equal Remuneration Convention was adopted by the General Conference of the ILO on June 29, 1951, and entered into force on May 23, 1953.

The Convention institutes the "principle of equal remuneration for men and women workers for equal value" (Article 12). According to the treaty, remuneration includes "the ordinary, basic or minimum wage or salary and any additional emoluments whatsoever payable directly or indirectly, whether in cash or in kind, by the employer to the worker and arising out of the worker's employment," while equal remuneration for men and women workers for work of equal value "refers to rates of remuneration established without discrimination based on sex" (Article 1). The treaty mandates that participating states ensure and promote the application of this remuneration standard either through national regulations, legally established machinery of wage determination, collective agreements between employers and workers, or a combination of these various methods. The Convention, however, permits differential rates between workers "which correspond, without regard to sex, to differences, as determined by such objective appraisal, in the work performed, shall not be considered as being contrary to the principle of equal remuneration for men and women workers for work of equal value" (Article 3).

Full text of the document can be accessed at http://www.ilo.org/ilolex/english/convdisp1.htm.

Discrimination (Employment and Occupation) Convention (no. 111)

The ILO Convention concerning Discrimination (Employment and Occupation) was adopted on June 25, 1958, and entered into force on June 15, 1960. The Convention contains five distinct articles that define discrimination and affirm antidiscrimination in labor practices.

According to the Convention, the term "discrimination" refers to "any distinction, exclusion or preference made on the basis of race, colour, sex, religion, political opinion, national extraction, or social origin, which has the effect of nullifying or impairing equality of opportunity or treatment in employment or occupation" (Article 1).

States that ratify the Convention are obliged to "declare and pursue a national policy designed to promote, by methods appropriate to national conditions and practice, equality of opportunity and treatment in respect of employment and occupation, with a view to eliminating any discrimination in respect thereof" (Article 2). States parties are also mandated to "repeal statutory provisions and modify any administrative instructions or practices, which are inconsistent with the policy" (Article 3).

Full text of the document can be accessed at http://www.ilo.org/ilolex/english/convdisp1.htm.

Minimum Age Convention (no. 138)

The Minimum Age Convention was adopted by the ILO on June 26, 1973, and entered into force on June 19, 1976.

The Convention targets the elimination of child labor and the states that ratify the Convention agree to implement national policies "designed to ensure the effective abolition of child labour" (Article 1). The Convention mandates declaration of "a minimum age for admission to employment" by each state party; no one younger than this age can be employed. The Convention further stipulates that the minimum age "shall not be less than the age of completion of compulsory schooling . . . and shall not be less than 15 years" (Article 2). However, a state "whose economy and administrative facilities are insufficiently developed" can avail itself of the provision to "initially limit the scope of application" (Article 5). Hence, in situations where states parties have economies and educational facilities that are insufficiently developed, the minimum age may be initially specified at fourteen years and further reduced to twelve years, the minimum age for light work (Articles 5 and 7). Exemptions for "young persons in schools for general, vocational or technical education or other training institutions" are accommodated (Article 6).

Full text of the document can be accessed at http://www.ilo .org/ilolex/english/convdisp1.htm.

Worst Forms of Child Labour Convention (no. 182)

The Worst Forms of Child Labour Convention was adopted by the ILO on June 17, 1999, and entered into force on November 10, 2000.

The treaty defines the "child" as "all persons under the age of 18" (Article 2) and mandates the elimination of exploitive and abusive child labor. The Convention acknowledges that "the effective elimination of the worst forms of child labour requires immediate and comprehensive action." Hence, ratifying members are expected to "take immediate and effective measures to secure the prohibition and elimination of the Worst Forms of Child Labour as a matter of urgency" (Article 1). The Convention affirms the "eradication of child slavery, trafficking of children in armed conflict, prostitution, pornography, forced or compulsory child labour, production and trafficking of drugs and hazardous work likely to harm the health, safety or morals of children" (Article 3).

States that are party to the Convention are obliged to establish or designate appropriate mechanisms to monitor the implementation of the Convention, and to that end they should prevent children's engagement in the worst forms of labor, take measures to remove children form the worst forms of labor, ensure children's access to free basic education, and take into consideration the "special situation of girls" (Article 7).

Full text of the document can be accessed at http://www.ilo .org/ilolex/english/convdisp1.htm.

Major Human Rights Documents of Regional Organizations

African Charter on Human and Peoples' Rights

The African Charter on Human and Peoples' Rights (also known as Banjul Charter) was adopted on June 27, 1981, by the members of the Organization of African Unity (which is now known as the African Union) and entered into force on October 21, 1986. It is known for its emphasis on group rights, along with individual rights, on social and economic rights, and on the relationship between rights and duties.

Preamble of the African Charter proclaims that "freedom, equality, justice and dignity are essential objectives for the achievement of legitimate aspirations of the African peoples . . . without distinction of any kind such as race, ethnic group, color, sex, language, religion, political or any other opinion, national and social origin, fortune, birth or other status." In addition to recognizing human rights and freedoms, member states are required to adopt legislative or other measures to ensure their realization. The Charter affirms that "human beings are inviolable" and prohibits "all forms of exploitation and degradation of man" (Article 4). The Charter establishes individuals' right to trial "within a reasonable time by an impartial court or tribunal" as well as "the right to be presumed innocent until proven guilty by a competent court or tribunal" (Article 7). Under the Charter, "the profession and free practice of religion" is guaranteed (Article 8), along with the following rights: to assemble freely with others, to have freedom of movement and residence within the borders of a state (providing the person abides by law), to leave any country including his own, to own property, to work under equitable and satisfactory conditions and to receive equal pay for equal work, to enjoy the best attainable state of physical and mental health as well as education and participation in cultural life. The family is acknowledged as "the natural unit and basis of society," and the protection of family and the "elimination of every discrimination against women" are affirmed (Article 18). The Charter also specifies an individual's duties "towards his family and society, the State and other legally recognized communities and the international community" (Article 27).

The Charter establishes an African Commission on Human and Peoples' Rights, which consists of eleven members, chosen "from among African personalities of the highest reputation" to oversee the implementation of its provisions (Article 31).

Full text of the document can be accessed at http://www.hrcr .org/Text/Regional/africa.html.

American Declaration of the Rights and Duties of Man

In 1948, at its Ninth International Conference, the Organization of American States proclaimed the American Declaration of the Rights and Duties of Man, in Bogotá, Colombia. The prologue of the Declaration asserts that "the international protection of the rights of man should be the principal guide of an evolving American law." The preamble of the Declaration recognizes the inter-relation of individual rights and duties "in every social and political activity of man." It further maintains that "the fulfillment of duty by each individual is a prerequisite to the rights of all." The Declaration has two chapters: the first focuses on the "rights" of man, the second on the "duties." The Declaration includes fundamental rights such as the right to life, liberty, and personal security; the right to equality before the law; the right to religious freedom and worship. Social, cultural, and political rights are enunciated, along with protection of honor, personal reputation, and private and family life. The Declaration's provisions also address the following rights: to a family and to its protection; to residence and movement; to the preservation of health and well-being; to education; to employment and fair remuneration; to social security; to benefits of culture; to a fair trial, to assembly, to own property, to association, to petition, and to be protected from arbitrary arrest. On the other hand, it stipulates individual duties that include: duties to society, children, and parents; to receive instruction; to vote; to obey the law; to serve the community and the nation; to pay taxes; and to refrain from political activities in a foreign country.

Full text of the document can be accessed at http://www .cidh.oas.org/Basicos/basic2.htm.

American Convention on Human Rights

The American Convention on Human Rights, also known as the "Pact of San Jose," was adopted by the General Assembly of the Organization of American States (OAS) on November 11, 1969, and entered into force on July 18, 1978.

The preamble of the Convention specifies its foundations in the Universal Declaration of Human Rights as well as the American Declaration of the Rights and Duties of Man. The Convention obliges the participating states to respect the rights and freedoms that are recognized in the Convention and "to ensure to all persons subject to their jurisdiction the free and full exercise of those rights and freedoms, without any discrimination for reasons of race, color, sex, language, religion, political or other opinion, national or social origin, economic status, birth, or any other social condition" (Article 1). The Convention enshrines the right to life. Although it does not abolish the death penalty, it includes several provisions to limit it. It calls for respect for one's right to physical, mental, and moral integrity; freedom from torture; freedom from all forms of degrading punishment or treatment; and freedom from slavery, forced or compulsory labor, and arbitrary arrest or imprisonment. The right to fair trial, privacy and compensation for miscarriage of judgment, peaceful assembly as well as freedom of conscience, religion, thought, expression, association, movement, and residence are recognized. Also included are the rights of the family and rights of the child. In addition to property and political rights, the Convention recognizes economic, social, and cultural rights and calls for their progressive development.

The Convention creates an Inter-American Commission on Human Rights, which includes seven persons of high moral character with recognized competence in the field of human rights. The Commission works on promoting respect for human rights and human rights advocacy. It monitors the implementation of the provisions of the Convention through a periodic reporting process and acceptance of petitions. Another enforcement agency created by the Convention is the Inter-American Court of Human Rights, which consists of seven judges who are nationals of the member states of OAS and elected in an individual capacity.

Full text of the document can be accessed at http://www .cidh.oas.org/Basicos/basic3.htm.

Additional Protocol to the American Convention on Human Rights in the Area of Economic, Social and Cultural Rights

The General Assembly of the Organization of American States adopted the Additional Protocol, also known as "Protocol of San Salvador," on November 17, 1988, to bring social, economic, and cultural rights under international legal protection. The Protocol entered into force on November 16, 1999.

The Protocol includes basic social and economic rights such as the right to work, remuneration that guarantees dignified and decent living conditions for workers and their families, safe and healthy work conditions, and freedom to organize trade unions and to strike. Also addressed are the right to social security, to health and a healthy environment, to adequate food and nutrition, and to education; additional provisions include a person's right to take part in the cultural and artistic life of the community and to enjoy the benefits of scientific and technological progress. The Protocol protects the right to establish a family and obliges the states parties to protect the family unit by taking certain measures, such as providing special care and assistance to mothers for a reasonable period before and after childbirth and guaranteeing adequate nutrition for children at the nursing stage and during school attendance years. The rights of the child and protection of the elderly and the handicapped are also addressed.

The Protocol obliges states parties to submit periodic reports on the progressive measures that they take to ensure the protection of human rights it sets forth. The reports are transmitted to the Inter-American Commission on Human Rights. The Protocol also stipulates that in "any instance in which the rights established in paragraph a) of Article 8 and in Article 13 [provisions on the right to trade unions and the right to education, respectively] are violated by action directly attributable to a State Party," the authority of the Inter-American Court of Human Rights may be invoked.

Full text of the document can be accessed at http://www.oas.org/main/main.asp?sLang=E&sLink=http://www.oas.org/juridico/english/treaties.html.

The Cairo Declaration on Human Rights in Islam

The Cairo Declaration on Human Rights in Islam was adopted at the Nineteenth Islamic Conference of Foreign Ministers, held in Cairo, Arab Republic of Egypt, in August 1990. According to its preamble, the Declaration was created "in contribution to the efforts of mankind to assert human rights, to protect man from exploitation and persecution, and to affirm his freedom and right to a dignified life in accordance with the Islamic Shari'ah."

The preamble indicates "that fundamental rights and freedoms . . . are an integral part of the Islamic religion and that no one shall have the right as a matter of principle to abolish them either in part or in whole." Article 1 affirms that "all men and women are equal in terms of basic human dignity and basic obligations and responsibilities, without any discrimination on the basis of race, colour, language, belief, sex, religion, political affiliation, social status or other considerations." The right to "both religious and worldly education" is recognized (Article 9). In addition to the right to medical care, employment, social benefits, fair wages for men and women, and the prohibition of exploitation, freedoms such as freedom of movement and expression are specified. The right to own property and the right to privacy are also acknowledged. The Declaration prescribes the legal rights and proper treatment of defendants including prohibition of "physical or psychological torture or to any form of maltreatment, cruelty or indignity" (Article 20). The Cairo Declaration stipulates the treatment of people during wartime and guarantees family rights including the right to marry. However, it reiterates repeatedly that rights are freedoms that will be recognized and respected as long as they are in accordance with the *Shari'ah*, the Islamic law.

Full text of the document can be accessed at http://www1 .umn.edu/humanrts/instree/cairodeclaration.html.

European Convention for the Protection of Human Rights and Fundamental Freedoms

The European Convention for the Protection of Human Rights and Fundamental Freedoms was opened for signatures by the Council of Europe on November 4, 1950, and entered into force on September 3, 1953. The Convention establishes the inalienable rights and freedoms of each citizen and obliges all states that have ratified the Convention to guarantee these rights.

The Convention ensures that "everyone's right to life shall be protected by law" (Article 1). In addition, it affirms that "no one shall be subjected to torture or to inhuman or degrading treatment or punishment" (Article 3). It calls for the protection of the right to liberty and security, freedom from slavery, servitude, and forced or compulsory labor. The Convention establishes the presumption of innocence until proven guilty, delineates procedures for effecting arrests, and confirms everyone's entitlement "to a fair and public hearing within a reasonable time by an independent and impartial tribunal established by law" (Article 6). The Convention also establishes respect for private and family life and institutes "the right to freedom of expression," which includes the "freedom to hold opinions and to receive and impart information and ideas without interference by public authority and regardless of frontiers" (Article 10).

To ensure observance of the provisions of the Convention, a European Commission of Human Rights was established. Moreover, the European Court on Human Rights, consisting of judges from member countries who sit on the court in their individual capacities, was established to enforce the Convention. In relation to this Convention, the Council of Europe has issued fourteen different protocols. Protocols allow amendments to the Convention and its adaptation to changing circumstances.

Full text of the document can be accessed at http://conventions.coe.int/Treaty/EN/CadreListeTraites.htm.

European Social Charter

The Council of Europe opened the European Social Charter for signature in Turin on October 18, 1961. The charter entered into force on February 26, 1965. Later, on May 3, 1996, the Council of Europe adopted a revised version of the Charter. The revisions were undertaken to preserve the indivisible nature of all human rights and to update and adapt the substantive content of the Charter by taking into account the fundamental social changes that have occurred since the text was adopted in 1961.

The Social Charter guarantees nineteen fundamental social and economic rights. The aims that states parties undertake to pursue, by all appropriate means, are determined in Part I of the Charter. The Charter stipulates that any state wishing to become a party to the agreement must agree to be bound by at least ten articles (out of 19) or forty-five numbered paragraphs of Part II of the charter. Seven of the articles are considered particularly significant: the right to work; the right to organize; the right to bargain collectively; the right to social security; the right to social and medical assistance; the right to the social, legal, and economic protection of the family; and migrant workers' and their families' right to protection and assistance. Of these seven, each state party must accept at least five.

The Charter contains provisions designed to ensure respect for the obligations undertaken. It establishes a supervisory system of national reports submitted every two years for examination by a committee of seven independent experts. The Governmental Committee then presents to the Committee of Ministers of the Council of Europe a report containing its conclusions, to which the report of the Committee of Independent Experts is appended. The Committee of Ministers may make any necessary recommendations to the governments concerned.

The 1996 revisions include several new rights and amendments. *New rights:* right to protection against poverty and social exclusion; right to housing; right to protection in case of termination of employment; right to protection against sexual harassment in the workplace and other forms of harassment; rights of workers with family responsibilities to equal opportunities and equal treatment; rights of workers' representatives in undertakings.

Amendments: reinforcement of the principle of nondiscrimination; improvement of gender equality in all fields covered by the treaty; better protection of maternity and social protection of mothers; better social, legal, and economic protection of employed children; better protection of handicapped people.

The full text of the document can be accessed at http://conventions.coe.int/treaty/en/Treaties/Html/163.htm.

European Convention for the Prevention of Torture and Inhuman or Degrading Treatment or Punishment

The Council of Europe adopted the European Convention for the Prevention of Torture and Inhuman or Degrading Treatment or Punishment, on November 26, 1987. The text was amended and entered into force on March 1, 2002.

The Convention is designed to establish a machinery to challenge the phenomenon of torture at its origin and prevent incidents of torture from occurring. Its preamble sets the purpose of the Convention as to strengthen the protection of persons deprived of their liberty and subjected to torture and inhuman or degrading treatment or punishment "by non-judicial means of a preventive character based on visits." The Convention, therefore, establishes a European Committee for the Prevention of Torture and Inhuman or Degrading Treatment or Punishment. The Committee shall "by means of visits, examine the treatment of persons deprived of their liberty with a view to strengthening, if necessary, the protection of such persons from torture and from inhuman or degrading treatment or punishment" (Article 1). Thus, the Convention directs the Committee to visit places of detention and to examine the treatment of detainees, and to seek improvements where necessary through cooperation with the state party concerned, as opposed to condemning that state for misconduct. This allows the Convention to create comprehensive protection against torture. An important element of the Convention is requiring the states parties to permit regular and impromptu visits by the committee, to any place within its jurisdiction, "where persons are detained by public authority" (Article 2).

The Committee is made up of members elected by the Committee of Ministers of the Council of Europe. The members of the Committee are elected for four-year terms and may be reelected twice.

Full text of the document can be accessed at http://www .cpt.coe.int/en/documents/ecpt.htm.

The Charter of Fundamental Rights of the European Union

Approved by the European Parliament, European Council, and the European Commission, the Charter was proclaimed on December 7, 2000, in Nice. Presently, the Charter is not a part of the European Union treaty, but it is incorporated as Part II of the Constitution of Europe, which is yet to be adopted.

In an attempt to consolidate fundamental human rights in a single document, the Charter draws together all personal, civil, political, economic, and social rights into a single text. The charter draws from the European Convention on Human Rights, the

Social Charter, the case law of the Court of Justice of the European Communities, national constitutional traditions, and the Community Charter of Fundamental Social Rights of Workers. It includes fifty-four articles listed under six main sections, dealing with dignity, freedoms, equality, solidarity, citizens' rights, and justice, as well as general provisions. While combining the traditional human rights into a single document, the Charter also addresses new concerns such as bio-ethics and protection of personal data.

Full text of the Charter can be accessed at http://europa.eu .int/comm/justice_home/unit/charte/index_en.html.

Helsinki Final Act/Helsinki Accords

The Helsinki Final Act, also known as the Helsinki Accords, is the final document of the Conference on Security and Cooperation in Europe, which opened in Helsinki on July 3, 1973, and continued in Geneva from September 1973 to July 21, 1975. The Helsinki Final Act was adopted in Helsinki on August 1, 1975. The Conference represented an extensive agreement encompassing a broad range of issues pertaining to political, economic, social, environmental, military, educational, cultural, and technological concerns. The states attending the Conference reaffirmed their commitment to peace, security, justice, and the continuing development of friendly relations. The participating states guaranteed respect for "the rights inherent in sovereignty" (Article 1-I) and the "inviolability of frontiers" (Article 1-III). In addition, they agreed to refrain "from the threat or use of force, peaceful settlement of disputes and non-intervention in internal affairs" (Article 1-V).

Article 1-VII of the Helsinki Accords addresses the "respect for human rights and fundamental freedoms, including the freedom of thought, conscience, religion or belief, for all without distinction as to race, sex, language or religion." It was specified that "in the field of human rights and fundamental freedoms, the participating States will act in conformity with the purposes and principles of the Charter of the United Nations and with the Universal Declaration of Human Rights. They will also fulfill their obligations as set forth in the international declarations and agreements in this field, including inter alia the International Covenants on Human Rights, by which they may be bound." Article 8 indicates that the "participating States will respect the equal rights of peoples and their right to self-determination."

Full Text of the text can be accessed at http://www.osce
.org/docs/english/1990–1999/summits/helfa75e.htm.

The Status of Countries on the Major UN and ILO Treaties

TABLE 7.1
The status of major international human rights instruments
(UN Conventions, as of May 1, 2005)

	GC 1948	CRD 1965	ICCPR 1966	ICESCR 1966	CEDAW 1979	CAT 1984	CRC 1989	CMW 1990
Afghanistan	•	•	•	•	•	•	•	
Albania	•	•	•	•	•	•	•	
Algeria	•	•	•	•	•	•	•	•
Andorra		□	□			•	□	•
Angola				•		•	•	
Antigua and Barbuda	•	•	•		•	•	•	
Argentina	•	•	•	•	•	•	•	□
Armenia	•	•	•	•	•	•	•	
Australia	•	•	•	•	•	•	•	
Austria	•	•	•	•	•	•	•	
Azerbaijan	•	•	•	•	•	•	•	•
Bahamas	•	•	•		•		•	
Bahrain	•	•			•	•	•	
Bangladesh	•	•	•	•	•	•	•	□
Barbados	•	•	•	•	•		•	
Belarus	•	•	•	•	•	•	•	
Belgium	•	•	•	•	•	•	•	
Belize	•	•	•	□	•	•	•	•
Benin		•	•	•	•	•	•	□
Bhutan		□	□		•		•	
Bolivia	•	•	•	•	•	•	•	•
Bosnia and Herzegovina	•	•	•	•	•	•	•	•
Botswana		•	•		•	•	•	
Brazil	•	•	•	•	•	•	•	
Brunei Darussalam							•	
Bulgaria	•	•	•	•	•	•	•	
Burkina Faso	•	•	•	•	•	•	•	•
Burundi	•	•	•	•	•	•	•	
Cambodia	•	•	•	•	•	•	•	□
Cameroon		•	•	•	•	•	•	
Canada	•	•	•	•	•	•	•	
Cape Verde		•	•	•	•	•	•	•

continues

TABLE 7.1   continued

	GC 1948	CRD 1965	ICCPR 1966	ICESCR 1966	CEDAW 1979	CAT 1984	CRC 1989	CMW 1990
Central African Republic		•	•	•	•		•	
Chad		•	•	•	•	•	•	
Chile	•	•	•	•	•	•	•	•
China	•	•	•	•	•	•	•	
Colombia	•	•	•	•	•	•	•	•
Comoros	•	•			•	•	•	□
Congo		•	•	•	•	•	•	
Congo, Dem. Rep. of the	•	•	•	•	•	•	•	
Costa Rica	•	•	•	•	•	•	•	
Côte d'Ivoire	•	•	•	•	•	•	•	
Croatia	•	•	•	•	•	•	•	
Cuba	•	•			•	•	•	
Cyprus	•	•	•	•	•	•	•	
Czech Republic	•	•	•	•	•	•	•	
Denmark	•	•	•		•	•	•	
Djibouti			•	•	•	•	•	
Dominica			•	•	•		•	
Dominican Republic	□	•	•	•	•	•	•	
Ecuador	•	•	•	•	•	•	•	•
Egypt	•	•	•	•	•	•	•	•
El Salvador	•	•	•	•	•	•	•	•
Equatorial Guinea		•	•	•	•	•	•	
Eritrea		•	•	•	•		•	
Estonia	•	•	•	•	•	•	•	
Ethiopia	•	•	•	•	•	•	•	
Fiji	•	•			•		•	
Finland	•	•	•	•	•	•	•	
France	•	•	•	•	•	•	•	
Gabon	•	•	•	•	•	•	•	□
Gambia	•	•	•	•	•	•	•	
Georgia	•	•	•	•	•	•	•	
Germany	•	•	•	•	•	•	•	
Ghana	•	•	•	•	•	•	•	•
Greece	•	•	•	•	•	•	•	
Grenada		□	□	•	•		•	
Guatemala	•	•	•	•	•	•	•	•
Guinea	•	•	•	•	•	•	•	•
Guinea-Bissau		□	□	•	•	•	•	□
Guyana		•	•	•	•	•	•	□
Haiti	•	•	•		•		•	
Honduras	•	•	•	•	•	•	•	•
Hungary	•	•	•	•	•	•	•	
Iceland	•	•	•	•	•	•	•	
India	•	•	•	•	•		•	

continues

TABLE 7.1 continued

	GC 1948	CRD 1965	ICCPR 1966	ICESCR 1966	CEDAW 1979	CAT 1984	CRC 1989	CMW 1990
Indonesia		•	•		•	•	•	□
Iran, Islamic Rep. of	•	•	•	•			•	
Iraq	•	•	•	•	•		•	
Ireland	•	•	•	•	•	•	•	
Israel	•	•	•	•	•	•	•	
Italy	•	•	•	•	•	•	•	
Jamaica	•	•	•	•	•		•	
Japan		•	•	•	•		•	
Jordan	•	•	•	•	•	•	•	
Kazakhstan	•	•	•	□	•	•	•	
Kenya		•	•	•	•	•	•	
Kiribati					•		•	
Korea, Dem. Rep.	•			•	•	•	•	
Korea, Rep. of	•	•	•	•	•	•	•	
Kuwait	•	•	•	•	•	•	•	
Kyrgyzstan	•	•	•	•	•	•	•	•
Lao People's Dem. Rep.	•	•	•	□	•		•	
Latvia	•	•	•	•	•	•	•	
Lebanon	•	•	•	•	•	•	•	
Lesotho	•	•	•	•	•	•	•	•
Liberia	•	•	•	•	•	•	•	□
Libyan Arab Jamahiriya	•	•	•	•	•	•	•	•
Liechtenstein	•	•	•	•	•	•	•	
Lithuania	•	•	•	•	•	•	•	
Luxembourg	•	•	•	•	•	•	•	
Macedonia, TFYR	•	•	•	•	•	•	•	
Madagascar		•	•	•	•	□	•	
Malawi		•	•	•	•	•	•	
Malaysia	•				•		•	
Maldives	•	•	•		•	•	•	
Mali	•	•	•	•	•	•	•	•
Malta		•	•	•	•	•	•	
Marshall Islands							•	
Mauritania		•	•	•	•	•	•	
Mauritius		•	•	•	•	•	•	
Mexico	•	•	•	•	•	•	•	•
Micronesia, Fed. Sts.					•		•	
Moldova, Rep. of	•	•	•	•	•	•	•	
Monaco	•	•	•	•	•	•	•	
Mongolia	•	•	•	•	•	•	•	
Morocco	•	•	•	•	•	•	•	•
Mozambique	•	•	•		•	•	•	
Myanmar	•				•		•	
Namibia	•	•	•	•	•	•	•	

continues

TABLE 7.1 continued

	GC 1948	CRD 1965	ICCPR 1966	ICESCR 1966	CEDAW 1979	CAT 1984	CRC 1989	CMW 1990
Nauru		□	□			□	•	
Nepal	•	•	•	•	•	•	•	
Netherlands	•	•	•					
New Zealand	•	•	•	•	•	•	•	
Nicaragua	•	•	•	•	•	•	•	•
Niger		•	•	•	•	•	•	
Nigeria		•	•	•	•	•	•	
Norway	•	•	•	•	•	•	•	
Oman		•	•				•	
Pakistan	•	•	•	□	•		•	
Palau							•	
Panama	•	•	•	•	•	•	•	
Papua New Guinea	•	•	•		•		•	
Paraguay	•	•	•	•	•	•	•	□
Peru	•	•	•	•	•	•	•	•
Philippines	•	•	•	•	•	•	•	•
Poland	•	•	•	•	•	•	•	
Portugal	•	•	•	•	•	•	•	
Qatar		•	•			•	•	
Romania	•	•	•	•	•	•	•	
Russian Federation	•	•	•	•	•	•	•	
Rwanda	•	•	•	•	•		•	
Saint Kitts and Nevis					•		•	
Saint Lucia		•			•		•	
Saint Vincent & the Grenadines	•	•	•	•	•	•	•	
Samoa (Western)					•		•	
San Marino		•	•	•	•	□	•	
São Tomé and Principe		□	□	□	•	□	•	□
Saudi Arabia	•	•	•		•	•	•	
Senegal	•	•	•	•	•	•	•	•
Serbia and Montenegro	•	•	•	•	•	•	•	□
Seychelles	•	•	•	•	•	•	•	•
Sierra Leone	•	•	•	•	•	•	•	□
Singapore	•				•		•	
Slovakia	•	•	•	•	•	•	•	
Slovenia	•	•	•	•	•	•	•	
Solomon Islands		•	•	•	•		•	
Somalia		•	•	•		•	□	
South Africa	•	•	•	□	•	•	•	
Spain	•	•	•	•	•	•	•	
Sri Lanka	•	•	•	•	•	•	•	•
Sudan	•	•	•	•		•	•	
Suriname		•	•	•	•		•	
Swaziland		•	•		•		•	

continues

TABLE 7.1 continued

	GC 1948	CRD 1965	ICCPR 1966	ICESCR 1966	CEDAW 1979	CAT 1984	CRC 1989	CMW 1990
Sweden	•	•	•	•	•	•	•	
Switzerland	•	•	•	•	•	•	•	
Syrian Arab Republic	•	•	•	•	•	•	•	•
Tajikistan		•	•	•	•	•	•	•
Tanzania, U. Rep. of	•	•	•	•	•		•	
Thailand		•	•	•	•		•	
Timor-Leste		•	•	•	•	•	•	•
Togo	•	•	•	•	•	•	•	□
Tonga	•	•	•				•	
Trinidad and Tobago	•	•	•	•	•		•	
Tunisia	•	•	•	•	•	•	•	
Turkey	•	•	•	•	•	•	•	•
Turkmenistan	•	•	•	•	•	•	•	
Tuvalu					•		•	
Uganda	•	•	•	•	•	•	•	•
Ukraine	•	•	•	•	•	•	•	
United Arab Emirates		•	•		•		•	
United Kingdom	•	•	•	•	•	•	•	
United States	•	•	•	□	□	•	□	
Uruguay	•	•	•	•	•	•	•	•
Uzbekistan	•	•	•	•	•	•	•	
Vanuatu					•		•	
Venezuela	•	•	•	•	•	•	•	
Viet Nam	•	•	•	•	•		•	
Yemen	•	•	•	•	•	•	•	
Zambia		•	•	•	•	•	•	
Zimbabwe	•	•	•	•	•		•	
TOTAL RATIFICATION								
SIGNATURES without ratification	136	170	170	151	180	146	192	34
	2	6	6	7	1	5	2	15

□ Convention signed; • Convention ratified
Source: *Human Development Report 2005.* New York: Oxford University Press, 2005, Table 32.
CMW data were obtained from the Office of the High Commissioner of Human Rights, www.ohchr.org/english/countries/ratification/13.htm (accessed November 5, 2005).
Notes:
GC- International Convention on the Prevention and Punishment of the Crime of Genocide
CRD-International Convention on the Elimination of All Forms of Racial Discrimination
ICCPR-International Covenant on Civil and Political Rights
ICESCR-International Covenant on Economic, Social and Cultural Rights
CEDAW-Convention on the Elimination of All Forms of Discrimination against Women
CAT-Convention against Torture and Other Cruel, Inhuman or Degrading Treatment or Punishment
CRC-Convention on the Rights of the Child
CMW-International Convention on the Protection of the Rights of All Migrant Workers and Members of Their Families

TABLE 7.2
The status of major international labor rights instruments
(ILO Conventions, as of May 1, 2005)

	Freedom of association & collective bargaining		Elimination of forced & compulsory labor		Elimination of discrimination in employment & occupation		Abolition of child labor	
	C 87	C 98	C 29	C 105	C 100	C 111	C 138	C 182
Afghanistan				•	•	•		
Albania	•	•	•	•	•	•	•	•
Algeria	•	•	•	•	•	•	•	•
Angola	•	•	•	•	•	•	•	•
Antigua and Barbuda	•	•	•	•	•	•	•	•
Argentina	•	•	•	•	•	•	•	•
Armenia		•	•	•	•	•		
Australia	•	•	•	•	•	•		
Austria	•	•	•	•	•	•	•	•
Azerbaijan	•	•	•	•	•	•	•	•
Bahamas	•	•	•	•	•	•	•	•
Bahrain			•	•		•		•
Bangladesh	•	•	•	•	•	•		•
Barbados	•	•	•	•	•	•	•	•
Belarus	•	•	•	•	•	•	•	•
Belgium	•	•	•	•	•	•	•	•
Belize	•	•	•	•	•	•	•	•
Benin	•	•	•	•	•	•	•	•
Bhutan								
Bolivia	•	•		•	•	•	•	•
Bosnia and Herzegovina	•	•	•	•	•	•	•	•
Botswana	•	•	•	•	•	•	•	•
Brazil		•	•	•	•	•	•	•
Brunei Darussalam								
Bulgaria	•	•	•	•	•	•	•	•
Burkina Faso	•	•	•	•	•	•	•	•
Burundi	•	•	•	•	•	•	•	•
Cambodia	•	•	•	•	•	•	•	•
Cameroon	•	•	•	•	•	•		•
Canada	•			•	•	•		•
Cape Verde	•	•	•	•	•	•		•
Central African Republic	•	•	•	•	•	•	•	•
Chad	•	•	•	•	•	•		•
Chile	•	•	•	•	•	•	•	•
China					•		•	•
Colombia	•	•	•	•	•	•	•	•
Comoros	•	•	•	•	•	•	•	•
Congo	•	•	•	•	•	•	•	•

continues

TABLE 7.2 continued

	Freedom of association & collective bargaining		Elimination of forced & compulsory labor		Elimination of discrimination in employment & occupation		Abolition of child labor	
	C 87	C 98	C 29	C 105	C 100	C 111	C 138	C 182
Congo, Dem. Rep. of the	•	•	•	•	•	•	•	•
Costa Rica	•	•	•	•	•	•	•	•
Côte d'Ivoire	•	•	•	•	•	•	•	•
Croatia	•	•	•	•	•	•	•	•
Cuba	•	•	•	•	•	•	•	
Cyprus	•	•	•	•	•	•	•	•
Czech Republic	•	•	•	•	•	•		
Denmark	•	•	•	•	•	•	•	•
Djibouti	•	•	•	•	•	•		
Dominica	•	•	•	•	•	•	•	•
Dominican Republic	•	•	•	•	•	•	•	•
Ecuador	•	•	•	•	•	•	•	•
Egypt	•	•	•	•	•	•	•	•
El Salvador			•	•	•	•	•	•
Equatorial Guinea	•	•	•	•	•	•	•	•
Eritrea	•	•	•	•	•	•	•	
Estonia	•	•	•	•	•			•
Ethiopia	•	•	•	•	•	•	•	•
Fiji	•	•	•	•	•	•	•	•
Finland	•	•	•	•	•	•	•	•
France	•	•	•	•	•	•	•	•
Gabon	•	•	•	•	•	•	•	•
Gambia	•	•	•	•	•	•	•	•
Georgia	•	•	•	•	•	•	•	•
Germany	•	•	•	•	•	•	•	•
Ghana	•	•	•	•	•	•		
Greece	•	•	•	•	•	•	•	•
Grenada	•	•	•	•	•	•	•	•
Guatemala	•	•	•	•	•	•	•	•
Guinea	•	•	•	•	•	•	•	•
Guinea-Bissau			•	•	•	•		
Guyana	•	•	•	•	•	•	•	•
Haiti	•	•	•	•	•	•		
Honduras	•	•	•	•	•	•	•	•
Hong Kong, China (SAR)								
Hungary	•	•	•	•	•	•	•	•
Iceland	•	•	•	•	•	•	•	•
India			•	•	•	•		
Indonesia	•	•	•	•	•	•	•	•
Iran, Islamic Rep. of			•	•	•	•		•

continues

TABLE 7.2 continued

	Freedom of association & collective bargaining		Elimination of forced & compulsory labor		Elimination of discrimination in employment & occupation		Abolition of child labor	
	C 87	C 98	C 29	C 105	C 100	C 111	C 138	C 182
Iraq		•	•	•	•	•	•	•
Ireland	•	•	•	•	•	•	•	•
Israel	•	•	•	•	•	•	•	
Italy	•	•	•	•	•	•	•	•
Jamaica	•	•	•	•	•	•	•	•
Japan	•	•	•		•		•	•
Jordan		•	•	•	•	•	•	•
Kazakhstan	•	•	•	•	•	•	•	•
Kenya		•	•	•	•	•	•	•
Kiribati	•	•	•	•				
Korea, Rep. of					•	•	•	•
Kuwait	•		•	•		•	•	•
Kyrgyzstan	•	•	•	•	•	•	•	•
Lao People's Dem. Rep.			•					
Latvia	•	•		•	•	•		
Lebanon		•	•	•	•	•	•	•
Lesotho	•	•	•	•	•	•	•	•
Liberia	•	•	•	•	•	•		
Libyan Arab Jamahiriya	•	•	•	•	•	•	•	•
Lithuania	•	•	•	•	•	•	•	•
Luxembourg	•	•	•	•	•	•	•	•
Macedonia, TFYR	•	•	•	•	•	•	•	•
Madagascar	•	•	•	•	•	•	•	•
Malawi	•	•	•	•	•	•	•	•
Malaysia		•	•	•	•		•	•
Maldives								
Mali	•	•	•	•	•	•	•	•
Malta	•	•	•	•	•	•	•	•
Mauritania	•	•	•	•	•	•	•	•
Mauritius		•	•	•	•	•	•	•
Mexico	•		•	•	•	•		•
Moldova, Rep. of	•	•	•	•	•	•	•	•
Mongolia	•	•			•	•	•	•
Morocco		•	•	•	•	•	•	•
Mozambique	•	•	•	•	•	•	•	•
Myanmar	•		•					
Namibia	•	•	•	•		•	•	•
Nepal		•	•		•	•	•	•
Netherlands	•	•	•	•	•	•	•	•
New Zealand		•	•	•	•	•		•

continues

TABLE 7.2   continued

	Freedom of association & collective bargaining		Elimination of forced & compulsory labor		Elimination of discrimination in employment & occupation		Abolition of child labor	
	C 87	*C 98*	*C 29*	*C 105*	*C 100*	*C 111*	*C 138*	*C 182*
Nicaragua	•	•	•	•	•	•	•	•
Niger	•	•	•	•	•	•	•	•
Nigeria	•	•	•	•	•	•	•	•
Norway	•	•	•	•	•	•	•	•
Occupied Palestinian Territories								
Oman			•					•
Pakistan	•	•	•	•	•	•		•
Panama	•	•	•	•	•	•	•	•
Papua New Guinea	•	•	•	•	•	•	•	•
Paraguay	•	•	•	•	•	•	•	•
Peru	•	•	•	•	•	•	•	•
Philippines	•	•		•	•	•	•	•
Poland	•	•	•	•	•	•	•	•
Portugal	•	•	•	•	•	•	•	•
Qatar			•			•		•
Romania	•	•	•	•	•	•	•	•
Russian Federation	•	•	•	•	•	•	•	•
Rwanda	•	•	•	•	•	•	•	•
Saint Kitts and Nevis	•	•	•	•	•	•	•	•
Saint Lucia	•	•	•	•	•	•		•
Saint Vincent and the Grenadines	•	•	•	•	•	•		•
Samoa (Western)								
San Marino	•	•	•	•	•	•	•	•
São Tomé and Principe	•	•			•	•		
Saudi Arabia			•	•	•	•		•
Senegal	•	•	•	•	•	•	•	•
Serbia and Montenegro	•	•	•	•	•	•	•	•
Seychelles	•	•	•	•	•	•	•	•
Sierra Leone	•	•	•	•	•	•		
Singapore		•	•	•	•			•
Slovakia	•	•	•	•	•	•	•	•
Slovenia	•	•	•	•	•	•	•	•
Solomon Islands			•					
Somalia			•	•		•		
South Africa	•	•	•	•	•	•	•	•
Spain	•	•	•	•	•	•	•	•
Sri Lanka	•	•	•	•	•	•	•	•
Sudan		•	•	•	•	•	•	•
Suriname	•	•	•	•				
Swaziland	•	•	•	•	•	•	•	•

continues

TABLE 7.2   continued

	Freedom of association & collective bargaining		Elimination of forced & compulsory labor		Elimination of discrimination in employment & occupation		Abolition of child labor	
	C 87	C 98	C 29	C 105	C 100	C 111	C 138	C 182
Sweden	•	•	•	•	•	•	•	•
Switzerland	•	•	•	•	•	•	•	•
Syrian Arab Republic	•	•	•	•	•	•	•	
Tajikistan	•	•	•	•	•	•	•	
Tanzania, U. Rep. of	•		•	•	•	•	•	•
Thailand			•	•	•		•	•
Timor-Leste								
Togo	•	•	•	•	•	•	•	•
Tonga								
Trinidad and Tobago	•	•	•	•	•	•	•	•
Tunisia	•	•	•	•	•	•	•	•
Turkey	•	•	•	•	•	•	•	•
Turkmenistan	•	•	•	•	•	•		
Uganda		•	•	•			•	•
Ukraine	•	•	•	•	•	•	•	•
United Arab Emirates			•	•	•	•	•	•
United Kingdom	•	•	•	•	•	•	•	•
United States				•				•
Uruguay	•	•	•	•	•	•	•	•
Uzbekistan		•	•	•	•	•		
Vanuatu								
Venezuela	•	•	•	•	•	•	•	
Viet Nam					•	•	•	•
Yemen	•	•	•	•	•	•	•	•
Zambia	•	•	•	•	•	•	•	•
Zimbabwe	•	•	•	•	•	•	•	•
TOTAL RATIFICATION	142	154	164	160	161	161	135	152

• Convention ratified; Convention denounced.

Source: From Human Development Report 2005 by United Nations Development Programme, copyright © 2005 by the United Nations Development Programme. Used by permission of Oxford University Press, Inc.

Note: ILO Membership includes two countries that lack statehood (Hong Kong and Palestine) but not the following states: Andorra, Dem. Rep. of Korea, Liechtenstein, Marshall Islands, Micronesia, Monaco, Nauru, Palau, and Tuvalu.

C87 - Freedom of Association and Protection of the Right to Organize Convention (1948).

C99 - Right to Organize and Collective Bargaining Convention (1949).

C29 - Forced Labour Convention (1930).

C105 - Abolition of Forced Labour Convention (1957).

C100 - Equal Remuneration Convention (1951).

C111 - Discrimination (Employment and Occupation) Convention (1958).

C138 - Minimum Age Convention (1973).

C182 - Worst Forms of Child Labour Convention (1999).

Appendix

Universal Declaration of Human Rights

G.A. res. 217A (III), U.N. Doc A/810 at 71 (1948).

PREAMBLE

Whereas recognition of the inherent dignity and of the equal and inalienable rights of all members of the human family is the foundation of freedom, justice and peace in the world,

Whereas disregard and contempt for human rights have resulted in barbarous acts which have outraged the conscience of mankind, and the advent of a world in which human beings shall enjoy freedom of speech and belief and freedom from fear and want has been proclaimed as the highest aspiration of the common people,

Whereas it is essential, if man is not to be compelled to have recourse, as a last resort, to rebellion against tyranny and oppression, that human rights should be protected by the rule of law,

Whereas it is essential to promote the development of friendly relations between nations,

Whereas the peoples of the United Nations have in the Charter reaffirmed their faith in fundamental human rights, in the dignity and worth of the human person and in the equal rights of men and women and have determined to promote social progress and better standards of life in larger freedom,

Whereas Member States have pledged themselves to achieve, in cooperation with the United Nations, the promotion of universal respect for and observance of human rights and fundamental freedoms,

Whereas a common understanding of these rights and freedoms is of the greatest importance for the full realization of this pledge,

Now, therefore,

The General Assembly,

Proclaims this Universal Declaration of Human Rights as a common standard of achievement for all peoples and all nations, to the end that every individual and every organ of society, keeping this Declaration constantly in mind, shall strive by teaching and education to promote respect for these rights and freedoms and by progressive measures, national and international, to secure their universal and effective recognition and observance, both among the peoples of Member States themselves and among the peoples of territories under their jurisdiction.

Article 1. All human beings are born free and equal in dignity and rights. They are endowed with reason and conscience and should act towards one another in a spirit of brotherhood.

Article 2. Everyone is entitled to all the rights and freedoms set forth in this Declaration, without distinction of any kind, such as race, colour, sex, language, religion, political or other opinion, national or social origin, property, birth or other status.

Furthermore, no distinction shall be made on the basis of the political, jurisdictional or international status of the country or territory to which a person belongs, whether it be independent, trust, non-self-governing or under any other limitation of sovereignty.

Article 3. Everyone has the right to life, liberty and security of person.

Article 4. No one shall be held in slavery or servitude; slavery and the slave trade shall be prohibited in all their forms.

Article 5. No one shall be subjected to torture or to cruel, inhuman or degrading treatment or punishment.

Article 6. Everyone has the right to recognition everywhere as a person before the law.

Article 7. All are equal before the law and are entitled without any discrimination to equal protection of the law. All are entitled to equal protection against any discrimination in violation of this Declaration and against any incitement to such discrimination.

Article 8. Everyone has the right to an effective remedy by the competent national tribunals for acts violating the fundamental rights granted him by the constitution or by law.

Article 9. No one shall be subjected to arbitrary arrest, detention or exile.

Article 10. Everyone is entitled in full equality to a fair and public hearing by an independent and impartial tribunal, in the determination of his rights and obligations and of any criminal charge against him.

Article 11.

1. Everyone charged with a penal offence has the right to be presumed innocent until proved guilty according to law in a public trial at which he has had all the guarantees necessary for his defence.
2. No one shall be held guilty of any penal offence on account of any act or omission which did not constitute a penal offence, under national or international law, at the time when it was committed. Nor shall a heavier penalty be imposed than the one that was applicable at the time the penal offence was committed.

Article 12. No one shall be subjected to arbitrary interference with his privacy, family, home or correspondence, nor to attacks upon his honour and reputation. Everyone has the right to the protection of the law against such interference or attacks.

Article 13.

1. Everyone has the right to freedom of movement and residence within the borders of each State.
2. Everyone has the right to leave any country, including his own, and to return to his country.

Article 14.

1. Everyone has the right to seek and to enjoy in other countries asylum from persecution.
2. This right may not be invoked in the case of prosecutions genuinely arising from non-political crimes or from acts contrary to the purposes and principles of the United Nations.

Article 15.

1. Everyone has the right to a nationality.

2. No one shall be arbitrarily deprived of his nationality nor denied the right to change his nationality.

Article 16.

1. Men and women of full age, without any limitation due to race, nationality or religion, have the right to marry and to found a family. They are entitled to equal rights as to marriage, during marriage and at its dissolution.
2. Marriage shall be entered into only with the free and full consent of the intending spouses.
3. The family is the natural and fundamental group unit of society and is entitled to protection by society and the State.

Article 17.

1. Everyone has the right to own property alone as well as in association with others.
2. No one shall be arbitrarily deprived of his property.

Article 18. Everyone has the right to freedom of thought, conscience and religion; this right includes freedom to change his religion or belief, and freedom, either alone or in community with others and in public or private, to manifest his religion or belief in teaching, practice, worship and observance.

Article 19. Everyone has the right to freedom of opinion and expression; this right includes freedom to hold opinions without interference and to seek, receive and impart information and ideas through any media and regardless of frontiers.

Article 20.

1. Everyone has the right to freedom of peaceful assembly and association.
2. No one may be compelled to belong to an association.

Article 21.

1. Everyone has the right to take part in the government of his country, directly or through freely chosen representatives.
2. Everyone has the right to equal access to public service in his country.
3. The will of the people shall be the basis of the authority of government; this will shall be expressed in periodic and genuine elections which shall be by universal and equal suffrage and shall be held by secret vote or by equivalent free voting procedures.

Article 22. Everyone, as a member of society, has the right to social security and is entitled to realization, through national effort and international co-operation and in accordance with the organization and resources of each State, of the economic, social and cultural rights indispensable for his dignity and the free development of his personality.

Article 23.

1. Everyone has the right to work, to free choice of employment, to just and favourable conditions of work and to protection against unemployment.
2. Everyone, without any discrimination, has the right to equal pay for equal work.
3. Everyone who works has the right to just and favourable remuneration ensuring for himself and his family an existence worthy of human dignity, and supplemented, if necessary, by other means of social protection.
4. Everyone has the right to form and to join trade unions for the protection of his interests.

Article 24. Everyone has the right to rest and leisure, including reasonable limitation of working hours and periodic holidays with pay.

Article 25.

1. Everyone has the right to a standard of living adequate for the health and well-being of himself and of his fam-

ily, including food, clothing, housing and medical care and necessary social services, and the right to security in the event of unemployment, sickness, disability, widow-hood, old age or other lack of livelihood in circum-stances beyond his control.
2. Motherhood and childhood are entitled to special care and assistance. All children, whether born in or out of wedlock, shall enjoy the same social protection.

Article 26.

1. Everyone has the right to education. Education shall be free, at least in the elementary and fundamental stages. Elementary education shall be compulsory. Technical and professional education shall be made generally available and higher education shall be equally accessi-ble to all on the basis of merit.
2. Education shall be directed to the full development of the human personality and to the strengthening of re-spect for human rights and fundamental freedoms. It shall promote understanding, tolerance and friendship among all nations, racial or religious groups, and shall further the activities of the United Nations for the main-tenance of peace.
3. Parents have a prior right to choose the kind of educa-tion that shall be given to their children.

Article 27.

1. Everyone has the right freely to participate in the cul-tural life of the community, to enjoy the arts and to share in scientific advancement and its benefits.
2. Everyone has the right to the protection of the moral and material interests resulting from any scientific, liter-ary or artistic production of which he is the author.

Article 28. Everyone is entitled to a social and international order in which the rights and freedoms set forth in this Declaration can be fully realized.

Article 29.

1. Everyone has duties to the community in which alone the free and full development of his personality is possible.
2. In the exercise of his rights and freedoms, everyone shall be subject only to such limitations as are determined by law solely for the purpose of securing due recognition and respect for the rights and freedoms of others and of meeting the just requirements of morality, public order and the general welfare in a democratic society.
3. These rights and freedoms may in no case be exercised contrary to the purposes and principles of the United Nations.

Article 30. Nothing in this Declaration may be interpreted as implying for any State, group or person any right to engage in any activity or to perform any act aimed at the destruction of any of the rights and freedoms set forth herein.

8

Organizations Working on Human Rights

Various organizations have been established with the mission of promoting human rights, preventing violations, or helping victims. Some humanitarian organizations, which do not focus on human rights, may also indirectly contribute to human rights advocacy. This chapter introduces information on some of the major organizations that are either international in their composition or take activities that transcend national borders, as well as on a few other human rights organizations that work primarily on human rights advocacy within the United States of America or in conflict zones where violations of the rights of entire nations have been on the international agenda for a long time.

International organizations can be grouped according to their relationship with states, as intergovernmental or nongovernmental organizations. States constitute the members of intergovernmental organizations; they provide funding and are involved in the governance of the organizations. Nongovernmental organizations (NGOs) are established by private individuals who share common concerns and a similar vision of human rights. Their relationship with states may vary, ranging from a close collaboration to being subject to repression. In addition to the nongovernmental organizations that include human rights within their missions, this chapter includes information on a few professional organizations that have human rights–related activities or sections. The information related to each organization included in this chapter has been obtained mainly from printed or online sources provided by the organization itself. Occasionally, the exact wording employed in such sources is used in describing the mission or activities of an organization. The quoted texts in this chapter denote such references that are incorporated from the organization's documents.

The list of organizations included here is far from being exhaustive. As there are numerous individuals who carry on human rights activism, often taking great personal risks, in every country there are several human rights organizations, local or national, that are active in their communities. Some professional organizations, such as bar associations or associations of medical professionals, tend to have human rights–related units or programs in several countries. In some countries there are also state agencies that work on human rights within the country or have programs with overseas missions, which involve monitoring or assisting human rights policies in other countries.

Intergovernmental Organizations

United Nations Agencies and Affiliates

Division for the Advancement of Women (DAW)
2 UN Plaza, DC2–12th Floor, New York, NY, 10017 USA
Fax: +1. 212. 963 3463
E-mail: daw@un.org
Website: http://www.un.org/womenwatch/daw

The Division for the Advancement of Women (DAW) is a UN agency that was established in 1946 as a section on the Status of Women of the Human Rights Division of the Department of Social Affairs. Following the equality principle of the United Nations Charter, the DAW is an advocate for and works on improving the status of women and achieving women's equality with men. It promotes women's full and equal participation in all aspects of human endeavor, with a special emphasis on their role in achieving and enjoying sustainable development, peace, and security, and in taking part in governance. Its mandate also includes taking measures "to stimulate the mainstreaming of gender perspectives both within and outside the United Nations system."

Publications: Publishes reports and monographs such as *Women Go Global; Women, Peace and Security; Gender Mainstreaming: An Overview.*

International Labour Organization (ILO)
4, route des Morillons CH-1211, Geneva 22 Switzerland
Phone: +41. 22. 799 6111
Fax: +41. 22. 798 8685
E-mail: ilo@ilo.org
Website: http://www.ilo.org

The ILO was founded in 1919 by the Treaty of Versailles, and after the Second World War, it became a specialized agency affiliated with the United Nations. Focusing on labor issues, it seeks the promotion of internationally recognized human and labor rights as well as social justice. It maintains a tripartite structure that includes workers, employers, and governments in its membership and these three participate in the governing organs of the ILO as equal partners. The ILO formulates conventions and recommendations for international labor standards with regard to basic labor rights such as freedom of association, the right to organize, collective bargaining, freedom from servitude and forced labor, and equality of opportunity and treatment. It also provides training and advisory services to labor unions and employers' organizations.

Publications: Confronting Economic Insecurity in Africa; Automotive Industry Trends Affecting Component Suppliers; Gender Roles and Sex Equality: European Solutions to Social Security Disputes; Renewing Labour Market Institutions and others.

UNICEF
UNICEF House, 3 United Nations Plaza, New York,
NY 10017 USA
Fax: +1. 212. 887 7465 and +1. 212. 887 7454
E-mail: information@unicefusa.org
Website: http://www.unicef.org

The United Nations Children's Fund (UNICEF) was created by the United Nations in 1946 to provide food, clothing, and health care to the children affected by World War II. It became a permanent agency of the UN in 1953 and assumed the role of promoting educational opportunities and removing obstacles to the healthy development of the world's children. It upholds the Convention on the Rights of the Child and works with other UN agencies, governments, and nongovernmental organizations to overcome poverty, violence, disease, and discrimination. The organization involves more than 7,000 people working in 157 countries around the world.

Publications: The State of the World's Children 2005; Progress for Children: A Report Card on Immunization (No. 3); *Investing in the Children of the Islamic World* (Full Report); *The Impact of Conflict on Women and Girls in West and Central Africa and the UNICEF Response* and others.

UNIFEM
United Nations Development Fund for Women
304 E. 45th Street,15th Floor, New York, NY 10017 USA
Phone: +1 .212. 906 6400
Fax: +1 .212. 906 6705
Website: http://www.unifem.org

The United Nations Development Fund for Women (UNIFEM) was established in 1976. It supports innovative programs and strategies that promote women's human rights, political participation, and economic security by providing financial and technical assistance. It promotes gender equality and works on gender mainstreaming within the UN and in its member nations by linking women's issues and concerns to national, regional, and global agendas.

Publications: Recent publications include *Pathway to Gender Equality: CEDAW, Beijing and the MDGs; Women and HIV/AIDS: Confronting the Crisis; Not a Minute More: Ending Violence against Women; Women, War and Peace.*

United Nations High Commissioner of Human Rights (UNHCHR)
8–14 Avenue de la Paix,1211 Geneva 10 , Switzerland
E-mail: InfoDesk@ohchr.org
Website: http://www.ohchr.org

Treaties and Commission Branch Office of the High Commissioner for Human Rights United Nations Office at Geneva
1211 Geneva 10 Switzerland
Fax: + 41. 22. 917 9011
E-mail: ngochr@ohchr.org

The Office of the United Nations High Commissioner for Human Rights (OHCHR) is the main human rights agency of the UN Secretariat. Its mission is "to protect and promote all human rights for all." The promotion of universal ratification and implementation of all human rights treaties of the United Nations is a goal that shapes the OHCHR programs and activities.

Publications: Fact Sheet booklets; special issue papers; educational material consisting of guides, manuals, and handbooks for indigenous peoples, minorities, professional groups, and educational institutions. Publications include *ABC—Teaching Human Rights: Practical Activities for Primary and Secondary Schools; Embedding Human Rights in Business Practice.*

United Nations High Commissioner of Refugees (UNHCR)
Case Postale 2500 CH-1211, Genève 2, Dépôt, Switzerland
Phone: +41. 22. 739 8111 (automatic switchboard).
Website: http://www.unhcr.ch

The Office of the United Nations High Commissioner for Refugees (UNHCR) was established in 1950 by the United Nations General Assembly, with the mandate of leading and coordinating the international community to protect refugees and resolve refugee problems worldwide. Safeguarding the rights and well-being of refugees constitutes its primary concern, and it "strives to ensure that everyone can exercise the right to seek asylum and find safe refuge in another State, with the option to return home voluntarily, integrate locally or to resettle in a third country."

Publications: Maps and handbooks, which include *Registration Handbook; Operations Management Handbook for UNHCR's Partners; The Global Appeal; The State of The World's Refugees 2000.*

United Nations Relief and Works Agency (UNRWA)
One United Nations Plaza, Room DC1–1265, New York, NY
10017 USA
Phone: + 1. 212. 963 2255 and +1. 212. 963 1234
Fax: + 1. 212 . 935 7899
Website: http://www.un.org/unrwa

The United Nations Relief and Works Agency for Palestine Refugees in the Near East was established by a UN General Assembly resolution, issued on December 8, 1949, to address the needs of the Palestinians who were displaced as a result of the 1948 Arab-Israeli conflict. The UNRWA began its operations on May 1, 1950, to fulfill its mission of developing and carrying out direct relief and works programs for Palestinian refugees. Unable to solve the Palestine refugee problem, the General Assembly has repeatedly renewed the UNRWA's mandate, and recently extended it until June 30, 2008. Currently, this agency is the main provider of basic education, health, relief, and social services to over 4.1 million registered Palestine refugees in the Middle East. *Publications:* Reports of the UNRWA Commissioner.

World Health Organization (WHO)
Avenue Appia 20, 1211 Geneva 27, Switzerland
Phone: + 41. 22. 791 2111
Fax: + 41. 22. 791 3111
Telex: 415 416
Telegraph: UNISANTE GENEVA
E-mail: info@who.int
Website: http://www.who.int/en/

The World Health Organization was established in 1948 by the UN General Assembly, as the UN's specialized agency for health. Its constitution sets the objective of the agency as the attainment by all peoples of the highest possible level of health and defines health "as a state of complete physical, mental and social well-being and not merely the absence of disease or infirmity."

Publications: Bulletin of the WHO; Eastern Mediterranean Health Journal; Pan American Journal of Public Health; World Health Report; Eastern Mediterranean Health Journal.

Other Intergovernmental Organizations

African Union (AU)
P.O. Box 3243, Addis Ababa, Ethiopia
Phone: +251. 1. 51 77 00 Fax: +251. 1. 51 78 44
Website: http://www.africa-union.org

Originally established as the Organization of African Unity in 1963, the AU is Africa's premier institution and principal organization for the promotion of accelerated socioeconomic integration of the continent, which will lead to greater unity and solidarity among African countries and peoples. Assuming its new name in July 2002, the African Union is based on the common vision of a united and strong Africa and on the need to build a partnership between governments and all segments of civil society—in particular, women, youth, and the private sector, in order to strengthen solidarity and cohesion among the peoples of Africa. As a continental organization it focuses on the promotion of peace, security, and stability on the continent as a prerequisite for the implementation of the development and integration agenda of the Union and sets the human rights standards for the continent.

Publications: Reports.

Organization for Security and Co-operation in Europe (OSCE)
Kärntner Ring 5–7,4th Floor, 1010, Vienna, Austria
Phone: +43. 1. 514 36 196
Fax: +43. 1. 514 36 105
E-mail:info@osce.org
Website: http://www.osce.org

The Organization for Security and Co-operation in Europe was originally started by thirty-five states on June 25, 1973, as the Conference for Security and Co-operation in Europe. The collaboration was later expanded and gained permanency, and as decided at the conference held in Budapest in 1994, it was re-named on January 1, 1995, the Organization for Security and Co-operation. Currently it involves fifty-five participating states from Europe, Central Asia, and North America. The OSCE has a comprehensive approach to security and deals with a wide range of security-related issues including arms control, preventive diplomacy, confidence- and security-building measures, human rights, democratization, election monitoring, and economic and environmental security. A document prepared by the OSCE, known as the Helsinki Final Act, includes provisions on the protection of human rights. It was adopted at its summit meeting on August 1, 1975, by the thirty-four polities attending the meeting, including the Holy See and the United States.

Publications: Handbooks, annual reports, thematic compilations, OSCE newsletter, OSCE magazine, and mission surveys.

Organization of American States (OAS)
General Secretariat, 1889 F Street NW, LL2, 8th Floor,
    Washington, DC 20006 USA
Phone: +1. 202. 458 6002
Fax: +1. 202. 458 3992
Website: http://www.oas.org

For the Inter-American Commission on Human Rights
E-mail: cidhoea@oas.org
Website: http://www.cidh.org

Established in 1948, the Organization of American States (OAS) brings together the countries of the Western Hemisphere. It works to strengthen cooperation among its members "to promote democracy, strengthen human rights, foster peace and security, expand trade, and address the complex problems caused by poverty, drugs and corruption." It involves a human rights system that allows the victims of human rights violations to seek justice that was denied in their own country. The Inter-American Commission on Human Rights, created in 1959 and based in Washington, D.C., and the Inter-American Court of Human Rights, located in San José, Costa Rica, are its main institutions of enforcement of regional law on human rights. The Commission accepts individual petitions and may recommend to the accused state measures the state can carry out to remedy the violation. In cases involving countries that accept the jurisdiction of the Inter-American Court, the Commission may forward a case to the Court, which can reach a binding decision. The Commission may also conduct investigations in member countries, at their invitation, to analyze and report on the status of human rights.

Publications: The organization's publications include the bimonthly magazine *Americas,* as well as numerous reports, books, and videos. Inter-American Commission of Human Rights publishes Annual Reports and Country Reports for over thirty countries.

The Council of Europe
Avenue de l'Europe 67075
Strasbourg Cedex, FrancePhone: +33. 3. 88 41 20 00
Fax: +33. 3. 88 41 27 45
E-mail: infopoint@coe.int
Website: http://www.coe.int

Founded in 1949, the Council of Europe is a continental political organization. It now brings together forty-six countries, including twenty-one countries from central and eastern Europe. It has granted observer status to five countries (the Holy See, the United States, Canada, Japan, and Mexico). Although it is distinct and separate from the European Union, there is a historical link between the two since no country has ever joined the Union without first belonging to the Council of Europe. In 1950, it adopted the Convention for the Protection of Human Rights and Fundamental Freedoms, which spells out civil and political rights as rights to be protected by the member states and sets up a mechanism for the enforcement of the obligations by contracting states. The Convention entrusts three institutions with this responsibility: the European Commission of Human Rights (1954), the European Court of Human Rights (1959), and the Committee of Ministers of the Council of Europe, which is composed of the Ministers of Foreign Affairs of the member states or their representatives. In 1961, the Council adopted the European Social Charter, which guarantees social and economic rights. Especially after 1989, the Council's "main job has become acting as a political anchor and human rights watchdog for Europe's post-communist democracies, assisting the countries of central and Eastern Europe in carrying out and consolidating political, legal and constitutional reform in parallel with economic reform, providing know-how in areas such as human rights, local democracy, education, culture and the environment."

Publications: A Decade Which Made History—The Council of Europe 1989–1999; Ireland and the Council of Europe; From Isolation towards Integration (2000), and others. They are posted on the website.

Nongovernmental Organizations

American Anti-Savery Group (AASG)
198 Tremont St., #421, Boston, MA 02116 USA
Phone: +1. 800. 884 0719
E-mail: info@iabolish.com
Website: http://www.iabolish.com

The American Anti-Slavery Group (AASG) was established in 1994 as "a human rights group dedicated to abolishing modern day slavery worldwide." It focuses on building public awareness, leading advocacy campaigns, and empowering survivors and activists.

Publications: Annual reports and press releases.

American Civil Liberties Union (ACLU)
125 Broad Street, 17th Floor, New York, NY 10004 USA

Phone: +1. 212. 344 3005
Website: http://www.aclu.org

The ACLU was established in 1920. Its mission is "to preserve the following protections and guarantees within the United States: the First Amendment rights—freedom of speech, association and assembly; the freedom of the press, and freedom of religion supported by the strict separation of church and state; the right to equal protection under the law—equal treatment regardless of race, sex, religion or national origin; the right to due process— fair treatment by the government whenever the loss of your liberty or property is at stake; and the right to privacy—freedom from unwarranted government intrusion into your personal and private affairs." The Union works also to extend these rights to those segments of the population that have "traditionally been denied their rights, including Native Americans and other people of color; lesbians, gay men, bisexuals and transgendered people; women; mental health patients; prisoners; people with disabilities; and the poor." It undertakes a wide range of activities, including lobbying politicians, educating the public, and litigation.

Publications: The ACLU issues reports on various issues including criminal justice; the death penalty; drug policy; free speech; HIV/AIDS; immigrant rights; international human rights; lesbian, gay, bisexual, and transgender rights; prisons; privacy and technology; racial justice; reproductive rights; voting rights; and human rights. They are posted on the organization's website.

Americans for Democratic Action (ADA)
1625 K. Street NW, Suite 210, Washington, DC 20006 USA
Phone: +1. 202. 785 5980
Fax: +1. 202. 785 5969
E-mail: adaction@ix.nergtcom.com
Website: http://www.adaction.org

The Americans for Democratic Action is an "independent liberal lobbying organization" that works mainly in the United States to promote human rights and social justice. Its founders included Eleanor Roosevelt, labor leader Walter Reuther, economist John Kenneth Galbraith, historian Arthur Schlesinger Jr., theologian Reinhold Niebuhr, and former U.S. vice president Hubert Humphrey. It promotes policies in the spirit of the New Deal through lobbying senators and representatives as constituent-advocates.

Publications: ADAction News and Notes, a weekly legislative update; *ADA Today,* a quarterly newsletter; and *Annual Voting Record.*

American Friends Service Committee (AFSC)

National Office, 1501 Cherry Street, Philadelphia, PA 19102 USA
Phone: +1. 215. 241 7000
Fax: +1. 215. 241 7275
E-mail: afscinfo@afsc.org
Website: http://www.afsc.org

The American Friends Service Committee was founded in 1917 by American Quakers with the goal of providing "conscientious objectors to war with a constructive alternative to military service," and today it "carries on a program of service, development, justice and peace under the direction of a Quaker Board and Corporation representing a wide spectrum of Quakers." Through its international headquarters in Philadelphia, its nine regional offices in the United States, and its program operations overseas, the organization works for the abolition of war and the fulfillment of human rights as essential twin goals of creating a nonviolent world in which all may live together. In the United States, the AFSC focuses on questions of exclusion and unequal opportunities in employment, education, administration of justice, land rights, welfare, and food programs. The organization also operates lending libraries with videos and films.

Publications: The AFSC has an extensive publications program, including leaflets, pamphlets, newsletters, and books. All of the publications are available online.

Amnesty International (AI)

17–25 New Inn Yard, London EC2A 3EA UK
Phone: +44. 20. 7814 6200
Fax: +44. 20. 7833 1510
Website: http://www.amnesty.org.uk

USA Office
5 Penn Plaza, 14th Floor, New York, NY 10001 USA
Phone: +1. 212. 807 8400
Fax: +1. 212. 627 1451

E-mail: aimember@aiusa.org
Website: http://www.amnesty.org

Established in 1961 as a British organization, Amnesty International has become the largest human rights organization in the world. Seeking a world in which every person enjoys all of the human rights enshrined in the Universal Declaration of Human Rights and other international human rights standards, its mission is to "undertake research and action focused on preventing and ending grave abuses of the rights to physical and mental integrity, freedom of conscience and expression and freedom from discrimination, within the context of its work to promote all human rights." Its activities have traditionally focused on freeing prisoners of conscience, ensuring fair trials and abolishing torture and execution; it also carries out letter-writing campaigns on behalf of persons in immediate danger as well as publicity programs designed to raise awareness of human rights violations. More recently, AI has expanded the scope of its work to address other issues, such as women's rights and violence against women.

Publications: Extensive publications include full-length books, an annual report on human rights in each country, country-specific reports, and special reports on such issues as female genital mutilation. They can be accessed online.

Anti-Defamation League (ADL)
823 United Nations Plaza, New York, NY 10017 USA
Phone: +1. 212. 490 2525
Fax: +1. 212. 885 5855
Website: http://www.adl.org

The Anti-Defamation League was launched in 1913 in response to anti-Semitism and discrimination against Jews. The organization defines its objective as "to stop, by appeals to reason and conscience and, if necessary, by appeals to law, the defamation of the Jewish people. Its ultimate purpose is to secure justice and fair treatment to all citizens alike and to put an end forever to unjust and unfair discrimination against and ridicule of any sect or body of citizens."

Publications: Weekly newsletters, reports, books, periodicals, and monographs focusing on topics such as prejudice, discrimination, and intergroup relations, multicultural education, political and social issues, and the Holocaust.

Anit-Slavery International
Thomas Clarkson House, The Stableyard, Broomgrove Road,
  London SW9 9TL UK
Phone: +44. 20. 7501 8920
Fax: +44. 20. 7738 4110
E-mail: info@antislavery.org
Website: http://www.antislavery.org

Anti-Slavery International, founded in 1839, "is the world's oldest international human rights organization." Working at local, national, and international levels, it seeks the elimination of slavery around the world by urging governments of countries with slavery to develop and implement measures to end it; lobbying governments and intergovernmental agencies to make slavery a priority issue; supporting research to assess the scale of slavery in order to identify measures to end it; working with local organizations to raise public awareness of slavery; and educating the public about the realities of slavery and campaigning for its end.

Publications: Its publications include *Slavery in Niger: Historical, Legal and Contemporary Perspective; L'esclavage au Niger; Slave: The True Story of a Girl's Lost Childhood and Her Fight for Survival; The Political Economy of New Slavery.*

Arab Association for Human Rights (HRA)
Mary's Well Street, P.O. Box 215, 16101 Nazareth, Israel
Phone: +972. 4. 6561923
Fax: +972. 4. 6564934
E-mail: hra1@arabhra.org
Website: http://www.arabhra.org

The Arab Association for Human Rights (HRA), an independent and grassroots organization, was established in 1988 and registered as a nonprofit organization in Israel in 1990. The organization's mandate is the protection and promotion of international human rights standards of the Palestinian Arab minority in Israel.

Publications: Reports, annual reports, press releases, and *Weekly Press Review.*

Asian Human Rights Commission (AHRC)
19/F Go-Up Commercial Building, 998 Canton Road, Kowloon,
  Hong Kong, China

Phone: +86. 852. 2698 6339
Fax: +86. 852. 2698 6367
Website: http://www.ahrchk.net

The AHRC is an international network that works on issues of human rights and social justice in Asia. Its long list of objectives includes "[to] protect and promote human rights by monitoring, investigation, advocacy, and taking solidarity actions." It emphasizes promotion of the rights of "people who have suffered discrimination in the past, such as women and children and minorities, including Dalits." In May 1998, it worked with several other NGOs and drafted an Asian Human Rights Charter. It also works toward the development of regional human rights mechanisms in Asia. It upholds the principles of the United Nations; sees a close link between human rights, development, and peace; and encourages the ratification of human rights instruments adopted by the United Nations.

Publications: Annual reports and books.

Association for Women's Rights in Development (AWID)
215 Spadina Ave., Suite 150, Toronto, Ontario M5T 2C7, Canada
Phone: +1. 416. 5943773
Fax: +1. 416. 594 0330
E-mail: awid@awid.org
Website: http://www.awid.org

The Association for Women's Rights in Development (AWID) was founded in 1982 as an international organization with members including researchers, academics, students, educators, activists, businesspeople, policymakers, and development practitioners. Its "mission is to connect, inform and mobilize people and organizations committed to achieving gender equality, sustainable development and women's human rights." It attempts to achieve changes in policies, institutions, and individual perceptions, and make them work toward improving the lives of women and girls everywhere by facilitating debates and building "the individual and organizational capacities of those working for women's empowerment and social justice."

Publications: Young Women and Leadership Glossary; Young Women Leadership Booklet # 1; Re-inventing Globalization; and conference/seminar reports, fact sheets, training materials and tools, occasional papers, and audiovisual resources, which can all be obtained online.

B'Tselem
8 HaTa'asiya St., 4th Floor, Jerusalem, Israel
Mailing address: P.O. Box 53132, Jerusalem 91531, Israel
Phone: +972. 2. 6735599
Fax: +972. 2. 6749111
E-mail: mail@btselem.org
Website: http://www.btselem.org

B'Tselem is the Israeli Center for Human Rights in the Occupied Territories. It was established in 1989 by a group of prominent academics, attorneys, journalists, and Knesset (Israeli parliament) members. Its activities and goals include "documenting and educating the Israeli public and policymakers about human rights violations in the Occupied Territories, combat the phenomenon of denial prevalent among the Israeli public, and help create a human rights culture in Israel."

Publications: Through No Fault of Their Own: Israel's Punitive House Demolitions in the al-Aqsa Intifada; Forbidden Roads: The Discriminatory West Bank Road Regime; Facing the Abyss: The Isolation of Sheikh Sa'ad Village—Before and After the Separation Barrier, and others that can be found online.

Canadian Human Rights Foundation (CHRF)
1425 René-Lévesque Blvd. West, Suite 407, Montréal, Québec,
   Canada H3G 1T7
Phone: +1. 514. 954 0382
Fax: +1. 514. 954 0659
E-mail: chrf@chrf.ca
Website: http://www.chrf.ca

The CHRF was established in 1967 by a group of Canadian scholars, jurists, and human rights advocates. It defines its mandate as advancing "democracy, human development, peace and social justice through educational programs." It emphasizes capacity-building programs in Canada and abroad and assists civil society organizations and government institutions to participate effectively in human rights debates, to challenge discriminatory attitudes and practices, and to advance important policy and legislative reforms to enhance human rights protection and fulfillment.
Publications: Annual Reports.

Carter Center
One Copenhill, 453 Freedom Parkway, Atlanta, GA 30307 USA

Phone: +1. 404. 420 5117
Fax: +1. 404. 420 5145
E-mail: carterweb@emory.edu
Website: http://www.cartercenter.org

Founded in 1982 by former U.S. president Jimmy Carter and his wife, Rosalynn Carter, the Carter Center works in partnership with Emory University on fighting disease, hunger, poverty, conflict, and oppression. Its programs and activities are designed to improve the quality of life for people living all around the world, and it has been active in more than sixty-five countries.

Publications: The center publishes annual reports, press releases, and other publications on health and peace programs. All of the publications can be found online.

Center for Constitutional Rights (CCR)
666 Broadway, 7th Floor, New York, NY 10012 USA
Phone: +1. 212. 614 6464
Fax: +1. 212. 614 6499
E-mail: info@ccr-ny.org
Website: http://www.ccr-ny.org

The Center for Constitutional Rights (CCR) was created in 1966 as a "legal and educational organization dedicated to protecting and advancing the rights guaranteed by the U.S. Constitution and the Universal Declaration of Human Rights." The CCR uses litigation to advance a wide range of human rights and tries to "empower poor communities and communities of color, to guarantee the rights of those with the fewest protections and least access to legal resources, to train the next generation of constitutional and human rights attorneys, and to strengthen the broader movement for constitutional and human rights."

Publications: The CCR publishes pamphlets and books, which are available online. Pamphlets include *Against War with Iraq: An Anti-War Primer; No War.* Books include *Against War with Iraq: An Anti-War Primer; Secret Trials and Executions: Military Tribunals and the Threat to Democracy.*

Center for Economic and Social Rights
162 Montague Street, 2nd Floor, Brooklyn, NY 11201 USA
Phone: +1. 718. 237 9145
Fax: +1. 718. 237 9147

E-mail: rights@cesr.org
Website: http://www.cesr.org

Established in 1993, the Center for Economic and Social Rights challenges economic injustice as a violation of international human rights law. Believing that economic and social rights are legally binding on all nations and can provide a universally accepted framework for strengthening social justice activism, the center carries out projects both in the United States and abroad. Its work combines research, advocacy, collaboration, and education.

Publications: It publishes articles, fact sheets, press releases, reports, and educational and training tools. They can be all accessed online.

Center for International Policy
1717 Massachusetts Avenue NW, Suite 802, Washington DC
    20036 USA
Phone: +1. 202. 232 3317
Fax: +1. 202. 232 3440
E-mail: cip@ciponline.org
Website: http://www.ciponline.org

Founded in 1975, in the wake of the Vietnam War, the center promotes a U.S. foreign policy based on international cooperation, demilitarization, and respect for human rights. The center carries out an extensive research and publication program on the implications of U.S. foreign aid, especially economic and military aid, to Cuba and Colombia as well as countries of Central America, Asia, Africa, and Latin America. It has worked for the demilitarization of Latin America and reform of the CIA.

Publications: The reports and the books published by the center, including *International Policy Report,* are available online.

Center for Law and Global Justice
University of San Francisco School of Law, 2130 Fulton Street,
    San Francisco, CA 94117 USA
Phone: +1. 415. 422 5922
E-mail: globaljustice@usfca.edu
Website: http://www.usfca.edu/law/globaljustice/

The Center for Law and Global Justice works on mechanisms that would challenge the process of globalization that tends to undermine economic self-determination and basic human freedoms, in the United States and abroad. It provides legal education and training that nurtures democratization, the protection of human rights, and sustainable economic growth. As a part of the University of San Francisco School of Law, the center shares the university's Jesuit ideals of promoting justice through education and service.

Publications: Legal education materials and judicial training materials.

Center for the Study of Human Rights

Columbia University, Mail Code: 3365, 420 West 118th Street,
   Room 1108 IAB, New York, NY 10027 USA
Phone: +1. 212. 854 2479
Fax: +1. 212. 316 4578
E-mail: cshr@columbia.edu
Website: http://www.columbia.edu/cu/humanrights

The Center for the Study of Human Rights was established in 1978, and thus constitutes one of the oldest university-based human rights institutions. The center focuses on the education and training of emerging human rights leaders. It promotes and employs an interdisciplinary approach in human rights education and research. Through its links to international human rights and nongovernmental organizations worldwide, the center sponsors an advocacy program and stimulates interaction among university faculty and students, human rights activists, policymakers, members of the business community, and other practitioners.

Publications: The center publishes annual and program reports, *RightsNews* online, and a series linking specific human rights issues to relevant documents, which include *Twenty-Five Human Rights Documents; Women and Human Rights: Basic Documents; Religion and Rights: Basic Documents.* Publications also include *Elements of Constitutionalism* and *The Rights of Man Today.*

Center for Victims of Torture (CVT)

717 East River Road, Minneapolis, MN 55455 USA
Phone: +1. 612. 436 4800
Fax: +1. 612. 436. 2600
E-mail: cvt@cvt.org
Website: http://www.cvt.org

Founded in 1985, the CVT provides services directly to torture survivors, including medical and psychological treatment and social services. It also trains health, education, and human services professionals who work with torture survivors and refugees; conducts research on the effects of torture and on effective treatment methods to ensure providing the best care to the clients; and is an advocate for public policy initiatives in Minnesota, in the United States, and worldwide that will help heal survivors and put an end to the practice of torture.

Publications: It publishes resource manuals for teachers, training videos, handbooks, classroom resources, and other materials, which can be found on the website.

Center of Concern
1225 Otis St. NE, Washington, DC 20017 USA
Phone: +1. 202. 635 2757
Fax: +1. 202. 832 9494
E-mail: coc@coc.org
Website: http://www.coc.org

Established in 1971, the Center of Concern holds "an ethical perspective based on Catholic social teaching." Its activities are "geared toward ending hunger, poverty, environmental decline and injustice in the United States and around the world." The center provides information and analysis on development issues, practical alternatives to current development policies, practical suggestions for personal action, and faith reflections on work for justice.

Publications: The center publishes a number of resources including *Center Focus,* a quarterly newsletter, articles, and papers. It also published *Rethinking Bretton Woods,* a five-volume series that includes material on development, the World Bank, the world's monetary system, and world trade. Educational resources, including links to sources appropriate for children and to lesson plans about human rights, are available on the website.

Committee of Concerned Scientists
145 West 79th Street, Suite 4D, New York, NY 10024 USA
Phone: +1. 212. 362 4441
E-mail: mnk.ccs@verizon.net
Website: http://www.libertynet.org/ccs/index.html

The Committee of Concerned Scientists is an independent organization of scientists, physicians, and engineers dedicated to the protection and advancement of the human rights and scientific freedom of colleagues throughout the world. It works toward achieving the following: "academic freedom for all scientists, physicians, engineers and scholars; freedom of exchange of scientific and other scholarly information, data and personnel; freedom of research, inquiry, publication and travel to and from scholarly and scientific meetings; freedom of association; freedom of emigration; recognition, implementation and preservation of human rights, individual and collective, without distinctions based on race, language, religion, sex or national origin; compliance by governments with provisions of international agreements they have signed pertaining to the human rights of scientists."

Publications: Annual reports.

Council on International and Public Affairs
777 United Nations Plaza, Suite 3C, New York, NY 10017 USA
Phone: +1. 212. 972 9877
Website: http://www.cipa-apex.org/programs.htm

The Council on International and Public Affairs was founded in 1954 and is a nonprofit research, education, and publishing group. With an emphasis on social and economic rights, it seeks to expand the study and public understanding of problems and affairs of the peoples of the United States and other nations of the world through conferences, research, seminars and workshops, publications, and other means. The council acts as U.S. secretariat for the Permanent People's Tribunal on Industrial Hazards and Human Rights Violations and focuses on corporate abuse of workers, communities, and the environment in the United States.

Publications: The council publishes books and videos on human rights issues. Recent books include *Greed and Good: Understanding and Overcoming the Inequality that Limits Our Life; Divided We Fall: The Story of the Paperworkers' Union and the Future of Labor; Myth America: Democracy vs. Capitalism* and other publications, which are available online.

Cultural Survival, Inc.
215 Prospect Street, Cambridge, MA 02139 USA
Phone: +1. 617. 441 5400

Fax: +1. 617. 441 5417
E-mail: culturalsurvival@cs.org
Website: http://www.cs.org

Founded in 1972 for the purpose of helping indigenous people survive and adapt to the world around them, Cultural Survival, Inc., is made up of indigenous people, ethnic minorities, academics interested in the Third World, research institutes and museums, government agencies, and other interested individuals. Cultural Survival sponsors projects designed to promote human rights for indigenous people and to help them become successful ethnic minorities. The organization maintains a library and speakers' bureau and also conducts seminars and research on problems confronting indigenous peoples.

Publications: Publications include *Cultural Survival Quarterly, Cultural Survival Voices, Cultural Survival Curriculum Resources, Weekly Indigenous News,* and annual reports. These and other publications can be found online.

Defence for Children International (DCI)
International Secretariat, 1 Rue de Varembé, P.O. Box 88, CH
   1211 Geneva 20, Switzerland
Phone: +41. 22. 734 05 58
Fax: +41. 22. 740 11 45
E-mail: dci.is@bluewin.ch
Website: http://www.dci-is.org

Defence for Children International (DCI) was born in July 1979 as an international children's rights movement. It promotes applying "a human rights-based approach to the multi-faceted problems faced by the world's children." A major contribution of the DCI was the mobilization of the NGO community to be involved in the drafting process of the Convention on the Rights of the Child. Since the adoption of the Convention by the UN General Assembly in 1989, its activities have focused on lobbying governments to ratify the Convention and monitoring its implementation by states parties.

Publications: Training manuals and reports.

Doctors Without Borders
International Office, Rue de la Tourelle, 39 1040 Bruxelles,
   Belgium
Phone: +32. 2. 280 18 81

Fax: +32. 2. 280 01 73
Website: http://www.msf.org

U.S. Headquarters
333 7th Avenue, 2nd Floor, New York, NY 10001–5004 USA
Phone: +1. 212. 679 6800
Fax: +1. 212. 679 7016
Website: http://www.doctorswithoutborders.org

Médecins Sans Frontières (MSF, also Doctors without Borders) was founded in 1971 by a small group of French doctors who believed that all people have the right to medical care regardless of race, religion, creed, or political affiliation and that the needs of these people supersede respect for national borders. Now an international organization with offices in eighteen countries, it delivers emergency aid to victims of armed conflict, epidemics, and natural and man-made disasters, and to others who lack health care because of social or geographical isolation. MSF provides primary health care, performs surgery, rehabilitates hospitals and clinics, runs nutrition and sanitation programs, trains local medical personnel, and provides mental health care. Through longer-term programs, MSF treats chronic diseases such as tuberculosis, malaria, sleeping sickness, and AIDS; assists with the medical and psychological problems of marginalized populations including street children and ethnic minorities; and brings health care to remote, isolated areas where resources and training are limited.

Publications: MSF publishes news alerts, special and annual reports, and books. It maintains an online Press Room, which provides current information.

European Council on Refugees and Exiles (ECRE)
ECRE Secretariat, 103 Worship Street, London EC2A 2DF UK
Phone: +44. 020. 7377 7556
Fax: +44. 020. 7377 7586
E-mail: ecre@ecre.org
Website: http://www.ecre.org

The ECRE functions as an umbrella organization for seventy-six refugee-assisting agencies in thirty European countries. It was established with the goal of promoting "the protection and integration of refugees in Europe based on the values of human dignity, human rights, and an ethic of solidarity." To achieve this goal, it advocates a human and generous asylum policy for Europe and helps networking of organizations and building institutional capacities.

Publications: Country reports, as well as reports such as *Report on Legal and Social Conditions for Asylum Seekers and Refugees in Western European Countries.* ECRE also publishes *ECRE Good Practice Guides.*

Freedom House
Washington Office, 1319 18th Street NW, Washington, DC
    20036 USA
Phone: +1. 202. 296 5101
Fax: +1. 202. 296 5078

New York Office
120 Wall Street, Floor 26, New York, NY 10005 USA
Phone: +1. 212. 514 8040
Fax: +1. 212. 514 8055
Website: http://www.freedomhouse.org

Founded over sixty years ago by Eleanor Roosevelt, Wendell Willkie, and other Americans concerned with the mounting threats to peace and democracy, Freedom House promotes democratic values and opposes dictatorships. It maintains a nonpartisan and broad-based membership, and its board of trustees is composed of leading Democrats, Republicans, and independents, as well as business and labor leaders, scholars, writers, and journalists. The organization and its members hold "the view that American leadership in international affairs is essential to the cause of human rights and freedom." The organization's annual surveys of civil and political liberties for all countries around the world have made it a frequently consulted source on measuring human rights and comparing countries with regard to their human rights practices.

Publications: Freedom in the World, The Annual Survey of Political Rights and Civil Liberties, and special reports.

Global Exchange
2017 Mission Street, #303 San Francisco, CA, 94110 USA
Phone: +1. 415. 255. 7296
Fax: +1. 415. 255. 7498
Website: http://www.globalexchange.org

Global Exchange was founded in 1988 to promote people-to-people ties around the world. As part of concern for worker rights around the world, the organization operates a fair trade store where the worker gets a fair percentage of the sales price of merchandise sold. Global Exchange has particular campaigns, including one to further corporate responsibility; country watches, and, uniquely, reality tours—participants tour areas and explore issues related to human rights. Besides the United States, the organization's Human Rights Programs extend to Brazil, Guatemala, Colombia, Cuba, Iraq, Mexico, and Palestine.

Publications: Global Exchange publishes an e-newsletter, which can be accessed online. Publications also include books, such as *Corporations Are Gonna Get Your Mama: Globalization and the Downsizing of the American Dream; 50 Years Is Enough: The Case against the World Bank and the International Monetary Fund.*

Global Fund for Women (GFW)

1375 Sutter Street, Suite 400, San Francisco, CA 94109 USA
Phone: +1. 415. 202. 7640
Fax: +1. 415. 202. 8604
E-mail: gfw@globalfundforwomen.org
Website: http://www.globalfundforwomen.org

The Global Fund for Women was established in 1988 to form an international network of "women and men committed to a world of equality and social justice [that] advocates for and defends women's human rights by issuing small grants to support women's groups around the world." The sponsored projects are aimed at improving the political situation of women, reducing poverty, increasing women's economic opportunities, enhancing reproductive health, securing lesbian rights, improving women's rights in the context of religious tradition, reducing violence against women, and helping organizations access the media. During its first ten years, the fund made grants of over $9,000,000 to over 1,000 organizations in 125 countries.

Publications: Publications feature online reports about international women's rights issues; *GFW* newsletter, *Raising Our Voice.* Strategic plans to advance women's rights, impact reports, and other materials are available online.

Global Policy Forum

777 UN Plaza, Suite 3D, New York, NY 10017 USA

Phone: +1. 212. 557. 3161
Fax: +1. 212. 557. 3165
E-mail: globalpolicy@globalpolicy.org
Website: http://www.globalpolicy.org

The Global Policy Forum was founded in 1993. Its mission includes monitoring policymaking at the United Nations, promoting accountability of global decisions, educating and mobilizing people to increase global citizen participation, and promoting peace and justice. The GPF focuses on the United Nations because it sees it as "the most inclusive international institution, offering the best hope for a humane and sustainable future" and attempts to democratize the policymaking processes by increasing citizen action and participation

Publications: The GPF publishes policy papers and topical reports such as *Report of the UN Millennium Project "Investing in Development."*

Human Rights Center at the University of Minnesota
Mondale Hall N-120, 229 19th Avenue, South Minneapolis,
    MN 55455 USA
Phone: +1. 612. 626. 0041/1–888-HREDUC8
Fax: +1. 612. 625. 2011
E-mail: humanrts@umn.edu
Website: http://www.umn.edu/humanrts

As an academic institution, the University of Minnesota Human Rights Center focuses on training. It assists human rights professionals and volunteers through five programs: (1) Applied Human Rights Research; (2) Educational Tools; (3) the Upper Midwest Human Rights Fellowship Program, the Humphrey Human Rights and Law Fellowships, and other Field/Training Opportunities; (4) the University of Minnesota Human Rights Library; and (5) Learning Communities and Partnerships. The University of Minnesota Human Rights Library houses a large collection of human rights documents, including several hundred human rights treaties and other primary international human rights instruments. The library's website provides access to more than four thousands links.

Human Rights Education Associates (HREA)
HREA–USA Office, P.O. Box 382396, Cambridge,
    MA 02238 USA

Visiting address: 97 Lowell Road, Concord, MA 01742 USA
Phone: +1. 978. 341 0200
Fax: +1. 978. 341 0201
E-mail: info@hrea.org
Website: http://www.hrea.org

Human Rights Education Associates (HREA) was established in 1996 in Amsterdam. It is an international nongovernmental organization that undertakes activities that involve promoting human rights learning, training of activists and professionals, development of educational materials and programming, and community building through online technologies. Collaborating with nongovernmental organizations, intergovernmental organizations, and governments interested in human rights education, the HREA provides assistance in curriculum and materials development, training staff, research, and organizational development.

Publications: Education and training materials and manuals.

Human Rights First
333 Seventh Avenue, 13th Floor, New York, NY 10165 USA
Phone: +1. 212. 845 5200
Fax: +1. 212. 845 5299
E-mail: pubs@humanrightsfirst.org
Website: http://www.humanrightsfirst.org

Originally founded as the Lawyers Committee for Human Rights in 1978, Human Rights First works in the United States and abroad with the goal of creating "a secure and humane world by advancing justice, human dignity and respect for the rule of law." It supports human rights activists who fight for basic freedoms and peaceful change at the local level, protects refugees in flight from persecution and repression, helps build a strong international system of justice and accountability, and tries to assure that human rights laws and principles are enforced in the United States and abroad.

Publications: It publishes reports of its fact-finding missions and conferences.

Human Rights Internet (HRI)
One Nicholas Street, Suite 300, Ottawa, Ontario K1N 7B7
    Canada
Phone: +1. 613. 789 7407
Fax: +1. 613. 789 7414

E-mail: hri@hri.ca
Website: http://www.hri.ca

Founded in 1976, the HRI is a leader in the exchange of information within the worldwide human rights community. Launched in the United States, the HRI now has its headquarters in Ottawa, Canada. The HRI communicates by phone, fax, mail, and the Internet with more than 5,000 organizations and individuals around the world working for the advancement of human rights.

Publications: It publishes the *Human Rights Internet Reporter,* as well as *Human Rights Tribune Magazine, Women's Guide,* an online source, electronic newsletter, annual reports, an occasional paper series, directories, and other special publications. The website includes a bookstore, where all HRI publications can be obtained.

Human Rights Watch
350 Fifth Avenue, 34th Floor, New York, NY 10118 USA
Phone +1. 212. 290 4700
Fax: +1. 212. 736 1300
E-mail: hrwnyc@hrw.org
Website: http://www.hrw.org

Human Rights Watch was founded in 1978 as Helsinki Watch (now Human Rights Watch/Helsinki). Originally it was a "response to a call for support from embattled groups in Moscow, Warsaw, and Prague that had been set up to monitor compliance with the human rights provisions of the Helsinki Accords [of 1975]." Later, it became a global operation with components of regional focus and adopted a broader definition of human rights. Human Rights Watch researchers conduct fact-finding investigations into human rights abuses in all regions of the world. The findings are published in dozens of books and reports every year. Its publications and other activities intend to inform the public about abuses and pressure governments to take measures to prevent violations. It also sponsors the Human Rights Film Festival.

Publications: In addition to an extensive books publication program, it produces numerous reports of its fact-finding missions. The HRW publications can be accessed or ordered online.

**Human Rights Information and Documentation Systems
  International (HURIDOCS)**
48, chemin de Montfleury CH-1290 Versoix, Switzerland

Phone: +41. 22. 755 52 52
Fax: +41. 22. 755 52 60
E-mail: info@huridocs.org
Website: http://www.huridocs.org/

HURIDOCS is a global network of human rights organizations. It was initiated in 1979 but formally established in 1982. Its mission is to improve "access to and the dissemination of public information on human rights through more effective, appropriate and compatible methods and techniques of information handling." It is an international organization that facilitates documentation and flow of information among human rights organizations, by providing training programs, teaching tools, and consultancy.
Publications: Annual reports.

Indian Law Resource Center
601 E Street SE, Washington, DC 20003 USA
Phone: +1. 202. 547 2800
Fax: +1. 202. 547 2803
E-mail: dcoffice@indianlaw.org
Website: http://www.indianlaw.org

The Indian Law Resource Center is a nonprofit law and advocacy organization established and directed by American Indians. The center is devoted to helping Indian nations, tribes, and other indigenous peoples to prevent destruction of their cultures and homelands. It works to establish national and international legal standards that uphold the human rights and dignity of indigenous peoples, protect Indian land and resources, and secure their authority for self-government and sustainable futures.
Publications: The center publishes articles and press releases about its work, which are available online.

Institute for Policy Studies (IPS)
733 15th St NW, Suite 1020, Washington DC, 20005, USA
Phone: +1. 202. 234 938
Fax: +1. 202. 387 7915
Website: http://www.ips-dc.org

Founded in 1963 as a transnational center for research, education, and social invention, the Institute for Policy Studies critically examines the assumptions and policies that define the U.S.

posture on domestic and international issues and offers alternative strategies and visions. It works with social movements to forge viable and sustainable policies to promote democracy, justice, human rights, and diversity. The IPS played key roles in the civil rights and anti-war movements in the 1960s, the women's and environmental movements in the 1970s, and the anti-apartheid and anti-intervention movements in the 1980s. Recently it has been working on the fair trade and environmental justice movements.

Publications: The institute's publications program includes books and reports that are available online.

Institute for the Study of Genocide
John Jay College of Criminal Justice, 899 10th Avenue,
    Room 325T, New York, NY 10019 USA
Phone: +1. 212. 582 2537
Fax: +1. 212. 491 8076
E-mail: info@isg-iags.org
Website: http://www.isg-iags.org

The Institute for the Study of Genocide, a nonprofit educational organization, was founded in 1982 to promote teaching and scholarship on the causes, consequences, and prevention of genocide. It provides support to scholars from various disciplines in conducting research, publishing findings, and applying findings to classroom teaching. It also maintains a library of resources pertaining to genocide.

Publications: The institute publishes the *ISG Newsletter* and occasional pamphlets on current issues relating to genocide, which can be accessed online.

Intercommunity Center for Justice and Peace (ICJP)
20 Washington Square North, New York, NY 10011 USA
Phone: +1. 212. 475 6677
Fax: +1. 212. 475 6969
E-mail: icjpny@aol.com
Website: http://www.icjpny.addr.com

The Intercommunity Center for Justice and Peace was established in 1974 with the mission of integrating "faith and justice in all areas of life," in order "to effect changes in societal structures toward the realization of a more human, just, and peaceful society." With such a mission, ICJP networks with a broad range of religious and community coalitions. It has forty-three member congregations.

Interights
Lancaster House, 33 Islington High Street, London N1 9LH UK
Phone: +44. 20. 7278 3230
Fax: + 44. 20. 7278 4334
E-mail: ir@interights.org
Website: http://www.interights.org

Interights was established in 1982. Based in the United Kingdom, "it works across the developing and developed world, with regional programs in Africa, South Asia, Central and Eastern Europe and the Commonwealth, and cross-cutting thematic programs focusing on equality, liberty and security and economic, social and cultural rights." Among its goals are "to enforce human rights through law, providing protection and redress, in particular regions and on issues of strategic focus; to strengthen human rights jurisprudence and mechanisms through the use of international and comparative law; and to empower legal partners and promote their effective use of law to protect human rights." It supports lawyers, judges, NGOs, and victims on the ground by tailoring activities in response to the needs of each group and region.

Publications: In addition to the periodicals, *INTERIGHTS Bulletin* and *Commonwealth Human Rights Law Digest*, publications include various handbooks on human rights advocacy.

International Action Center
39 West 14th St., #206 New York, NY 10011 USA
Phone: +1. 212. 633 6646
Fax +1. 212. 633 2889
E-mail: iacenter@action-mail.org
Website:http://www.iacenter.org

International Action Center was founded by Ramsey Clark, former U.S. attorney general. Focusing on promoting peace, solidarity, and truth, the activities of the center intend to affect the domestic and international policies of the United States government.

Publications: It publishes books, including *Wars of the 21st Century: New Threats New Fears; A Right to Be Hostile: The Boondocks Treasury; We Want Freedom: A Life in the Black Panther Party.* All publications can be obtained online.

International Alert
346 Clapham Road, London SW9 9AP UK
Phone: +44. 20. 7627 6800
Fax: +44. 20. 7627 6900
Website: http://www.international-alert.org/

International Alert was established by a group of human rights advocates in 1985 as a result of their concerns over human rights violations and their connection to ethnic conflict and genocide. It works with an understanding that "the denial of human rights often led to internal armed conflicts which in turn undermined efforts to protect individual and collective human rights and to promote sustainable development." Emphasizing peace-building efforts, it focuses on areas affected or threatened by armed conflict—more recently in the Great Lakes region of Africa, West Africa, the Caucasus, Colombia, Sri Lanka, Nepal, and the Philippines.

Publications: Its publications include a range of advocacy training and awareness raising tools.

International Alliance of Indigenous and Tribal Peoples of the Tropical Forests (IAITPTF)
6/1 Moo 1, Suthep Road, Suthep Sub-district, Muang District, Chiang Mai 50200, Thailand
Phone: +66, 53. 904 037
Fax: +66. 53. 277 645
E-mail: iait@loxinfo.co.th
Website: http://www.international-alliance.org

The International Alliance of Indigenous and Tribal Peoples of the Tropical Forests was established in 1992, during a conference of indigenous peoples, held in Malaysia. As a global network of organizations representing indigenous and tribal peoples living in tropical forest regions (Africa, the Asia-Pacific, and the Americas), the Alliance's mission includes "the promotion of the full recognition of the rights of indigenous peoples, development of indigenous and tribal people, their participation in decision-making processes, enabling them in their dealings with the UN and multilateral development banks and agencies, and establishment of networks and worldwide solidarity among them."

Publications: Thematic brochures and reports.

International Alliance of Women (IAW)
10 Queen Street, Melbourne VIC 3000, Australia
E-mail: iaw.iwnews@toddsec.com
Website: http://www.womenalliance.com

The IAW has its origins in a 1902 Washington meeting of suffragists from eleven countries, who established the International Alliance of Women for Suffrage and Legal Citizenship. After changing its name a few times, the Alliance acquired its current name in 1946 with the subtitle "Equal Rights—Equal Responsibilities," which has became the Alliance's motto. The Alliance "affirms that full and equal enjoyment of human rights is due to all women and girls" and "maintains that a prerequisite to securing these rights is the universal ratification and implementation without reservation of the Convention on the Elimination of All Forms of Discrimination against Women (CEDAW)." In addition to lobbying UN officials and agencies, it works on stimulating communication and cooperation among its members.

Publications: A monthly newsletter, newsflashes, and action sheets.

International Association for Religious Freedom (IARF)
2 Market Street, Oxford OX1 3ET, UK
Phone:+44. 1865. 202 744
Fax: +44. 1865. 202 746
E-mail: hq@iarf.net
Website: http://www.iarf.net

The International Association for Religious Freedom is a United Kingdom–based charity organization. It works for freedom of religion and belief at a global level and encourages interfaith dialogue and tolerance. It has over ninety affiliated member groups in approximately twenty-five countries. They cover a wide range of faith traditions, including Christianity, Buddhism, Islam, Shintoism, Hinduism, and Sikhism.

Publications: World newsletter is published twice a year. The organization also publishes books.

International Association of Official Human Rights Agencies (IAOHRA)
444 North Capitol Street, Suite 408, Washington, DC 20001 USA
Phone: +1. 202. 624 5410

Fax: +1. 202. 624 8185
E-mail: iaohra@sso.org
Website: http://www.sso.org/iaohra/

The IAOHRA was established in 1949 to assist official human rights agencies. It has maintained "the goals of (1) promoting civil and human rights around the world, by providing leadership in the development and enforcement of laws at all levels of government, protecting the civil and human rights of all persons, (2) fostering human and inter-group relations, and (3) enhancing human rights practices under law." The association offers extensive services and training for personnel of state and local human rights agencies throughout the United States and Canada. Currently, its membership includes approximately 160 human rights agencies in these two countries. It conducts workshops and seminars for human rights administrators and promotes development of state legislation through its technical assistance workshops for state and regional planning agencies.

International Centre for Transitional Justice (ICTJ)
20 Exchange Place, 33rd Floor New York, NY 10005 USA
Phone: +1. 917. 438 9300
Fax: +1. 212. 509 6036
E-mail: info@ictj.org
Website: http://www.ictj.org

The International Center for Transitional Justice was founded in 2001. It provides assistance to countries in their attempts to establish accountability for past mass atrocities and human rights abuses. It works with governments and nongovernmental organizations—at local, national, and international levels—and "provides documentation, comparative data, legal and policy analyses, and strategy guidelines in seeking truth and justice."

Publications: A bimonthly newsletter, *Transitional Justice in the News*; reports; and articles that are posted on its website.

International Commission of Jurists (ICJ)
P.O. Box 216, 1219 Châtelaine, Geneva, Switzerland
Phone: +41.22. 979 3800
Fax: +41. 22. 979 3801
E-mail: info@icj.org
Website: http://www.icj.org

Founded in Berlin in 1952, the International Commission of Jurists is "dedicated to the primacy, coherence and implementation of international law and principles that advance human rights." It is composed of sixty eminent jurists who are representatives of the different legal systems of the world. The ICJ uses its legal expertise to ensure that "international law adheres to human rights principles and that international standards are implemented at the national level."

Publications: Publications include titles such as *Military Jurisdiction and International Law: Military Courts and Gross Human Rights Violations; Yearbook of the International Commission of Jurists; Attacks on Justice: The Harassment and Persecution of Judges and Lawyers.* All publications can be obtained online.

International Council on Human Rights Policy
48, chemin du Grand-Montfleury, P.O. Box 147 CH-1290,
 Versoix ,Geneva, Switzerland Tel: +41. 22. 775 33 00
Fax: +41. 22. 775 33 03
E-mail: ichrp@international-council.org
Website: http://www.ichrp.org

International Council on Human Rights Policy was established in Geneva in 1998 with the goals of providing "a forum for applied research, reflection and forward thinking on matters of international human rights policy," identifying "issues that impede efforts to protect and promote human rights," and proposing "approaches and strategies that will advance that purpose." It works with nongovernmental, governmental, and intergovernmental agencies to stimulate cooperation among them to improve human rights policies.

Publications: The council produces reports and briefing papers that provide policy recommendations.

International Federation for Human Rights (FIDH)
17 Passage de la main d'or, Paris 75011, France
Phone: +331. 43. 55 25 18
Fax: +331. 43. 55 18 80
Website: http://www.fidh.org/

Fédération Internationale des Ligues des Droits de l'Homme (FIDH), established in 1922, is one of the oldest human rights organizations. Its current mandate is "to contribute to the respect of all the rights defined in the Universal Declaration of Human

Rights." It functions as a network of 141 international non-governmental organizations and local groups that promotes the Universal Declaration of Human Rights. It investigates human rights violations, observes trials, and provides training programs in over 100 countries. It enjoys consultative status with the United Nations, UNESCO, and the European Council and holds observer status with the African Commission of Human and Peoples' Rights. In addition to its four statutory priorities—protecting human rights and assisting victims, mobilizing the community of states, supporting local NGOs' capacity, and raising awareness—its current thematic priorities include protecting human rights defenders; defending women's rights; seeking justice for victims; promoting respect of human rights in the fight against terrorism; and advocating economic globalization respectful of human rights.

International Freedom of Expression Exchange (IFEX)
The IFEX Clearing House, 489 College Street, Suite 403, Toronto,
  Ontario, Canada, M6G 1A5
Phone: +1. 416. 515 9622
Fax: +1. 416. 515 7879
E-mail: ifex@ifex.org
Website: http://www.ifex.org

The International Freedom of Expression Exchange was founded in 1992. Composed of more than twenty-five member organizations from all over the world that support freedom of expression, it operates as an information clearinghouse to coordinate the work of members, thereby reducing overlap among activities to make them more effective in their shared objective. IFEX also runs an outreach program that provides information, financial and technical assistance, and international support and recognition to fledgling groups that work on freedom of expression.

Publications: In addition to the Action Alert Network, IFEX publishes the *Communique,* a weekly publication about current free expression issues that is available by e-mail or surface mail in English, Spanish, and French.

International Helsinki Federation for Human Rights
Wickenburggasse 14, 1080 Vienna, Austria
Phone: +43. 1. 408 88 22
Fax: +43. 1. 408 88 22 50

E-mail: office@ihf-hr.org
Website: http://www.ihf-hr.org

The International Helsinki Federation for Human Rights was created by the organizations that were established after the Helsinki Final Act (1975) to protect human rights throughout Europe, North America, and Central Asia. Thus, its primary goal is to monitor countries' compliance with the human rights provisions of the Helsinki Final Act and its follow-up documents. Its Vienna-based secretariat serves as a liaison among forty-two Helsinki member committees and associated human rights groups, provides support, and represents them at the international political level. It gathers and analyzes information on human rights conditions in states that are members of the Organization for Security and Cooperation in Europe (OSCE), and disseminates its findings to governments, intergovernmental organizations, nongovernmental organizations, and the public at large.

Publications: Annual reports and press releases.

International League for Human Rights
228 E 45th Street, 5th Floor, New York, NY 10017 USA
Phone: +1. 212. 661 0480
Fax: +1. 212. 661 0416
E-mail: info@ilhr.org
Website: http://www.ilhr.org

Established in 1941, the League's special mission has been defending individual human rights advocates who have risked their lives to promote the ideals of a just and civil society in their homelands. It is based in New York but holds representation in Geneva and dozens of affiliates and partners around the world. The International League has special consultative status at the United Nations, the Council of Europe, and the International Labour Organization, and also contributes to the Africa Commission and the Organization for Security and Cooperation in Europe (OSCE).

Publications: It publishes reports that are available online.

International Rescue Committee, Inc.
122 East 42nd Street, New York, NY 10168-1289 USA
Phone: +1. 212. 551 3000
Fax: +1. 212. 551 3180

E-mail: irc@theirc.org
Website: http://www.intrescom.org

The International Rescue Committee was established in 1933 to provide "relief, rehabilitation, protection, post-conflict development, resettlement services and advocacy for those uprooted or affected by violent conflict and oppression." Active globally, the Committee's services range from emergency aid to rebuilding communities; reuniting separated families; rehabilitating health care, education, water, and sanitation systems; and strengthening the capacity of local organizations.

Publications: Annual reports and books.

International Service for Human Rights (ISHR)
Case/P.O. Box 16 CH-1211, Geneva 20, Switzerland
Phone: +41. 22. 733 51 23
Fax: +41. 22. 733 08 26
Website: http://www.ishr.ch

The International Service for Human Rights (ISHR) was established in Geneva in 1984 by members of various nongovernmental organizations for the purposes of promoting "the development, strengthening, effective use, and implementation of international and regional law and mechanisms for the protection and promotion of human rights." It provides information, training, and support to human rights defenders from around the world. It also monitors activities and issues reports on the UN and other international and regional human rights mechanisms.

Publications: Human Rights Monitor, provides review of all UN human rights meetings; *HR-Documentation-DH; Info-Pack; HR-Dossier-DH,* and manuals. They can be accessed online.

International Society for Peace and Human Rights (ISPHR)
U of A, Box 40 2–900, 8900–114 Street, Edmonton, AB
    Canada T6G 2J7
E-mail: alisonazer@shaw.ca
Website: http://www.peaceandhumanrights.org

The International Society for Peace and Human Rights is "a global network of caring individuals working together for peace, human rights and the environment." Based in Canada, the ISPHR works with representatives in all regions of the world to ensure the protection of both peoples and their environment.

Karamah: Muslim Women Lawyers for Human Rights
Phone: +1. 202. 234 7302/7303
Fax: +1. 202. 234 7304
E-mail: karamah@karamah.org
Website: http://www.karamah.org

Karamah was established in 1993 to support the human rights of Muslims in the United States of America and internationally, through education, grassroots advocacy, and activism. An important goal of the organization is the transformation of "the conception of women's status within Islamic communities to both improve the treatment of women and to ensure that women take an active part in governing their lives." It undertakes programs and activities that focus on educating younger generations of Muslim women about their rights. It also organizes events and conferences to inform the non-Muslim community and increase public awareness about the civil rights of Muslims.
Publications: Press releases and statements.

Kurdish Human Rights Project (KHRP)
2 New Burlington Place, London W1S 2HP UK
Phone: +44.20. 7287 2772
Fax: +44. 20. 7734 4927
E-mail: khrp@khrp.org
Website: http://www.khrp.org

The Kurdish Human Rights Project was founded in London in 1992 to promote the protection of "the human rights of all persons in the Kurdish regions of Turkey, Iraq, Iran, Syria and elsewhere" irrespective of race, religion, sex, political persuasion, or other beliefs or opinions.
Publications: Reports and manuals.

MADRE
121 West 27th Street, # 301 New York, NY 10001 USA
Phone: +1. 212. 627 0444
Fax: +1. 212. 675 3704
E-mail: madre@madre.org
Website: http://ww.madre.org

MADRE is an international women's human rights organization that was established in 1983 and works in partnership with women's groups in conflict areas worldwide. Its programs and activities cover a wide range of issues, such as armed conflict and forced displacement; women's health and reproductive rights; economic justice and community development; indigenous peoples' rights and resources, food security, and sustainable development; human rights advocacy; youth; and U.S. foreign policy. In its efforts to improve women's conditions and rights, MADRE provides resources and training to its affiliated organizations.

Publications: Madre Speaks, a quarterly newsletter.

Meiklejohn Civil Liberties Institute
P.O. Box 673 Berkeley, CA 94701 USA
Phone: +1. 510. 848 0599
Fax: +1. 510. 848 6008
E-mail: info@mcli.org
Website: http://www.mcli.org

Meiklejohn Civil Liberties Institute was founded in 1965 with the goal of promoting "social change by increasing the recognition and use of existing human rights and peace law at the local, national, and international levels." With activities covering various issues, ranging from the right to education to ensuring government accountability, it functions as both a research and training center and a repository of history.

Publications: It publishes a quarterly newsletter, *Human Rights Now,* as well as books.

Minority Rights Group International
54 Commercial Street, London E1 6LT UK
Phone: +44. 20. 7422 4200
Fax: +44. 20. 7422 4201
E-mail: minority.rights@mrgmail.org
Website: http://www.minorityrights.org

Minority Rights Group International (MRG) has been active for over thirty years. Working on behalf of nondominant ethnic, religious, and linguistic communities, it seeks to secure the rights of these groups worldwide as it promotes cooperation and understanding among communities.

Publications: Country and workshop reports, training manuals, as well as minority group materials such as *Unheard Indigenous Voices: The Kihals in Pakistan; Kenya's Castaways: The Ogiek and National Development Processes; Indigenous Peoples and Poverty: The Cases of Bolivia, Guatemala, Honduras and Nicaragua.*

National Center for Policy Alternatives
1875 Connecticut Avenue NW, Suite 710, Washington,
   DC 20009 USA
Phone: +1. 202. 387 6030
Fax: +1. 202. 986 2539
E-mail: info@cfpa.org
Website: http://www.cfpa.org

Founded in 1975 as a progressive, nonpartisan, nonprofit, public policy center focusing on innovation at the state and local levels, the National Center for Policy Alternatives provides policymakers with field-based services, national resources, and connections to advocates and experts and serves as a catalyst for innovative public policy in the United States. Although its focus is on state and local policy, its program areas include human rights issues such as family and work, women's rights, housing, and environmental security.

Publications: The Center for Policy Alternatives publishes a wide variety of material, including issue briefings, books, and reports.

Peace Brigades International (PBI)
International Office,The Grayston Centre, 28 Charles Square,
   London N1 6HT UK
Phone: + 44. 20. 7324 4628
E-mail: info@peacebrigades.org

U.S. Office
428 8th St. S.E., 2nd Floor, Washington DC 20003 USA
Phone: +1. 202. 544 3765
Fax: +1. 202. 544 3766
E-mail: info@pbiusa.org
Website: http://www.peacebrigades.org/usa.html

Peace Brigades International is a grassroots organization dedicated to exploring and implementing nonviolent approaches to peacekeeping and to the protection of basic human rights. By sending teams of volunteers into areas of political repression and conflict, the PBI seeks to enlarge the space for local activists to work for social justice and human rights and provides protective international accompaniment for individuals and organizations who have been threatened by political violence or who are otherwise at risk. It trains volunteers from all over the world, operates a speakers' bureau, sends short-term delegations to all sides of conflicts, and has a public education campaign.

Publications: The Project Bulletin and annual reports.

People's Rights Fund, Inc.
39 West 14th Street, #206, New York, NY 10011 USA
Phone: +1 .212. 633 6646
Fax: +1. 212. 633 2889
E-mail: donations@peoplesrightsfund.org
Website: http://www.peoplesrightsfund.org

Established in 1986, the People's Rights Fund, Inc., provides funding for educational programs on peace, civil rights, civil liberties, economic inequality, and anti-repression and social justice issues. It allocates grants to fund conferences, meetings, seminars, classes, and speaking tours, as well as for publications that would disseminate information not found in the daily print or electronic media.

Physicians for Human Rights (PHR)
Two Arrow Street, Suite 301, Cambridge, MA 02138 USA
Phone: +1. 617. 695 0041
Fax: +1. 617. 301 4250
E-mail: phrusa@phrusa.org
Website: http://www.phrusa.org

Physicians for Human Rights (PHR) was established in 1986. Subscribing to a philosophy that human rights are essential preconditions for the health and well-being of all people, it promotes health by protecting human rights. Thus, it employs medical expertise and scientific methods to investigate and expose violations of human rights worldwide and works toward stopping violations. It supports institutions that hold perpetrators of human rights abuses accountable for their actions. It educates health professionals and students in medical, public health, and nursing programs and organizes them to become active in supporting a movement for human rights and creating a culture of human rights in the medical and scientific professions.

Publications: Members receive the *Physicians for Human Rights Record* three times a year and *Medical Action Alerts*. The organization also publishes reports of fact-finding missions.

Physicians for Social Responsibility (PSR)
1875 Connecticut Avenue NW, Suite 1012, Washington,
  DC 20009 USA
Phone: +1. 202. 667 4260
Fax: +1. 202. 667 4201
E-mail: psrnatl@psr.org
Website: http://www.psr.org

Physicians for Social Responsibility was established in 1961. It is a public policy organization with 24,000 members drawn from medical and public health professions and concerned citizens. It works for nuclear disarmament, a healthful environment, and an end to the epidemic of gun violence.

Publications: PSR maintains an online pressroom, which provides updated media resources on environmental, public health, security, and violence prevention issues.

Redress
3rd Floor, 87 Vauxhall Walk, London SE11 5HJ UK
Phone: +44. 20. 7793 1777
Fax: +44. 20. 7793 1719
E-mail: info.redress.org
Website: http://www.redress.org

Established in 1992, Redress works to rebuild the lives and livelihoods of torture survivors and their families all around the world to help them become active and contributing members of society again. Its ultimate goal, however, is to eradicate the practice of torture worldwide.

Publications: Reports include *Ensuring the Effective Participation of Victims before the International Criminal Court Comments and Recommendations regarding Legal Representation for Victims; National and International Remedies for Torture: A Handbook for Sudanese Lawyers; The Reparation Report; The Protection of British Nationals Detained Abroad; A Discussion Paper concerning Consular and Diplomatic Protection,* and many more that can be obtained online.

Reporters Without Borders
International Secretariat, 5 rue Geoffroy-Marie, 75009
  Paris, France
Phone: +33. 1. 44 83 84 84
Fax: +33. 1. 45 23 11 51

E-mail: rsf@rsf.org
Website: http://www.rsf.org

Reporters without Borders has been active for two decades as a public interest association that advocates the freedom of press and people's right to be informed. It works for press freedom worldwide, and with the conviction that imprisoning or killing a journalist is like eliminating a key witness and threatening everyone's right to be informed, the association fights such practices. It defends journalists and other media contributors and professionals who have been imprisoned or persecuted for doing their work. It speaks out against the abusive treatment and torture, censorship, and laws designed to restrict press freedom, and it works to improve the safety of journalists worldwide, particularly in war zones. Lately, it has started to assess the overall press freedom in countries around the world, to assign annual scores of press freedom, and to publicize the results by ranking the countries.

Publications: Télérama, which reports major attacks on press freedom in five continents, can be obtained online.

Simon Wiesenthal Center (SWC)
1399 South Roxbury, Los Angeles, CA 90035 USA
Phone: +1. 800. 900 9036
Fax: +1. 310. 772 7654
Website: http://www.wiesenthal.com

The Simon Wiesenthal Center was established in 1977 as "an international Jewish human rights organization dedicated to preserving the memory of the Holocaust by fostering tolerance and understanding through community involvement, educational outreach and social action." However, it also works on contemporary issues including racism, anti-Semitism, terrorism, and genocide and promotes tolerance. While its headquarter is in Los Angeles, it also maintains offices in New York, Toronto, Miami, Jerusalem, Paris, and Buenos Aires.

Publications: The center produces a quarterly newsletter, *Response*, and other publications.

Southern Poverty Law Center
400 Washington Avenue, Montgomery, AL 36104 USA
Phone: +1. 334. 956 8200

Fax: +1. 334. 264 0629
Website: http://www.splcenter.org

Founded in 1971, the Southern Poverty Law Center was originally a small civil rights law firm. Today, it is internationally active and known for its education programs on promoting tolerance, litigation of white supremacists, and tracking of hate
groups. The center's legal department fights all forms of discrimination.

Publications: Publications include *SPLC Report* and teaching
materials as part of the Teaching Tolerance program.

Statewatch
P.O. Box 1516, London N16 0EW UK
Phone: +44. 20. 8802 1882
Fax: + 44. 20. 8880 1727
E-mail: office@statewatch.org
Website: http://www.statewatch.org

Statewatch is a European network of lawyers, academics, journalists, researchers, and community activists from thirteen countries. Founded in 1991, Statewatch encourages investigative jour-
nalism and publication of critical research in Europe on states'
conduct in regard to justice, home affairs, civil liberties, accountability, and openness.

*Publications: Statewatch Bulletin; Statewatch European Monitor;
Researching the European State: A Critical Guide; Handbook: State-
watching the New Europe; IRR European Race Audit.*

Survival International
6 Charterhouse Buildings, London EC1M 7ET UK
Phone: + 44. 20. 7687 8700
Fax: + 44. 20. 7687 8701
E-mail: info@survival-international.org
Website: http://www.survival-international.org

Survival International was founded in 1969 as an international
organization to protect tribal peoples worldwide from massacres,
repression in the name of "economic growth," and racial oppression. With supporters from eighty-two countries, it educates the
public on indigenous peoples' rights and works with local indigenous organizations. It focuses especially on tribal people that

are considered most vulnerable due to their very recent contact with the outside world.

Survivors International
703 Market Street, Suite 301, San Francisco, CA 94103 USA
Phone: +1. 415. 546 2080
Fax: +1. 415. 546 2084
E-mail: info@survivorsintl.org
Website: http://www.survivorsintl.org

Survivors International was founded in 1986 to serve the population of refugees and immigrants who had survived torture or the trauma of armed conflict and war in their home countries. It provides essential psychological and medical services to survivors of torture who have fled from around the world to the San Francisco Bay Area, with the goal of helping them to reestablish healthy and productive lives.

Publications: Torture and Its Consequences: A Challenge to Clinical Neuropsychology; Principles of Documenting Psychological Evidence of Torture; Treatment of Survivors of Political Torture: Administrative and Clinical Issues, among others. They can be found on the organization's website.

United European Network Against Nationalism, Racism,
Fascism and In Support of Migrants and Refugees
POSTBUS 413 NL-1000 AK, Amsterdam, Netherlands
Phone: +31. 20. 683 4778
Fax: +31. 20. 683 4582
E-mail: info@unitedagainstracism.org
Website: http://www.unitedagainstracism.org

The United European Network Against Nationalism was established in 1992 through anti-racist youth seminars. It works as a voluntary cooperation of more than 560 organizations from 49 European countries to increase public awareness about all forms of racism and organize continentwide campaigns to protect the rights of refugees and migrants and to end racism, nationalism, and discrimination.

Publications: Information leaflets and annual reports.

Victorian Foundation for Survivors of Torture, Inc. (VFST)
P.O. Box 96 Parkville, Victoria 3052 Australia
Phone: +61. 3. 9388 0022

Fax: +61. 3. 9387 0828
Website: http://www.survivorsvic.org.au

The VFST was founded in 1987 in Victoria to meet the needs of people who were "tortured or traumatized in their countries of origin, in other countries, or while fleeing those countries." The foundation's assistance to the survivors takes various forms including counseling, advocacy, family support, group work, psycho-education, information sessions, and complementary therapies.

Publications: The foundation has a wide variety of publications that address issues such as refugee health, food and nutrition, and schools, and they can be found on their website.

World Organisation Against Torture (OMCT)
International Secretariat, P.O. Box 21 8, rue du Vieux-Billard
 CH-1211 Geneva 8, Switzerland
Phone: +41. 22. 809 4939
Fax: +41. 22. 809 4929
E-mail: omct@omct.org
Website: http://www.omct.org

Europe Office
Rue du Marteau 19 B-1000, Bruxelles—Belgique
Phone/Fax : +32 2 218 37 19
E-mail: omcteurope@omct.org

OMCT's network was established in 1986, and initially comprised forty-eight organizations. The World Organisation against Torture (OMCT) is a coalition of nearly 300 local, national, and regional human rights organizations. It works to prevent arbitrary detention, torture, summary and extrajudicial executions, forced disappearances, and other forms of violence. With a holistic approach to human rights, the network has also instituted programs on racism, children's rights, violence against women, and social and economic rights.

Publications: SOS-Torture, a bilingual English/French periodical, and thematic reports.

World Policy Institute
New School University, 66 Fifth Avenue, 9th Floor, New York,
 NY 10011 USA

Phone: +1. 212. 229 5808
Fax: +1. 212. 229 5579
E-mail: wpi@newschool.edu
Website: http://www.worldpolicy.org

Founded in 1948, the World Policy Institute is a not-for-profit research and educational organization; it works for the development of U.S. foreign policies that support peace, global security, human development, and the rights of all peoples to self-determination. It supports research fellows; operates the Arms Trade Resource Center, which offers research and public education on preventive diplomacy and control of international arms transfers; and is involved in the North American Project, which explores democracy, human rights, and environmental quality in the context of North American economic integration.

Publications: World Policy Journal and various reports.

Professional Organizations

AAAS's Science and Human Rights Program
American Association for the Advancement of Science, 1200
   New York Avenue NW, Washington, DC 20005 USA
Phone: +1. 202. 326 6400
Fax: +1. 202. 289 4950
E-mail: webmaster@aaas.org
Website: http://shr.aaas.org/

American Association for the Advancement of Science is an international professional organization dedicated to advancing science around the world by serving as an educator, leader, spokesperson, and professional association. Founded in 1848, AAAS serves some 262 affiliated societies and academies of science, serving 10 million individuals. Its Science and Human Rights Program works to protect the human rights of scientists, to advance scientific methods and skills for documenting and preventing human rights abuses, to develop scientific methodologies for monitoring the implementation of human rights, to foster greater understanding and support of human rights among scientists, and to conduct research on human rights issues.

Publications: AAAS publishes a number of online and print materials.

APSA Organized Section on Human Rights
Website: http://www.apsanet.org/humanrights

Established in 1903, the American Political Science Association (APSA) is a professional organization for the study of political science and serves more than 15,000 members in over 80 countries. In November 2000, a group of 200 human rights scholars established an Organized Section on Human Rights "to encourage scholarship and facilitate exchange of data and research findings on all components of human rights (e.g., civil, political, economic, social, cultural, environmental), their relationship, determinants and consequences of human rights policies, structure and influence of human rights organizations, development, implementation and impact of international conventions, and changes in the international human rights regime." In its effort to advance research on human rights, the section grants best doctoral thesis and best book awards on an annual basis.

Publications: It posts its newsletter on its webpage, along with some other information about its activities and links to human rights sources.

IPSA Research Committee on Human Rights
1590, av. Docteur-Penfield, Bureau 331, Montreal, QC H3G 1C5
 Canada
Tel. : +1. 514. 848 8717
Fax : +1. 514. 848 4095
Website: http://www.ipsa-aisp.org

International Political Science Association was founded as a professional organization in 1949 under UNESCO sponsorship. It holds world conferences every third year to stimulate scholarship and research exchange among its international members of scholars and national organizations. It embodies various study groups and research committees that work on special issues and themes in political science. Its members, who are engaged in human rights research, established a Study Group in Human Rights in 1980. In 1987, the group acquired Research Committee status. The committee organizes specialized conferences and holds panel discussions at the world conferences of the IPSA.

Pen International
9/10 Charterhouse Buildings, Goswell Rd., London
 EC1M 7AT UK

Phone: +44. 20. 7253 4308
Fax: +44. 20. 7253 5711
Website: http://www.internationalpen.org.uk/

PEN America Center
588 Broadway, Suite 303, New York, NY 10012 USA
Phone: +1. 212. 334 1660
Fax: +1 .212. 334 2181
E-mail: pen@pen.org
Website: http://www.pen.org

International PEN, the worldwide association of writers, was founded in 1921 to promote friendship and intellectual cooperation among writers everywhere; to emphasize the role of literature in the development of mutual understanding and world culture; to fight for freedom of expression; and to act as a powerful voice on behalf of writers harassed, imprisoned, and sometimes killed for their views. It has grown to include centers on six continents—with a total membership of more than 10,000—which sponsor International PEN Congress, held at least once a year. Among the activities, programs, and services sponsored by the headquarters and the five branches are public literary events, literary awards, outreach projects to encourage reading, assistance to writers in financial need, and international and domestic human rights campaigns on behalf of the many writers, editors, and journalists censored, persecuted, or imprisoned because of their writing.

Publications: PEN has a substantial publications program, including *PEN America Literary Journal, PEN Newsletter,* a bimonthly newsletter, and books.

9

Research and Data Sources

This chapter provides lists of selective sources of information that would enable further study of and research on human rights. Although sources overlap in terms of their content, they are classified as

Directories
Dictionaries
Encyclopedias
Yearbooks
Reference Books and Bibliographies
Journals and Periodicals
Internet Sites and Networks
Datasets and Statistical Sources
Film Distributors and Media Sources

Most sources have websites or can be accessed through other websites, and web addresses are provided when available. While there was an effort to incorporate most recent sources, some earlier publications are included with the intention of guiding the interested researcher to some earlier materials that have become "classics."

Directories

Central and Eastern European Internet Directory for Human Rights **(CEEHR)**
Website: http://www.ceehr.euv-frankfurt-o.de/hr

Provides a comprehensive collection on links and sites with reference to human rights issues in Europe and the newly independent states (NIS).

Directory of Scientific Society Action on Human Rights
American Association for the Advancement of Science (AAAS).
Website: http://shr.aaas.org/scisocs/

Organized by the Science and Human Rights Program of the AAAS, this Internet directory offers descriptions, contact information, and websites for scientific and professional organizations' human rights committees and activities.

Human Rights Organizations and Periodicals Directory. 11th Ed. Berkeley: Meiklejohn Civil Liberties Institute, 2003. 254 pp. ISBN 00980579
Website: http://mcli.org/law/federal/human_rights_organizations.html

Includes information on over 800 groups, periodicals, and other sources for teachers, students, and researchers seeking information on improving human rights in the United States. Provides a federal agencies guide, a list of internships, and subject and geographic indices.

The List. Human Rights Internet (HRI). Ottawa, Ontario 2000.
Website: http://www.hri.ca/publications/directories.shtml

This work replaces four regional directories prepared by HRI and provides a listing of over 2,500 organizations concerned with human rights and social justice issues worldwide. The majority of these entries are nongovernmental organizations (NGOs), but also included are governmental bodies, national institutions, and intergovernmental agencies.

Thematic Directory. Geneva: United Nations, 1998. 69 pp.

Bilingual (English and French), a directory for all bodies comprising the UN human rights machinery. UN Document Symbol: [ST/HR/NONE/98/51]

World Directory of Human Rights Research and Training Institutions. 6th edition. Paris: UNESCO Directories series, 2003. 374 pp. Website: http://unesdoc.unesco.org/images/0013/001321/132133m.pdf

Prepared on the basis of information received by UNESCO in response to a questionnaire, it includes lists of regional, national, and international institutions, cooperation programs, human rights periodicals, specialists, and institutions providing scholarships.

An Online Directory on academic degree programs in human rights
Website: http://www.du.edu/gsis/hr_prog_survey/index.html

Based on a survey conducted in 2003, the list includes academic human rights programs in various countries. The information on programs is organized geographically in four separate lists for the United States, Canada, Latin America, and Europe.

Dictionaries

Dictionary of International Human Rights Law. Edited by John Gibson. Lanham, MD: Scarecrow Press, 1996. 225 pp. ISBN: 081083118X.

Covers sixty-four rights in international treaties; divided into five categories: civil and political rights; legal rights; economic, social, and cultural rights; collective rights; and declaratory rights. Each entry contains the treaty definition, other sources and treaties, an expanded definition, historical landmarks in the development of the right, and cross-references. Includes an extensive bibliography.

Handbook of International Human Rights Terminology. 2nd edition. Edited by H. Victor Conde. Lincoln: University of Nebraska Press, 2004. 394 pp. ISBN: 0803215347 or 0803264399.

Contains over 400 new commonly used key terms and acronyms as well as updates and corrections to terms that have taken on new meaning since the publication of the original. Also includes information on new treaty instruments and citations of important human rights instruments.

Historical Dictionary of Human Rights and Humanitarian Organizations. Edited by Robert Gorman and Edward Mihalkanin. Lanham, MD: Scarecrow Press, 1997. 296 pp. ISBN: 0810832631.

Includes a time line of human rights events and entries for conventions, concepts, and organizations. Organization entries include contact information. Also has cross-references, an extensive bibliography, and selected human rights documents.

Encyclopedias

Encyclopedia of Human Rights Issues since 1945 Winston E. Langley. Westport, CT: Greenwood Press, 1999. 368 pp. ISBN: 0313301638.

Features more than 400 entries on incidents and violations, instruments and initiatives, countries, and human rights activists.

Encyclopedia of the United Nations and International Agreements. Edmund Osmanczyk. Washington, D.C.: Taylor and Francis, 1990. 1059 pp. ISBN: 0415939208.

A compendium of political, economic, and social information related to the United Nations, it contains many references to and some texts of human rights documents and covenants.

The Encyclopedia of Human Rights. 2nd edition. Edward Lawson. New York: Taylor and Francis, 1996. 1715 pp. ISBN: 1560323620.

Long articles on countries, organizations, and topics. Includes the texts of major documents, bibliography, chronological list of documents, and index.

Concise Encyclopedia of Democracy. Washington, D.C.: Congressional Quarterly, Inc., 2000. 488 pp. ISBN: 1568024266.

Features more than 300 entries covering concepts, countries, and individuals. Includes new entries on the U.S. Constitution and general government practices that meet the National Standards in Civics and Government, as well as 150 maps, photographs, charts, and timelines.

International Encyclopedia of Human Rights: Freedoms, Abuses, and Remedies. Robert L. Maddex. Washington, D.C.: CQ Press, 2000. 450 pp. ISBN: 1568024908.

Includes entries that define and describe concepts and terms, text excerpts of documents, charts depicting global comparisons, essays on organizations, and biographies of activists and theorists.

Yearbooks

Country Reports on Human Rights Practices. Washington, D.C., 1979–. Annual.
Website: http://www.state.gov/g/drl/hr/

Annual reports submitted to the Committee on Foreign Relations (U.S. Senate) and Committee on Foreign Affairs (U.S. House of Representatives) by the U.S. Department of State. Provides an assessment of human rights conditions by country.

Human Development Report, United Nations (national, regional, and global)
Yearbook of the United Nations, 1946– . New York, UN, Annual.
Website: http://hdr.undp.org/reports

Prepared by the United Nations Development Programme, addresses human development issues at global, regional, and national levels. In addition to the Human Development Index, it provides data on various development and human rights–related statistics and analysis of issues. *Global:* Published annually, presents agenda-setting data and analysis and calls international attention to issues and policy options that put people at the center of strategies to meet the challenges of development today. Includes tables on development and human rights indicators by country. *Regional:* Promotes regional partnerships for influencing change and addresses region-specific human development approaches to human rights, poverty, education, economic reform,

HIV/AIDS, and globalization. *National:* Country-based reports address development and human rights issues; data for different geographic locations within the country are provided.

Human Rights in Developing Countries—Yearbook 1996. Edited by Peter Baehr, Lalaine Sadiwa, and Jacqueline Smith in cooperation with Annelies Bosch. Kluwer Law International and Nordic Human Rights Publications. 1996. 425 pp. ISBN: 904112906. Website: http://www.humanrights.dk/publications/all

Contains contributions on the right to development in the development assistance policies of Norway and the European Union. It also contains reports on seven countries—Bhutan, Egypt, El Salvador, Ethiopia, India, Mexico, and Uganda—which assess human rights trends, covering civil and political as well as economic, social, and cultural rights during the period 1993–1995.

Israel Yearbook on Human Rights. Edited by Yoram Dinstein. Tel Aviv: Tel Aviv University. Annual. Website: http://www.kluwerarbitration.com

The yearbook contains articles by different scholars describing aspects of human rights, with particular emphasis on problems relevant to the state of Israel and the Jewish people. It also includes documentary material relating to Israel and the occupied territories.

Yearbook on Human Rights. New York: UN, since 1946. Website: https://unp.un.org

Reports on national developments, activities of supervisory bodies, international developments in the UN system. Covers political and security questions; human rights; economic and social questions; legal questions; institutional, administrative, and budgetary questions; and intergovernmental organizations related to the United Nations.

Reference Books and Bibliographies

Bennett, James. *Political Prisoners and Trials: A Worldwide Annotated Bibliography, 1900 through 1993.* Jefferson, NC: McFarland, 1995. 363 pp. ISBN: 0786400234.

Over 3,500 entries, including magazine articles, monographs, and reports arranged by country, and an extensive index.

Brownlie, Ian, and Guy S. Goodwin-Gill, eds. *Basic Documents on Human Rights*. New York: Oxford University Press, 2002. 916 pp. ISBN: 019924944X.

Provides a collection of key documents of human rights, accompanied by an authoritative commentary and annotation.

Thomas P. Fenton. *Human Rights: A Directory of Resources*. New York: Orbis, 1989. 156 pp. ISBN: 0883445344.

Includes annotated bibliography of books and articles, reference works, yearbooks and country reports series, periodicals, pamphlets, and audiovisuals, as well as a directory of organizations.

Michael Freeman. *Human Rights: An Interdisciplinary Approach*. Key Concepts. Cambridge, UK: Polity Press, 2002. 201 pp. ISBN: 0745623565.

Provides information on the conceptualization and origin of human rights, theories, advances in various disciplinary approaches, and the impact of globalization.

Human Rights in Latin America, 1964–1980: A Selective Annotated Bibliography. Compiled and edited by Hispanic Division. Washington: U.S. Government Printing Office, 1983. 257 pp. ISBN: 0844404152.

A selective annotated bibliography. Includes information on general publications as well as chapters on countries.

Ishay, Micheline. *The History of Human Rights: From Ancient Times to the Globalization Era*. Berkeley, CA: University of California Press, 2004. 459 pp. ISBN: 0520234960.

Provides a historical overview of the development of international human rights concepts and documents with references to texts, cultural traditions, and events.

Ishay, Micheline. *The Human Rights Reader: Major Political Essays, Speeches and Documents from the Bible to the Present*. New York: Routledge Press, 1997. 518 pp. ISBN: 0415918499.

Traces the historical lineage and discursive tradition of human rights by providing excerpts from texts.

Kinnard, Cynthia. *Antifeminism in American Thought: An Annotated Bibliography.* Boston: G. K. Hall, 1986. 321 pp. ISBN: 0816181225.

Contains 1,331 annotated entries for books, articles, and pamphlets, eighteenth century to the present. Arranged by broad topics, subdivided chronologically.

Lauren, Paul Gordon. *The Evolution of International Human Rights: Visions Seen.* 2nd edition. Philadelphia: University of Pennsylvania Press. 2003. 392 pp. ISBN: 081221854X.

Provides comprehensive and exhaustively researched history of human rights ideas and the institutions to implement those ideas that has been written to date.

Levinson, David et al., eds. *The Wilson Chronology of Human Rights.* Bronx, NY: H. W. Wilson, 2003. 573 pp. ISBN: 0824209729.

Provides a chronological history of human rights struggles and violations from ancient times in nine chapters covering topics such as "Civil Rights," "Children's Rights," "Gay Rights," and "Refugee Rights."

Stanek, Edward. *A Bibliography of Periodicals and Other Serials on Human Rights.* Monticello, IL: Vance Bibliographies, 1991. 9 pp. ISBN: 0792007662.

A list of periodicals in the human rights fields. Not annotated.

Steiner, Henry, and Philip Alston. *International Human Rights in Context: Law, Politics, Morals.* 2nd edition. New York: Oxford University Press, 2000. 1497. ISBN: 0198298498.

Includes edited versions of primary materials, ranging from intergovernmental or NGO reports to treaties, resolutions, and decisions as well as excerpts from secondary readings in law, legal theory, international relations, moral and political theory, and anthropology.

Symonides, Janusz, and Darlene R. Stille, eds. *Human Rights: International Protection, Monitoring, Enforcement.* Hampshire, UK: Ashgate, 2003. 416 pp. ISBN: 0754623017.

Expert analyses of human rights protection and monitoring by the United Nations, International Labour Organization, UNESCO, and regional human rights regimes.

Tobin, Jack, and Green, Jennifer. *Guide to Human Rights Research.* Cambridge, MA: Harvard Law School Human Rights Program, 1994. 228 pp. ISBN: 1879875020.

Annotated bibliography of reference works, books, series, and periodicals—arranged by topics. Includes information on computer resources and the Internet. Includes name and topical index.

Human Rights Bibliography: United Nations Documents and Publications, 1980–1990. New York: United Nations, 1993. 5 vols. 2048 pp. ISBN: 9211003776.

This five-volume bibliography lists author, subject, title, and United Nations document numbers by category in over 9,000 entries.

Human Rights on CD-ROM 1999: Bibliographical References to United Nations Documents and Publications. New York: United Nations Publications, 2003.

Contains 14,000 bibliographical references to UN documents and publications, from 1980 to 1994. Includes full text of ninety-five international instruments.

National Human Rights Institutions: A Handbook on the Establishment and Strengthening of National Institutions for the Promotion and Protection of Human Rights. New York: United Nations, 1995. 55 pp. ISBN: 9211541158.

The United Nations and Human Rights, 1945–1995. New York: United Nations, 1995. 536 pp. UN Document Symbol: DPI/1676.

Provides an overview of the United Nations involvement in the development of international human rights and reproduces major UN documents pertaining to human rights.

United Nations Reference Guide in the Field of Human Rights.
New York: United Nations, 1993. 124p. ISBN: 9211540976.

Provides sales numbers for purchasing materials published on human rights by the United Nations since 1948. Entries are arranged by categories of rights, and an index in the back gives country access.

Wannoters, Gregory. *Human Rights in Theory and Practice: A Selected and Annotated Bibliography.* Metuchen, NJ: Scarecrow Press, 1995. 459 pp. ISBN: 0810830108.

Annotated information on philosophical foundations of human rights, cultural relativism, cross-cultural perspectives, human rights and religious traditions, basic human needs, development and security, human rights and foreign policy, international law, organizations and human rights, group and individual rights, women and human rights, and emerging human rights issues. Includes four separate indexes.

Weinberg, Meyer. *World Racism and Related Inhumanities: A Country by Country Bibliography.* Westport, CT: Greenwood Press, 1992. 1048 pp. ISBN: 0313281092.

References include racism, slavery, class domination, sexism, national oppression, imperialism, colonialism, and anti-Semitism. More than 12,000 entries that span 135 countries and cover ancient history to the present. Not annotated.

Journals and Periodicals

This section includes information on major periodicals that focus on human rights issues and events. However, since human rights as a field of study is interdisciplinary, the researcher should also consult journals specializing in international law and social sciences, many of which publish articles on human rights or related issues.

Asia-Pacific Journal on Human Rights and the Law
233 Spring Street, New York, NY 10013
Website: http://www.springeronline.com

Published in conjunction with the Asia-Pacific Centre for Human Rights and the Prevention of Ethnic Conflict, School of Law, Murdoch University, Australia; offers scholarly articles of comparative, international, and national research dealing specifically with issues of law and human rights in the Asia-Pacific region.

Cultural Survival Quarterly
Quarterly
Cultural Survival, Inc., 96 Mount Auburn Street, Cambridge, MA 02138
Website: http://www.culturalsurvival.org

Promotes the rights, voices, and visions of indigenous people.

Columbia Human Rights Law Review
Semiannual
Columbia University School of Law, 435 West 116th Street, New York, NY 10027
Website: http://www.columbia.edu/cu/hrlr}

Established in 1968 and run by students at Columbia University School of Law. Provides analyses and discussions of human rights and civil liberties under both domestic and international law.

Covert Action Quarterly (formerly titled Covert Action Information Bulletin)
Quarterly
Covert Action Publications, Inc., 1500 Massachusetts Avenue, NW, Suite 732, Washington, D.C. 20005
Website: http://www.covertactionquarterly.org

Published since 1978; offers investigative reporting and examines materials related to the workings of government and the media, as well as the relations between the two.

East European Human Rights Review
P.O. Box 951361, Lake Mary, FL. 32795
Website: http://bwp-bookcenter.com

Focuses on the transformation of legal systems in eastern and central Europe; publishes contributions from authors worldwide, which provide comparative discussion of both national and international aspects of human rights.

Human Rights Review
Quarterly
Transaction Publisher, 390 Campus Drive, Somerset, NJ 07830
Website: http://www.transactionpub.com

Aims at integrating social scientific information and historical perspective. Covers topics such as international law and national sovereignty; the relationship of personal rights to public responsibilities; different standards of measurement of political systems; the role of economic development or backwardness in establishing normative structures of human rights; and the place of foreign intervention in mandating a human rights agenda in transitional regimes.

Harvard Civil Rights–Civil Liberties Law Review
Semiannual
Publications Center, Harvard Law School, 1541 Massachusetts
    Avenue, Cambridge, MA 02138
Website: http://www.law.harvard.edu/students/orgs/crcl

Founded in 1966 as an instrument to advance personal freedoms and human dignities; seeks to catalyze progressive thought and dialogue through publishing innovative legal scholarship from various perspectives and in diverse fields of study.

Harvard Human Rights Journal
Annual
Pound Hall, 403 Harvard Law School, Cambridge, MA 02138
Phone: 617. 495. 8318
E-mail: hlshrj@law.harvard.edu
Website: http://www.law.harvard.edu/students/orgs/hrj

Published annually by Harvard Law School students and includes scholarly articles and analytical essays.

Human Rights Brief
Tri-yearly
4801 Massachusetts Avenue NW, Room 630, Washington,
    D.C. 20016–8181
Website: http://www.wcl.american.edu/hrbrief

Published by Washington College of Law; offers articles related to international human rights and humanitarian law and authored by practitioners around the world.

Human Rights Case Digest
233 Spring Street, New York, NY 10013
Website: http://www.springerlink.com

All significant cases before the European Court of Human Rights are summarized, with a statement on the relevant violation, the principal facts of the case, details of the proceedings, a summary of the judgment, and the composition of the chamber.

Human Rights and Human Welfare
Quarterly
University of Denver, 2201 South Gaylord Street,
    Denver, CO 80209
E-mail:hrhw@du.edu
Website: http://www.du.edu/gsis/hrhw

An Internet journal provided by an International Consortium of eight human rights centers throughout the world. Publishes essays on significant contemporary debates in the area of human rights, defined broadly, using current books and other publications as centerpieces or points of departure, as well as working papers.

Human Rights Law Review
Semiannual
School of Law, University of Nottingham, Nottingham NG7
    2RD, UK Website: http://www.nottingham.ac.uk/law/hrlc

Publishes academic research articles and book reviews. Includes a section titled "United Nations and Regional Human Rights Systems: Recent Practice"

Human Rights Tribune
Tri-yearly
One Nicholas Street, Suite 300, Ottawa, Ontario K1N 7B7
    Canada
Website: http://www.hri.ca

Human Rights Internet (HRI). Offers analysis of human rights issues, news, and reports from nongovernmental organizations (NGOs) working in the field as well as news and reports from other key actors like the United Nations, other intergovernmental organizations, and government agencies.

Human Rights Quarterly
Quarterly
Johns Hopkins University Press, Journals Publishing Division,
  2715 North Charles Street, Baltimore, MD 21218
Website: http://muse.jhu.edu/journals/human_rights_
  quarterly

This interdisciplinary journal publishes articles written by experts from around the world, as well as book reviews on a wide range of human rights issues and policies.

Index on Censorship
Quarterly
6–8 Amwell Street, London EC1R 1UQ UK
Website: http://www.indexoncensorship.org

Founded in 1972 by a team of writers, journalists, and artists in defense of the basic human right of free expression. Publishes a wide range of opinion, analysis, comment, and reportage from all corners of the world. Provides a log of free expression issues in several countries in its index section.

The International Journal of Children's Rights
Quarterly
P.O. Box 9000, 2300 PA, Leiden, The Netherlands
Website: http://www.brill.nl

Focusing on both critical leadership and practical policy development, includes articles written from the perspectives of a broad range of disciplines and analyzing children's rights and their impact on the concept and development of childhood.

International Journal of Human Rights
Quarterly
Taylor & Francis Inc., including Routledge, Inc., 29 West 35th
  Street, New York, NY 10001
Website: http://www.tandf.co.uk/journals

Publishes research articles and essays on a broad spectrum of human rights issues: human rights and the law, race, religion, gender, children, class, refugees and immigration, genocide, torture, capital punishment, and the laws of war and war crimes.

Journal of Human Rights
Quarterly
Wellesley College, 106 Central Street Wellesley, MA 02481
Website: http://www.wellesley.edu/JournalofHumanRights

Publishes interdisciplinary and scholarly analysis on the theory and practice of human rights as well as new empirical approaches to the study of human rights.

Protection Project Journal of Human Rights and Civil Society
1717 Massachusetts Ave. NW, Washington D.C. 20036
Website: http://www.protectionproject.org

A new journal that aims to provide a forum for scholarly analysis of critical contemporary human rights issues within the prism and from the perspective of civil society and practitioners in the nongovernmental sector.

SUR International Journal on Human Rights
Biannually
Rua Pamplona, 1197 Casa 4, São Paulo, SP 01405–030 Brasil
Website: http://www.surjournal.org/eng

Published in English, Portuguese, and Spanish, it is the journal of SUR, which is a network of academics working together to strengthen the voice of universities in the south on human rights and social justice, and to create stronger cooperation between them and the United Nations.

Women's Rights Law Reporter
123 Washington Street, Newark, New Jersey 07102
Website: http://www.pegasus.rutgers.edu/~wrlr

Founded in 1970 by feminist activists, legal workers, and law students, the *Women's Rights Law Reporter* is a legal periodical in the United States focusing exclusively on the field of women's rights law. Examines legislative developments, significant federal and state court cases, judicial doctrines, litigation strategies, the lives and careers of prominent women jurists, the legal profession, and other areas of law or public policy relating to women's rights, at the intersection of race, class, gender, and sexuality.

WorldViews: A Quarterly Review of Resources for Education and Action (formerly World Views: A Quarterly Review)
Quarterly
World Views, 1515 Webster, Oakland, CA 94612
Website: http://worldviews.igc.org/

Published since 1984, provides reviews of print and audiovisual resources from and about the Third World, offering new perspectives on critical world affairs.

Yale Human Rights and Development Law Journal
Yale Law School, P.O. Box 208215, New Haven, CT 06520–8215
Phone: 203. 432. 9693
Website: http://www.yale.edu/yhrdlj

Focusing on the tension and congruence between human rights and development, publishes analysis and writings that draw upon various academic disciplines, such as political science, public policy, economics, health, and sociology.

Internet Sites and Networks

Asia-Pacific Forum of National Human Rights Institutions
Website: http://www.asiapacificforum.net

The Forum is an independent nonprofit organization that supports, through regional cooperation, the establishment and development of national institutions to protect and promote the human rights of the peoples of the region.

Human Rights Web
Website: http://www.hrweb.org

Includes human rights legal and political documents, history of human rights, information about human rights organizations, and other related resources.

Human Rights Network International (HRNi)
HRNi ULB – CP, 132 Avenue F.-D. Roosevelt, 50 1050
  BRUXELLES, Belgium
Fax: 32. 2. 650. 40. 07
E-mail: hrni@ulb.ac.be
Website: http://www.hrni.org/index_flash.html

HRNi is a network of specialists designed to mobilize the academic community to lead research programs in the field of human rights and democracy. It encourages contact among researchers to promote research and the exchange of ideas and specialized information. Its website, in both English and French, includes information on the theory and practice of human rights.

International Federation for Human Rights (FIDH)
Website: http://www.fidh.org

A network of human rights defenders, it provides news and links to various human rights organizations around the world. It also issues a newsletter that can be subscribed to and received via e-mail. The website is maintained in English, French, Spanish, and Arabic.

National Human Rights Institutions Forum
Website: http://www.nhri.net

An international forum for researchers and practitioners in the field of national human rights institutions. The website includes text of major global and regional documents, information on and from national human rights institutions, bibliography and research materials, and capacity-building and training resources.

United Nations Documentation: Research Guide
Website: http://www.un.org/rights

Includes information about the United Nations High Commissioner for Human Rights; the universal declaration of human rights, treaties, documents and research guides, and other information related to human rights.

University of Minnesota Human Rights Library
Website: http://www1.umn.edu/humanrts

Offers human rights documents and materials (more than 21,000 documents), human rights search engines, mirror sites, other information at the University of Minnesota Human Rights Library.

University of Pennsylvania Human Rights Research Guide
Website: http://gethelp.library.upenn.edu/guides/polisci/humrts.html

Provides information on human rights dictionaries, bibliographies, indexes, catalogs, documents, and other statistics.

Women's Human Rights Resources (WHRR)
Website: http://www.law-lib.utoronto.ca/Diana

Free, online library designed to help researchers, students, teachers, and human rights advocates to locate authoritative and diverse information on women's international human rights.

Datasets and Statistical Sources

Digital Sources

Armed Conflict Database (ACD)
Website: http://acd.iiss.org/armedconflict/MainPages/dsp_WorldMap.asp

Compiled by the International Institute of Strategic Studies (IISS), Defence Analysis Department, the ACD provides an interactive and user-friendly source of information on seventy armed conflicts. The database covers international and internal armed conflicts as well as terrorism. It offers year-on-year analysis of conflicts, their political status, number of fatalities, weapons being used, and the costs ($US) accrued. It can be accessed by subscribers only.

CIRI Human Rights Data Set
Website: http://www.humanrightsdata.com

The Cingranelli and Richards (CIRI) Human Rights Data Set contains standards-based quantitative information on government respect for 13 internationally recognized human rights for 195 countries, annually from 1981 to 2004. The dataset contains measures of government human rights practices and public policies, including democratization, economic and military aid, structural adjustment policies, and humanitarian intervention.

Democide Statistics
Website: http://www.hawaii.edu/powerkills/SOD.CHAP23.HTM

Compiled by R. J. Rummel, the dataset includes counts of deaths in genocide and mass murders committed by 141 different regimes worldwide during the twentieth century.

Eurostat
Website: http://epp.eurostat.cec.eu.int

Available in three languages—English, French, and German—the webpage provides statistical data on European Union and European Council member countries on various human rights–related issues, including good governance, sustainable development, social conditions, and the environment.

Freedom in the World. Freedom House, 1978–.
Website: http://www.freedomhouse.org/research/

Produced annually, it presents articles, charts, tables, ratings, and maps. Has summaries evaluating political rights and civil liberties in 191 nations and 58 related territories.

Governance Datasets and Indicators (a directory)
Website: http://www.worldbank.org/wbi/governance/
govdatasets/external.html

Several datasets and databases on human rights violations, democracy, and other aspects of governance compiled by various scholars and institutions, including one prepared by the World Bank Institute, are presented in a table on the webpage of the World Bank Institute.

Political Terror Scale
Website: http://www.unca.edu/politicalscience/faculty-staff/
gibney.html

Developed by Mark Gibney and Steven Poe, this five-point scale measures the political terror level for 179 countries annually for the years between 1980 and 2003.

Polity IV Project: Political Regime Characteristics and
Transitions, 1800–2003
Website: http://www.cidcm.umd.edu/inscr/polity/index.htm

Originally designed by Ted Robert Gurr, now managed by Monty G. Marshall and Keith Jaggers, Polity IV contains coded annual information on regime and authority characteristics for all independent states (with greater than 500,000 total population) in the global state system and covers the years 1800–2003.

Project Diana: Online Human Rights Archive
Website: http://www.yale.edu/lawweb/avalon/diana/index.html

Managed by Yale University Law School, the website includes information on human rights court cases and various human rights documents.

Protest and Coercion Data
Website: http://lark.cc.ku.edu/~ronfran/data/

Compiled by Ronald Francisco, this dataset contains events data on protests as well as government coercion including arrests of dissidents, trials, censorship, and other civil and political rights violations in twenty-eight European countries from 1980 through 1995.

Refugees and Internally Displaced People
Website:
http://garnet.acns.fsu.edu/~whmoore/RefugeeandInternally DisplacedPersonFlows.htm

Compiled by Will H. Moore, Christian Davenport, Steven C. Poe, and Stephen M. Shellman, the dataset covers the period 1952–1995 and includes information on refugee and migration counts.

It can be obtained from Inter-University Consortium for Political and Social Research (ICPSR) as Study # 1288, at http://www.icpsr.umich.edu/

Print Sources

Arat, Zehra F. *Democracy and Human Rights in Developing Countries.* Boulder, CO: Lynne Rienner, 1991. See also Authors Guild Backprint.com edition. (Lincoln, NE: iUniverse, Inc, 2003).

Claude, Richard, and T. B. Jabine, eds. *Human Rights and Statistics: Getting the Record Straight.* Philadelphia: University of Pennsylvania Press, 1992.

Humana, Charles. *World Human Rights Guide.* New York: Oxford University Press, 1992. 393 pp.

Taylor, Charles L., ed. *Indicator Systems for Political, Economic and Social Analysis.* Cambridge, MA: Oelgesthlanger, Gunn, and Hain, 1980.

Taylor, Charles L., and David A Jodice. *World Handbook of Political and Social Indicators.* 3rd ed. New Haven, CN: Yale University Press, 1983.

Film Distributors and Media Sources

There are few nonprint materials on human rights as such, but there are many on human rights–related issues such as hunger, imprisonment and torture, disappearances and political killings, refugees, the rights of women, and labor rights. The following are selected film producers and distributors that tend to focus on documentary or featured film productions that have human rights relevance.

ABC News Videos
P.O. Box 51790, Lavonia, MI 48151
Phone: 800. 225. 5222
Website: http://www.abcnews.go.com

A&E Television Networks
Online Store http://www.aetv.com

American Friends Service Committee
1501 Cherry Street, Philadelphia, PA 19102
Phone: 215. 241. 7000
Website: http://www.afsc.org

Amnesty International
5 Penn Plaza, 14th Floor, New York, NY 10001
Phone: 212. 807. 8400
Website: http://www.amnesty.org

Ashley Eames, Buffalo Road, Wentworth, NH 03282
Phone: 603. 764. 9948

California Newsreel
Order Department, P.O. Box 2284, South Burlington, VT 05407
Phone: 877. 811. 7495
Website: http://www.newsreel.org

Cambridge Documentary Films
P.O. Box 390385, Cambridge, MA 02139
Phone: 617. 484. 3993
Website: http://www.cambridgedocumentaryfilms.org

Carousel Film & Video
250 Fifth Avenue, Suite 2004, New York, NY 10036
Phone: 800. 683. 1660
Website: http://www.carouselfilms.com

CBS Video
P.O. Box 2284, South Burlington, VT 05407
Phone: 800. 848. 3256
Website: http://www.cbs.com

Church World Service
28606 Phillips Street, P.O. Box 968, Elkhart, IN 46515
Phone: 219. 264. 3102
Website: http://www.churchworldservice.org/

Cinema Guild
130 Madison Avenue, New York, NY 10016
Phone: 212. 685. 6242
Website: http://www.cinemaguild.com

EcuFilm
810 12th Avenue South, Nashville, TN 37203
Phone: 800. 251. 4091
Website: http://www.ecufilm.org

Filmakers Library
124 East 40th Street, New York, NY 10016
Phone: 212. 808. 4980
Website: http://www.filmakers.com/

Films for the Humanities & Sciences
Films Media Group
P.O. Box 2053, Princeton, NJ 08453
Phone: 800. 257. 5126
Website: http://www.films.com

First Run/Icarus Films
32 Court Street, 21st Floor, Brooklyn, NY 11201
Phone: 718. 488. 8900
Website: http://www.frif.com

Franciscan Communications Inc.
1229 Santee Street, Los Angeles, CA 90069
Phone: 213. 746. 2916

Human Rights Watch International Film Festival
350 Fifth Avenue, 34th Floor, New York, NY 10118
Phone: 212. 290. 4700
Website: http://www.hrw.org

IDERA Films
1037 West Broadway, Suite 400, Vancouver, British Columbia,
    Canada V6H 1E3
Phone: 604. 738. 8815

Ladyslipper (Audio resources)
P.O. Box 3124, Durham, NC 27705
Phone: 919. 683. 1570
Website: http://www.ladyslipper.org

Maryknoll World Productions
P.O. Box 308, Maryknoll, NY 10545
Phone: 800. 227. 8523
Website: http://www.maryknoll.org

Media Guild
11722 Sorrento Valley Road, Suite E, San Diego, CA 92121
Phone: 619. 755. 9191

Mennonite Central Committee
P.O. Box 500, 21 South 12th Street, Akron, PA 17501
Phone: 717. 859. 1151
Website: http://www.mcc.org

National Labor Committee
540 West 48th St., 3rd Floor, New York, NY 10036
Phone: 212. 242. 3002
Website: http://www.nlcnet.org

PBS
P.O. Box 791, Alexandria, VA 22313

Phone: 800. 328. 7271
Website: http://www.pbs.org

Simon Wiesenthal Center
1399 South Roxbury Drive, Los Angeles, CA 90035
Phone: 800. 900. 9036
E-mail: information@wiesenthal.net
Website: http://www.wiesenthal.com

Social Studies School Service
10200 Jefferson Boulevard, Room 15, P.O. Box 802,
    Culver City, CA 90232
Phone: 800. 421. 4246
Website: http://www.socialstudies.com

Tolerance
c/o The Southern Poverty Law Center, 400 Washington Ave.,
    Montgomery, AL 36104
Phone: 334. 956. 8200
Website: http://www.tolerance.org

United Nations Publications Sales Section
2 United Nations Plaza, Room D.C.2–853, New York, NY 10017
Phone: 212. 963. 8302; 800. 253. 9646
Website: https://unp.un.org

Wellspring Media
419 Park Avenue South, New York, NY 10016
Phone: 212. 686. 6777
Website: http://www.wellspring.com

Women Make Movies
462 Broadway, Suite 500WS, New York, New York 10013
Phone: 212. 925. 0606
Website: http://www.wmm.com

World Council of Churches
150 route de Ferney, P.O. Box 2100 1211, Geneva 2, Switzerland
Phone: 41. 22. 791. 6111
Website: http://www2.wcc-coe.org

Glossary

Accession Act of a country in ratifying or becoming a state party to an international treaty after the treaty has entered into force.

Adoption of an international declaration or convention Consensus reached by a majority (usually more than one-half) of the states that are members of the international organization to accept the language of a proposed declaration or convention.

Collective rights See *Group rights.*

Convention An international agreement among states dealing with a specific subject, such as the rights of children. Also referred to as a treaty, covenant, accord, or pact.

Covenant See *Convention.*

Crimes against humanity The most egregious crimes, such as apartheid, genocide, and summary executions, committed at times of war or peace, for which criminal liability is imposed by domestic or international tribunals.

Cultural liberty Ability to choose freely the extent to which one wishes to engage in the practice and preservation of the traditions of one's cultural heritage.

Cultural relativism The notion that ethical and moral standards are relative to what a particular society or culture believes to be good or bad; as applied to the concept of human rights, because the importance of a particular cultural idea varies from one society to another, it is impossible to have a common, universally applicable set of human rights.

Declaration, international An international document that highlights an issue and sets forth principles and goals to be upheld by the adopting organization and its members, though the declaration is not legally binding.

Derogation Partial abrogation of a law or treaty; in case of human rights treaties, a state party would be relieved of the obligation to honor certain treaty provisions concerning human rights only temporarily and under extraordinary conditions.

Dignity   The quality of being worthy of esteem or respect.

Entering into force   The date when a law or treaty becomes effective, starts to be applied.

Ethnic cleansing   The systemic effort to remove a specific population (e.g., as determined by race, religion, sexual orientation) from a specific area, through means ranging from forced migration to extermination.

Ethnocentrism   The evaluation of other groups according to the values and standards of one's own ethnic group, usually with the conviction that one's own race or culture is superior to all others.

Exceptionalism   A pattern of assertions that a subject, especially a nation, is exempt from universally held assumptions and does not conform to a pattern or norm.

Gender   Culturally defined meanings and identity attached to the (biologically) different sexes within social systems.

Generations of rights   A debatable classification of different types of rights into categories according to their "age"—when they became internationally accepted norms—as first, second, and third generations of rights.

Gini Index   A measure of the distribution of materials (e.g., income, land) throughout a society; used to assess equality/inequality within the society, by using a scale ranging from 0 (perfect equality) to 1 or 100 (perfect inequality).

Globalization   A process that involves the creation of a single/integrated market, increased human mobility and interaction across borders, and the development of common values and norms.

Group rights   Rights claimed by a group of individuals or communities (e.g., a people's right to self-determination).

Human Development Index (HDI)   A composite measure of societal advancement, developed and used by the United Nations Development Programme to rank countries with regard to the level of wealth, education, and longevity attained by their population. It ranges from 0 to 1, from the lowest to the highest levels of achievement.

Indigenous people   Cultural groups and their descendants who inhabited a given territory or region before its colonization or annexation and have a historical continuity or association with the region.

Individual rights   Rights claimed by individuals (e.g., the right to vote, right to work, and freedom from torture or imprisonment).

Intergovernmental organization (IGO)   Organizations established by a group of states around some common goals.

International Bill of Rights   The collective content of three core international human rights documents: the Universal Declaration of Human Rights (1948); the International Covenant on Economic, Social, and Cultural Rights (1966); and the International Covenant on Civil and Political Rights (1966).

Laissez-faire economy or state   A socioeconomic system based on private economic enterprises that operate free from government involvement or subject to minimal intervention by the state.

Micro-enterprises   Small, entrepreneurial operations run by individuals or a group of individuals.

Misogyny   The hatred of women as a sexually defined group.

Multinational corporation (MNC)   See *Transnational corporation.*

Multinational enterprise (MNE)   See *Transnational corporation.*

Negative rights   Rights, the enjoyment of which is argued to depend on nonaction by other individuals or the state.

Neo-liberalism   The belief that social and economic progress should be driven by private enterprise and the market economy, with minimal government interference; based on the tenets of classical liberal theory.

Nongovernmental organization (NGO)   An organization that is not part of a government or state agency and pursues social missions and goals.

Nonintervention in international politics   The concept that no state has the right to intervene in the affairs of another state.

Norm   A shared belief or pattern of behavior expected within a particular society.

Normative standards, international   With regard to international law, conventions and declarations set standards that, once accepted by a portion of the international community, are applicable as a standard of behavior for all countries, even in countries that are not signatories or parties to those agreements.

Pact   See *Convention.*

Patriarchy   The social system of male domination over females and the ideology that sustains such a system.

Positive rights   Rights, the enjoyment of which is argued to depend upon action and effort by the state and society.

Protocol   The first copy of a treaty or other such document before its ratification, as well as the additional clauses and procedures adopted in relation to a convention after it enters into force (e.g., the Optional Protocol to the Convention on the Elimination of All Forms of Discrimination against Women).

Racism   The constructed notion that uses mainly biological differences (e.g., skin color, hair texture, facial features) to create categories of peoples as inferior and superior for purposes of discrimination and to justify the domination of one group over another.

Ratification   The action taken by a state to become a party to a convention, which then obliges the state to uphold and implement the provisions of the convention.

Refoulement   The process by which a country returns a potential immigrant to his or her home country, or a third country, where the individual's life or freedom may be under threat.

Reservations, treaty   Exceptions specified by a country at the time it signs or ratifies a treaty to exempt itself temporarily from some provisions of the treaty.

Sanctions, international   Conditions imposed on a state party that is in violation of its commitment to a charter or treaty.

Signature, treaty   A state's approval of a treaty or convention, which expresses the state's support for the convention's adoption but falls short of binding the state to implement the provisions of the convention.

Social structure   The pattern of social relationships and behaviors in a group, organization, or society.

Sovereignty   The right of a state to self-determine its internal and external affairs without interference from another state.

Special rapporteurs of the UN   Individuals who use their expertise to gather information on member states on specific human rights issues and other specialized areas that concern the United Nations and to issue reports and recommendations based on their findings.

State   A defined territory whose sovereignty is recognized by other states, and whose sovereign government decides the laws and behaviors that are to be followed within its borders.

States parties   Countries that have ratified a convention and are thus bound by its terms.

Structural Adjustment Programs/Policies (SAPs)   Conditions set by the World Bank and the International Monetary Fund to be fulfilled by member countries that seek loans in order for them to be granted a loan.

Transnational corporation (TNC)   A large private business corporation that spans multiple countries, while the headquarters in the parent country issues management decisions and controls profits. Also referred to as a multinational corporation (MNC) or a multinational enterprise (MNE).

Treaty   See *Convention*.

Treaty body   A committee comprised of independent experts that monitors the implementation of a treaty, usually through the review of periodic reports submitted by the states that are party to that treaty.

Universalism   The principle that holds that norms and policies are applicable to all individuals equally and without exception to their characteristics, status, or location (e.g., human rights apply to all human beings regardless of their individual characteristics or the society or country to which they belong).

Index

About the Author

Zehra F. Kabasakal Arat is professor of political science and women's studies at Purchase College of the State University of New York. Her research and publications address a wide range of topics related to human rights, with an emphasis on democracy, development, and women's rights, as expressed in some of her book titles: *Democracy and Human Rights in Developing Countries; Deconstructing Images of "the Turkish Woman,"* and *Non-State Actors in the Human Rights Universe*. One of her recent research projects examines the history and politics of the Republic of Turkey; the findings will be published in a book, tentatively titled *Human Rights Discourse and Practices in Turkey*.